INSIGHT GUIDES

Vienna

```
D0169740
```

APA PUBLICATIONS

Part of the Langenscheidt Publishing Group

L

ABOUT THIS BOOK

Editorial

Project Editor
Jane Ladle
Editorial Director
Brian Bell

Distribution

UK & Ireland
GeoCenter International UK Ltd
The Viables Centre
Harrow Way
Basingstoke
Hants RG22 4BJ
Fax: (44) 1256-817988

United States
Langenscheidt Publishers, Inc.
46–35 54th Road
Maspeth, NY 11378
Fax: (718) 784-0640

Worldwide
APA Publications GmbH & Co.
Verlag KG Singapore Branch, Singapore
38 Joo Koon Road
Singapore 628990
Tel: (65) 865-1600
Fax: (65) 861-6438

Printing

Insight Print Services (Pte) Ltd
38 Joo Koon Road
Singapore 628990
Tel: (65) 865-1600
Fax: (65) 861-6438

© 1998 Apa Publications GmbH & Co
Verlag KG Singapore Branch, Singapore
All Rights Reserved
First Edition 1988
Third Edition 1998

CONTACTING THE EDITORS

Although every effort is made to provide accurate information in this publication, we live in a fast-changing world and would appreciate it if readers would call our attention to any errors or outdated information that may occur by writing to us at:
Insight Guides, P.O. Box 7910, London SE1 8ZB, England. Fax: (44 171) 620-1074. e-mail: insight@apaguide.demon.co.uk

Vienna is indisputably one of Europe's most interesting and beautiful cities. Such is the enthusiasm of the team at Insight for Austria's capital that we have also produced *Insight Compact Guide: Vienna*, the ideal reference guide to use on the spot, and *Insight Pocket Guide: Vienna*, which highlights personal recommendations and includes a full-size pull-out map.

Both these smaller books complement this volume but do not replace it, for the flagship *Insight Guide: Vienna* is the only detailed portrait of the city's culture.

How to use this book

This is far more than just a guidebook. Aided by the distinctive new series design, it combines highly informative, entertaining and well-written text with an exciting photo-journalistic approach. It thereby conveys an understanding of the essential nature of the city, and guides readers through its sights and attractions.

◆ To understand Vienna today, you need to know something of its past. The first section covers the city's political and cultural **History**, as well as its **People**, plus special **Features** on what makes it unique.
◆ The main **Places** section provides a full run-down of all the attractions worth seeing. The principal places of interest are co-ordinated by number with full-colour maps.

◆ The **Travel Tips** listings section is a practical reference guide to travel, hotels, restaurants, shops and festivals, plus the German language. Information may be located quickly by using the index printed on the back cover flap – and the flaps are designed to serve as bookmarks.
◆ **Photographs** are chosen not only to illustrate geography and buildings, but also to convey the many moods of the city and the everyday activities of its people.

The contributors

The project editor given the task of recruiting the original team was **Wilhelm Klein**, a Frankfurt-based author. Klein describes himself as a "Viennese in exile", one of the many citizens of the Austrian capital who left their native city in the 1950s and 1960s in order to seek their fortunes elsewhere. He maintained close contact with Vienna during his absence and was familiar with recent publications on the city.

This new edition was overseen by **Jane Ladle**, who has also edited guidebooks to her home city London and to the British regions. She was helped and advised by opera-lover and Insight regular, **Douglas Amrine**, who did the picture edit; and by **Eckhard Zimmermann**, who commissioned new material and wrote the picture stories for the "Insight on..." features.

The main photographer is **Christian Hager**, another "Viennese in exile". Producing the pictures for this book enabled Hager to rediscover his native city.

Fellow citizens maintain that **Dr Felix Czeike** has turned over every single stone in Vienna city centre, and that he is as familiar with the city's long history as the rest of us are with the present day. A university professor and the president of a number of historical associations in Austria, he has written nearly 50 books and contributed more than 700 articles to newspapers and periodicals. His chapters on Viennese history and the city centre are a highlight of this book.

The introduction, *City of my Dreams*, was written by **Dr Lonnie R. Johnson**, an American who, in 1983, was awarded a doctorate by the University of Vienna. He co-wrote *Vienna: The Past in the Present* and *Introducing Austria: A Guide of Sorts*. He is married to a Viennese and has made the city his adoptive home.

The brand-new features in this edition, on *Music* and *Culture*, were written by **Karin Schiefer**, who was born in Steyr, Upper Austria. She also updated the other chapters. Schiefer is now based in

Vienna and writes for German and Austrian magazines on film, literature, art, music, fashion and travel.

Journalist **Dr Jutta Kohout**, who studied history and political sciences in Vienna, and whose articles have appeared in *Stern*, *Geo* and *Cosmopolitan*, wrote the chapters *The Viennese* and *Where to Eat, Drink and Be Merry*. She knows Vienna inside out: the pubs, museums, discos, theatres and balls.

Dr Günter Treffer, who studied in Innsbruck, Vienna and at the University of Pennsylvania, contributed the last three chapters on the suburbs and outlying regions. He is a typical Viennese cosmopolitan: utterly European, but at home anywhere in the world. He has worked as editor and publisher for a number of renowned publishing houses and has written books about Vienna, its surroundings and its history.

Finally, **Tobias Streitferdt** updated the **Travel Tips** for this edition, and the book was proof-read and indexed by **Lynn Bresler**.

A parting thought ...
"The nostalgic city with a streak of gentle hopelessness, where Freud discovered sex", is how television travel reporter Alan Whicker describes Vienna in *The Best of Everything*. *Insight Guide: Vienna* endeavours to put into words the often contradictory elements that give this proud city its wonderful atmosphere.

Map Legend

▬▬ ▪▪	International Boundary
– – – –	Province/ State Boundary
⊖	Border Crossing
•▪▪	National Park/ Reserve
– – – –	Ferry Route
Ⓤ	U-Bahn
✈	Airport
🚌	Bus Station
Ⓟ	Parking
❶	Tourist Information
✉	Post Office
† ⚲ ♂	Church/Ruins
☾ ♣	Mosque
✡ ⚑	Synagogue
♂ ♂	Castle/Ruins
∴	Archaeological Site
∩	Cave
★	Place of Interest

The main places of interest in the *Places* section are coordinated by number with a full-colour map (e.g. ❶) and a symbol at the top of every right-hand page tells you where to find the map.

INSIGHT GUIDES
Vienna

CONTENTS

Tempting display at Café Demel

VIENNA, CITY OF MY DREAMS

The Viennese may be blasé about their heritage, but a restoration drive has revitalised the city's splendour

If you get too close to one of the masterpieces in the world-famous collection of Vienna's Kunsthistorisches Museum, a guard will request you to step back. He himself seems oblivious to the picture's beauty, and the Viennese often seem to regard their city with a similar disinterest. Familiar with a beauty which enchants foreigners, they go about their daily routines without paying undue attention to the spectacular setting. Yet, in a *Heuriger* wine tavern, you can sometimes see their cynicism evaporate as they proclaim in song: "Vienna, Vienna, just you alone, you are the city of my dreams."

Until the 1980s, despite – or perhaps because of – its imposing ensembles of historic buildings, many of them completed long before the turn of the century, Vienna faced the world with a grey countenance which mostly turned black on rainy days. This has changed radically in recent years. In a mammoth operation, the authorities have had the façades of entire streets and squares cleaned and restored. In the inner city the Baroque façades gleam once more in original splendour, and the palaces on the outskirts are bright with a new coat of Maria Theresa-yellow paint. The main squares have been redesigned; where appropriate, gaps in the building have been filled by prizewinning designs by the world's leading architects.

Needless to say, all this activity was accompanied by much controversy and public discussion, revealing the ambivalent relationship between the Viennese and their city. Now that St Stephen's Square and St Michael's Square have received their facelifts, the storm has died down. Most Viennese have accepted the fact that they now live in a modern city, one which has not remained static since the 1920s.

Behind the scenes, too, there have been many changes. In the early 1970s many apartments still had no running water. Renovated and modernised, the lovely old flats in the historic buildings between the Gürtel and the Ringstrasse are attractive places to live, and their owners would not want to exchange tradition for modernity.

In the past Vienna was the capital city not only of the Austrians but also of the Czechs, Slovaks, Poles, Ruthenians, Ukrainians, Hungarians, Romanians, Serbs, Croats, Slovenians and Italians. Today, Vienna's politicians never tire of singing the praises of their city's merits as a modern metropolis. They stress its importance as the home of a number of United Nations organisations, an assortment of other international agencies, and its role as a neutral meeting ground for East and West. But it's Vienna's imperial past that interests most visitors. Virtually all the facets of the Habsburg era are on display, from the apartments of the Hofburg to the summer palace of Schönbrunn, from the Vienna Boys' Choir to the Spanish Riding School. Combining ancient and modern, Vienna has an anachronistic and eclectic appeal.

PRECEDING PAGES: the Vienna Boys' Choir; University arcades; the Opera Ball; in the park of the Schönbrunn Palace.
LEFT: Art Nouveau relief

Decisive Dates

BEGINNINGS: 4TH CENTURY BC–10TH CENTURY AD

Approx. 400BC Celts establish the settlement of Vindobona on the site of today's Hoher Markt.
15BC The Romans conquer the Alpine and Danube regions. The Limes and numerous garrisons secure the borders of the province of Pannonia. The most important garrison in the Vienna area, Carnuntum, is protected by the military camp of Vindobona, which contains 6,000 soldiers. A residential area is later built to the east of the camp with a population of 20,000.
Approx. AD400 The mass migration of tribes passes

through the Vienna Basin. Vindobona is destroyed by the Visigoths. In 433 the Romans are forced to surrender the whole of Pannonia to the Huns.
955 The German emperor Otto I beats the Huns on the Lechfeld and drives them back eastwards.

THE BABENBERG ERA: 976–1246

976 As administrator of the new Ottonian eastern march, Otto I puts the Babenbergs in power in Vienna.
1155 Vienna, strategically located at the junction of the Danube and the trading route across the Alps known as the Bernsteinstrasse, becomes the seat of Heinrich II Jasomirgott. He extends the city and founds several churches, including St Stephen's Cathedral.
1192–1200 During a Crusade, Duke Leopold V takes Richard the Lionheart prisoner. He uses the ransom money to extend Vienna still further and reinforce its fortifications.
1221 Vienna receives municipal and staple rights, requiring foreign merchants to offer their goods for sale in the city.
1246 Death of Frederick II, the last of the Babenbergs.

THE HABSBURG ERA (PRE-IMPERIAL) : 1278–1804

1278 Rudolf I of Habsburg, elected Holy Roman Emperor five years previously, wins the struggle for the Austrian succession.
1358–65 Rudolf IV the "Founder" commissions the Gothic additions to St Stephen's Cathedral, and founds Vienna University.
1421 The Vienna Geserah: the Jewish population is driven out of the city and over 200 Jews are murdered.
1493–1519 Cleverly exploiting several marital alliances, Maximilian I extends the Habsburg domains to include the Netherlands, Burgundy and Spain, and also makes preparations for the unification of Austria, Bohemia and Hungary. Vienna, hitherto merely a border city, now becomes the capital of an enormous empire.
1529 The Turks almost reach Vienna but are forced to withdraw after the early onset of winter. The Viennese extend their fortifications.
1551 Protestantism spreads, and by the late 16th century three quarters of Vienna's population are Protestant. The Catholic Habsburgs summon the Jesuits to Vienna. Under Rudolf II the Protestants are systematically persecuted and exiled.
1618–48 Vienna undergoes a period of economic recession as a result of the Thirty Years' War. The Swedish army withdraws without a fight, however.
1679 Plague outbreak in Vienna, claiming the lives of at least 75,000 people.
1683 The Turks reach Vienna again. The 250,000-strong Turkish army faces just 17,000 defenders. Although the situation seems hopeless, the Imperial army arrives to assist the Viennese and decisively drives the Turks away. This victory marks the rise of a young man from the House of Savoy: Prince Eugene, who becomes the advisor of three emperors under whom Vienna gains international acclaim and astonishing prosperity. The city is filled with Baroque architecture, and becomes a magnet for the world's greatest architects, painters and sculptors.
1698 The "so-called" suburbs (the present city districts II–IX and XX) are incorporated in the precincts charter of Emperor Leopold and surrounded by the Linienwall fortifications along the present-day ring road (1704).
1740 Maria Theresa ascends the imperial throne. Together with her son and co-regent Joseph II she ushers in a series of domestic reforms. Vienna becomes

the scene of unprecedented architectural activity.

1780 Joseph II becomes sole regent. Influenced by the Enlightenment, he attempts to introduce numerous radical changes, several of which are rejected by the Viennese.

1792 Franz II suppresses the growing dissatisfaction with the aid of his secret police. The wars of coalition begin against revolutionary France.

THE AUSTRIAN EMPIRE: 1804–1918

1804 Franz founds the Austrian Empire after Napoleon has crowned himself Emperor of the French. Two years later, however, Napoleon forces him to abdicate from the German imperial throne – marking the end of the Holy Roman Empire.

1814–15 The Congress of Vienna is convened, at which Europe's princes and statesmen rearrange the political map. Under chancellor Metternich, who nips any liberal or nationalist feeling in the bud, Austria slowly sinks into the deathly stillness of the Restoration.

1848 The March Revolution: radical Viennese citizens, students and workers call for the abolition of censorship and for participation in executive decisions. Imperial troops crush the uprising. The 18-year-old Franz Joseph I ascends the imperial throne.

1857 The bastions are removed and the new Rings are built around Vienna. Expanding to include several of its surrounding municipalities, the city greatly increases in size and is given the right of self-administration.

1873 World Exhibition held in Vienna.

1895 Under its mayor Dr Karl Lueger, Vienna becomes a modern metropolis with hospitals, gas, electricity and its own tram network.

1896 The giant Ferris Wheel is installed in the Prater.

1914 The assassination in Sarajevo of Franz Ferdinand, the heir to the imperial throne, ushers in World War I. The death of Franz Joseph in 1916 marks the end of an epoch.

POST-IMPERIAL VIENNA: FROM 1918

1918 The Republic of Austria is declared, ending the double monarchy. Karl I goes into exile. Austria shrinks to a twelfth of its original size.

1922 Vienna becomes one of the Federal States of Austria.

1927 Burning of the Palace of Justice in riots.

PRECEDING PAGES: view of Vienna, 1483.
ABOVE LEFT: Maximilian I and his family.
ABOVE RIGHT: Karl Lueger, reforming mayor of Vienna 1897–1910.

1934 Bloody fights between Social Democratic paramilitary troops and the Conservative Christian government, which is eager to end the Socialists' reign over "Red Vienna". Chancellor Dollfuss prohibits the SPÖ and the trades unions, and is murdered shortly afterwards during an attempted coup by the National Socialists.

1938 On the Heldenplatz, Hitler announces the Anschluss: Austria's annexation by Nazi Germany.

1944–5 Bombing raids by the Allies destroy 30 percent of Vienna. The city is taken by the Red Army, and divided into four occupation zones.

1955 The victorious powers sign the Austrian Staatsvertrag (State Treaty) in the Belvedere, and the

country is given back its freedom. Vienna becomes a diplomatic watershed between East and West.

1969 Work begins on the city's U-Bahn system.

1972 Kurt Waldheim becomes Secretary General of the United Nations. Later, as President of Austria, he is accused of being involved in war-time atrocities.

1979 Vienna becomes the third seat of the United Nations Organization after New York and Geneva. Vienna International Centre is opened.

1989 The end of the Cold War increases the diplomatic importance of Vienna. Its economic, social and cultural life profits from the new communication possibilities.

1995 Austria joins the European Union.

1997 Vienna Philharmonic Orchestra changes its rules to allow the first woman to join its ranks.

FROM ROMAN FORTRESS TO UNITED NATIONS CITY

Vienna has grappled with Habsburg imperialism as well as Nazism.
But it has also flourished during "golden ages" of achievement in the arts

Although the area around Vienna has been inhabited for many thousands of years, the actual history of the city begins when the Romans advanced into the Celtic Kingdom of Noricum. Here, the Romans built a line of fortifications along the banks of the Danube, as a protection against the German tribes. The main camp in this area was Carnuntum, at the point where the road from Poland to the Adriatic crossed the Danube.

The second flanking fortification was where part of Vienna's city centre is now, at Vindobona, next to a Celtic settlement that lay in a good strategic position. A civilian town grew up next to the camp. Somewhere around AD 400 the fort was destroyed by Germanic tribes.

The Roman walls remained intact until the 12th century and up till that time had protected the developing settlement, which had its centres to the north of the Hoher Markt (Berghof and St Rupert's Church), at St Peter's and at Maria am Gestade. Fortified villages grew up outside the gates, among them trading settlements between Wollzeile and Fleischmarkt and near where the Weihburggasse is today.

The Babenberg era

Vienna was first described as *civitas* (town) in 1137. In 1147, St Stephen's Cathedral was consecrated, in 1155, the House of Babenberg set up its residence in Vienna (Am Hof), and in 1189, Frederick Barbarossa rested in Vienna on his way to the Crusades. Towards the end of the 12th century, an expansion of the city took place that would shape the development of Vienna for centuries to come. A new circular wall surrounded it. The district around the Neuer Markt was built in the time of Duke Leopold VI to absorb the trade in goods coming north from Venice. At that time the whole area between the Kärntner Strasse, Graben and Kohlmarkt was built up.

LEFT: Rudolf IV, the Founder.
ABOVE: Heinrich II (1141–77) travelling to the Holy Land

By the beginning of the 13th century Vienna had evolved into a fully developed city with a centre and suburbs. It was the most important city north of the Alps after Cologne. Leopold encouraged trade, gave Vienna city rights in 1221 (at the head of the city council was a city magistrate), invited Catholic orders, whose churches (Teutonic Order of Knights, Dominicans and Minorites) can still be seen today, into the city, and founded St Michael's Church. Vienna developed into an important trading and cultural centre, praised by the Minnesinger poets.

After the death of Duke Frederick II in the battle of the Leitha (1246), the Bohemian King Przemysl Ottokar II and the King of Hungary, Bela IV, both laid claim to the Austrian inheritance. The Viennese aristocracy backed Ottokar, whose policies of support for the cities seemed to offer them advantages.

The Habsburgs takeover

In 1273, a German king was elected, Rudolf I of the house of Habsburg, who ended the quarrel by giving Austria and Styria to his sons Albrecht I and Rudolf II after the defeat and death of Ottokar in the battle of Dürnkrut in 1278. The Viennese were placated in 1278 with a city charter. But Albrecht reduced the economic privileges of the city considerably in 1281, and provoked a rebellion by the citizens which was put down with great difficulty in 1288. In 1296, the city's rights were reduced even further and the political activities, even of the aristocracy, were considerably reduced.

The Habsburgs completed the new castle begun by Ottokar II (the Swiss wing of the Hofburg) and encouraged completion of the Herrenviertel district (Herrengasse). Despite their efforts the Viennese citizens remained mistrustful for a long time. However, from the beginning of the 14th century, Vienna's supremacy over other cities in the Habsburg domains was undisputed.

The 14th century brought the consolidation of Habsburg rule, running parallel with the completion of the Old City: the building of the Gothic choir of St Stephen's, the building of the Church of the Augustinians next to the Burg, and the "jewel of Gothic architecture", the church of Our

THE GOTHIC CITY

In the 16th century, the Gothic style of architecture was largely superseded in Europe by the Renaissance style. Yet, in Vienna, the absence of the Imperial court from the city in this period spelled a dearth of new building (an exception being the city fortifications of 1529). Therefore, narrow, high-gabled town houses still predominate, with the spires of Gothic churches – most of which survive today – soaring above them. Gothic styles in the Viennese arts are typical for the 14th to the early 16th century.

Lady of the River Bank. The dominant personality among the nobility was Duke Rudolf IV, the Founder, who laid the foundation stone of the tower of St Stephen's (1359). He founded the University in 1365 and instigated economic and social reforms. In 1396, the Dukes passed an order in council which gave craftsmen and tradesmen equal standing with the great patrician families and saved Vienna from the bloody civil wars that convulsed many German cities at this time.

We can already form a clear picture of Vienna in the 15th century. The humanist Aeneas Silvius Piccolomini (later Pope Pius II) left a description of the city, and authentic drawings were produced in 1470 and 1490. It was not a good time for the mayors, however. Following the example of other German Imperial cities, they wanted to pursue independent policies. Konrad Vorlauf was executed in 1408 for being on the losing side during an internecine Habsburg struggle, and Konrad Holzer, a popular hero, suffered the same fate in 1463 as a result of bad tactics. The unfortunate persecution of the Jews in 1421, which was set in motion for the most trivial reasons and yet led to the destruction of the Jewish quarter; the confused events of the 1440s and 1450s, when the Emperor Frederick III quarrelled with his brother Albrecht VI, and was besieged by the Viennese in the Hofburg in 1462, even though he had presented them with a new coat of arms in 1461; the occupation of Vienna by the King of Hungary, Matthew Corvinus (1485–90) – these are the principal milestones of an eventful century.

First Turkish Siege

In the 16th century, the whole of Europe was shaken by the Protestant teachings of Martin Luther and the threat of a Turkish invasion. In 1529, the Turks, led by Sultan Suleiman, reached the walls of Vienna for the first time, and the city only survived due to the early onset of winter. After this, Ferdinand I deliberately moved his residence to Vienna in 1533. Noticeable social and architectural changes followed the settlement of court personnel and the increased presence of nobility.

The rest of the 16th century was marked by the building of the Renaissance wall with its bastions, which was completed in the 1560s. The image of the walls with their *glacis* (area in which building was prohibited) in front and the unregulated course of the Danube appeared in many pictures produced in the following years. On the other side of the *glacis* the suburbs developed, mainly inhabited by craftsmen and tradesmen, and further out by peasants. Since all financial and labour resources went to the building of the walls, there are few Renaissance buildings within the city area.

Reformation and Counter-Reformation

In the second half of the century, disputes with the Protestants became more and more acrimo-

nious. In the 1570s, under the tolerant Emperor Maximilian II, Vienna was almost 80 percent Protestant and, for a short time, the city even had a Lutheran mayor. Maximilian's successor, Rudolf II, moved the Imperial residence to Prague, and Vienna temporarily lost its position of precedence. Emperor Ferdinand II rigorously suppressed Protestantism, his motives being mainly political rather than religious.

Thanks to the fanatical involvement of the Jesuits, the first half of the 17th century saw an overwhelming victory for the Counter-Reformation. Under Cardinal Melchior Khesl, a number of orders were invited to Vienna. Their churches

remain among the attractions of the city today. The Carmelites and the hospital order of the Brothers of Mercy settled in Leopoldstadt. The Augustinians built the Church of St Rochus on the Landstrasse, the Paulites settled on the Wieden, as did the Servites in the Rossau – and that's to name just a few. In the city centre new churches were built by the Franciscans, the Dominicans and the Capuchins (including the crypt where the Habsburgs are buried). The Scottish Church gained a Baroque façade and the Jesuits built an impressive church next to the Old University which they ran. The Ghetto in Leopoldstadt was assigned to the Jews in 1625, but religious bigotry closed it again as early as 1671.

LEFT: Vienna in the 15th century.
RIGHT: Kärntner Strasse, around 1470

Turks at the Gates

Sultan Suleiman the Magnificent's first attempt to conquer the Holy Roman Empire had ended in 1526 at the Hungarian border. Three years later, however, a vast Turkish army returned to take Vienna. They reached its walls with only minimal opposition and laid siege. "On the third day", a message to the motley defenders promised, "we will breakfast within your walls".

Turkish sappers moved their trenches forward and tunnelled under the walls to lay mines. As the days turned to weeks, the Viennese commander

side the city on 13 July 1683. A few days later, Vienna was surrounded, and the Emperor and many of his subjects had fled. Would the 17,000 defenders, led by Mayor Johann Andreas von Liebenberg and City Commander Ernst Rudiger von Starhemberg, be able to hold out against 250,000 troops?

By September, the city's situation was desperate. Mines had torn great gaps in the wall, ammunition and provisions were low, casualties were higher than expected, epidemics broke out, Liebenberg died. But the Turks were also flagging. The Viennese only just managed to fight off the final large-scale attack by the Janissaries on 6 September, in which the Löwel bastion collapsed. At last, unhin-

was emboldened to signal the Turks: "Your breakfast is getting cold". So was the weather, and faced with the problems of feeding 250,000 mouths in frozen conditions 1,126 km (700 miles) from home, the aggressors summarily struck camp and left.

The war peaked in the 1670s. The Sultan had renewed his alliance with France, whilst the Pope, together with Leopold I, had gained military help from the Empire. In 1682, Imre Thököli, the leader of the Hungarian army which had rebelled against Habsburg domination, asked the Turks for help. This provided the latter with the excuse to send a vast army. In 1683 the king of Poland joined the Papal–Imperial alliance, tipping the balance for the defenders.

The advance guard of Grand Vizier Kara Mustapha's forces ranged against Vienna arrived out-

dered by the Turks, the relief force arrived on the Kahlenberg, a hill in the Vienna Woods, unaccountably left unoccupied by Kara Mustapha. On 12 September 1683, it went into attack along a broad front.

Perhaps the battle would not have ended in quite such a clear-cut victory if Kara Mustapha hadn't made the fatal mistake of simultaneously storming the walls once again. After bitter fighting, the Turkish front, pressed by the Polish cavalry, began to give way. Soon the Turks were trying to save themselves in headlong flight, leaving uncounted piles of spoil for the victors. The Pummerin, the great bell of St Stephen's, was cast from the melted-down bronze of captured Turkish guns.

ABOVE: the Turkish siege of Vienna, 1683

The "advance of the monasteries" occurred at the same time as the emergence of the Roman Baroque style in architecture. Its high point was reached in the façade of the Kirche Am Hof, which bears the strongest resemblance to Roman models. The early Baroque style (circa 1600–80) was dominated by Italian architects, sculptors and painters. The building of palaces was secondary to that of churches.

The Thirty Years' War (1618–48) passed Vienna by almost without trace – the Swedish army once approached the city (1645) but did not attack. The mayor and the city council became increasingly dependent on the rulers, and no

a "Mecca of the arts". Nobility and commoners burst out of the fortified city into the airy suburbs and outskirts. Vienna had never before seen such building frenzy.

The era of the high Baroque (circa 1685–1750) is characterised by a passion for building which had its roots in both the spiritual and temporal worlds. The court, aligning itself with European power struggles, the church, strengthened by the defeat of Protestantism, the nobility, which had acquired massive wealth – the need to impress which had seized all the upper echelons of society led to the wish to glorify recent victories. In these times of uncertain currency and few oppor-

noteworthy political disputes developed. Daniel Moser, the most prominent head of the city, was a loyal follower of Emperor Ferdinand II.

Second Turkish Siege

The last years of the 17th century saw a number of important events: a catastrophic outbreak of the plague (1679) and the second siege by the Turks (1683). The victory over the Turks is marked by a change in the architecture of the city. The "Imperial city", freed from military threat, developed as the residence of Karl VI (1711–40) and his daughter Maria Theresa (1740–80) into

ABOVE: the Kohlmarkt, 1784

tunities for economic investment, this was also a lucrative way of investing capital.

The Baroque style, with its celebration of life, its stress on the eternal, and its splendour and show, offered the ideal conditions. The city centre began to change fundamentally, the suburbs were improved. A Baroque metropolis of European stature arose out of this symbiosis of the temporal and the spiritual, involving all branches of the arts. Under Leopold I (1659–1705), the first of the "Baroque Emperors", Vienna became a centre for European music and theatre.

The architectural style of the high Baroque was no longer in the hands of the Italians, but in those of two great contemporary architects,

Johann Bernhard Fischer von Erlach and Johann Lukas von Hildebrandt. Fischer, with a touch of genius, knew how to transform the Baroque of the south into an art form that suited the Viennese mentality. His best works were created for the Emperor: the National Library in the Josefsplatz, the Bohemian State Chancellery in the Judenplatz, and the Royal Stables. His most notable work is the Church of St Charles, commissioned by Karl VI during the plague of 1713. He also built palaces for the nobility, for the Batthyány-Strattman, Schwarzenberg and Trautson families, among others. Some buildings were completed after his death in 1723, by his

son Joseph Emanuel, who also designed the Imperial Chancellery Wing of the Hofburg.

Hildebrandt, the second great individualist of this era, worked mainly for Prince Eugene of Savoy (Belvedere, Winter Palace) and for the nobility, which overwhelmed him with contracts (the palaces of Schönbrunn, Harrach and Daun-Kinsky). For the court, he created the Secret Chancellery (now the Federal Chancellery) as well as St Peter's and the Church of the Piarists.

The city administration had the Town Hall built in the Wipplingerstrasse, and the Arsenal by Anton Ospel. Sculptors (such as Georg Raphael Donner and Balthasar Permoser), fresco painters (such as Daniel Gran, who decorated the National Library, Franz Anton Maulpertsch, who painted the Church of the Piarists, and Johann Michael Rottmayr, responsible for the Church of St Charles), as well as countless craftsmen were responsible, together with the architects, for the image of "Viennese Baroque".

Under Maria Theresa, who commissioned the building of Schönbrunn Palace, Vienna developed into the capital of an absolutist centralised state. The mayors were demoted to assistants to the rulers, the citizens lost interest in local politics.

Culture and science were considerably influenced by the French, who came to Vienna in the entourage of Maria Theresa's husband Franz Stephan (Emperor Franz I). Franz also intervened actively in economic policy to encourage domestic production. From the 1750s onwards, the Baroque style, also under French influence, was gradually transformed into Rococo – the most noticeable example in the city centre being the Hall of the Old University.

Emperor Joseph II (1780–90), who as his mother's co-ruler was responsible for making Vienna a garrison city, has gone down in history as the initiator of massive reforms. The "Edict of Tolerance", the dissolution of some monasteries (which caused Pope Pius VI to make a rapid trip to Vienna), and the reforms to the magistracy – highly influential in Vienna – which completely abolished city autonomy, are the most remarkable measures taken by his government.

Also, laws were passed to further science, technology and education, and the Hofburg Theatre was founded as a national drama company. The run up to the new century is marked by the French Revolution, Napoleon's claims to power and the defeat of Rococo by neo-classicism.

Hard times

The 19th century had a turbulent start. Napoleon invaded Vienna twice (1805 and 1809) and resided in Schönbrunn. The battle of Aspern in 1809 was his first defeat, but could not influence the outcome of the war. The Emperor Franz II had acceded to the Austrian crown in 1804 and laid down the crown of the Holy Roman Empire in 1806. Meanwhile the population suffered from housing shortages and rising costs of living.

LEFT: architect Johann Bernhard Fischer von Erlach.
RIGHT: Maria Theresa as a young woman.

The enormous sums of military expenditure had thrown the state finances into disorder, and in 1811 this led to state bankruptcy and a currency collapse, from which Vienna's economy took more than 20 years to recover. Because of this, the city lost its value as a partner for its rulers and was put under strict control. The mayors were forced to obey orders and their status was eroded in the eyes of the population.

The Congress of Vienna

Yet, superficially, the position of Vienna appeared more gorgeous than ever. In 1814–15 the Congress of Vienna, attended by statesmen and

diplomats from all over Europe, met here. The splendid celebrations lasted for months, prompting the slogan "The Congress is dancing" to be coined. The period until 1848, dominated by State Chancellor Metternich, is classified either as Vormärz or Biedermeier, according to one's political point of view. Vormärz equals police state, censorship, loss of civil rights. Biedermeier refers to middle-class comfort and the blossoming of the arts.

The first notable buildings in the neo-classical style were created, among them the Albertina, the Technical University and the Mint. More and more often the survival of the Renaissance fortifications was called into question. The area of

the bastion blown up by the retreating French in 1809 provided the site for two public parks, the Burggarten and Volksgarten. In 1817, the remaining bastions were opened up as promenades and the fortified character of the city was lost. Making use of private transport, the citizens could take outings into the surrounding countryside, particularly into the Vienna Woods.

A few suburbs developed into summer and health resorts. Innovations came in the 1820s and 1830s: 1823 saw the opening of the Danube steamship company, 1828 the building of the first gasworks, 1835 the first exhibition of manufactured goods, and 1837 the opening of the first railway, which was rapidly followed by others. The swift spread of the steam engine also led to the replacement of outdated forms of manufacture by early industrial factories.

The 1848 Revolution

The economic revolution made social problems worse. Poor working conditions, low wages, rising prices, appalling housing conditions and a lack of political rights finally led to the revolution of 1848, in which the middle and working classes at times fought together for the same aims. After the repression of the revolution by the military, there was a period of neo-absolutism.

In 1850, the government decided to combine the suburbs (as far as today's Gürtel) with the city centre for administrative purposes. The city was divided into eight districts (*Bezirke*) and now had a population of 431,000. In 1857, the Emperor Franz Joseph ordered the demolition of the fortifications and the building development of the surrounding *glacis*. The creation of the "Ringstrasse Zone" occupied the most famous architects in Europe for decades. It was a work of civic architecture whose homogeneous nature was unparalleled anywhere in Europe.

In 1861, the community council (Gemeinderat) was re-elected for the first time since the Vormärz. However, less than 1 percent of the population, all privileged property owners, was elegible to vote. In the 1860s and 1870s, considerable improvements were made to the city's infrastructure in addition to the Ringstrasse project. The water supply was improved, the course of the Danube regulated, and the Central Cemetery created. In addition the new Town Hall was built and a new park, the Stadtpark, opened.

LEFT: Graf Latour being lynched in 1848

The Biedermeier Culture

The Biedermeier lifestyle is not a half-forgotten cultural-historical memory. It lives on in the daily lives of the Viennese. Typically Viennese songs will be heard at night, not only in the world-famous *Heurigen*, but also in the little *Beisl* (bistros) of the city suburbs.

Together with the Viennese dialect and a marked desire to avoid conflict, this community singing forms the basis for the traditional Viennese lifestyle. It represents a flight from reality; just as people built houses and villas with ornamental façades, but they also built the first big apartment blocks. In sculpture, Zauner and Marchesi made monuments to the rulers, and Klieber produced his well-crafted ornamental sculptures.

Painting was a favourite art form of the Biedermeier: Waldmüller's landscape and genre paintings; Amerling's sought-after society portraits; Kriehuber's portrait lithography (the art he founded); Daffinger's miniatures; and Fendi's striking portraits of children. However, social problems often appear in the subject matter. Music was dominated by Beethoven and Schubert and by the "fathers" of the Viennese waltz, Strauss and Lanner. The Gesell-

had to come to terms with new ideas during the period of unrest following the Napoleonic wars, so the Biedermeier way of life is a protective haven today.

"Biedermeier" is made up of the adjective *bieder*, meaning worthy, respectable, and a little boring, and the common surname Meier. A rough translation would be "good citizen Meier". The style echoed the conflict between Classicism and Romanticism which raged throughout Europe in the first half of the 19th century. During this period, the middle classes were kept out of politics and could hardly engage in trade either. They withdrew to their private sphere and, in their salons, concentrated on culture. Architects, Kornhäusel among them,

schaft der Musikfreunde (Society of the Friends of Music) and the Vienna Philharmonic Orchestra, together with composers and music publishers, laid the foundations of Vienna's musical greatness.

Franz Grillparzer (1791–1872), the leading poet and dramatist of the day, has been compared to Goethe and Schiller. His work looks back to the classical dramatists, but contains a new realism. Grillparzer, Ferdinand Raimund and Johann Nestroy dominated literature. Theatre blossomed and entertainment venues were much patronised. A busy social life and a comfortable home made for a cultivated lifestyle. Furniture (many pieces designed by Danhauser), paintings, porcelain and silver, clocks and painted glass from the period can be seen in museums and antique shops today.

ABOVE: Franz Schubert (painting by Moritz von Schwind)

After expansion to the south of the city (1874) various suburbs (districts 11 to 19) were incorporated in 1892. But practical developments were left to the city council, already dominated in 1895 by the Christian Socialist Party led by Mayor Karl Lueger (1897–1910). There were radical changes of economic direction (the building of the city gasworks and electricity stations, the communal ownership and electrification of the trams), further improvements to the water supply, and also the first policies for dealing with social and health problems. These developments continued to be financed by loans, so that the city ran up debts of alarming proportions.

In 1905, Lueger incorporated Florisdorf (Vienna 21) on the opposite side of the Danube, simultaneously declaring a green belt of meadows and woodland around the city. Vienna soon had more than 2 million inhabitants. The Social Democrats in opposition demanded a universal franchise, but were knocked back.

The second half of the 19th century was architecturally influenced by Historicism, from which the Viennese Secessionism split off. The work of notable representatives of the Second Viennese School of Medicine (Billroth, Hyrtl, Skoda and others) and the blossoming of other sciences (Sigmund Freud and others) made Vienna world-famous. The great composers, the "Golden" and "Silver" ages of Viennese operetta, the excellent ensembles of the Court Opera, opened in 1869, and the Court Theatre, which moved into the theatre on the Ringstrasse in 1888, the innumerable poets, painters and sculptors, as well as the Künstlerhaus (from which the Secession broke off in 1897), the Musikverein, the art academies and other institutions – all of them, financed by nobility and the upper middle classes, shaped the times which have gained legendary fame as "Ringstrasse Era" and "fin de siècle".

Red Vienna

After the end of World War I, profound political and social changes took place. The general franchise, introduced in 1919, gave the Socialists an absolute majority in the city council, which has been interrupted (forcibly) since then only by Fascism (1934-45). Vienna was also split off from the Federal State of Lower Austria and, since 1922, it has been both city and Federal State.

The period up to 1934 is known throughout Europe as "Red Vienna". Vienna's achievements in the field of communal housing and in programmes for improving health and easing social problems aroused the interest of other European cities. Mayor Karl Seitz and City Councillor Julius Tandler became famous outside Austria's borders, synonymous with the successes of the socialist administration, which would not be moved off course either by repressive measures of the government or by the world economic crisis.

The Nazi era

Escalations in paramilitary confrontation led to civil war in February 1934. It was the first struggle between democratic and Fascist forces in Europe. The Austrian Nationalist victors, under

---

THE RINGSTRASSE ERA

Important figures in the Viennese arts in the latter part of the 19th century included:
- **architects:** Theophil Hansen, Heinrich Ferstel, Karl Hasenauer, Anton Fernkorn. (Secessionist architects Otto Wagner and Joseph Maria Olbrich were active in the 1890s too)
- **composers:** Anton Bruckner, Johannes Brahms, Gustav Mahler, Johann Strauss (father and son), Franz Léhar
- **poets:** Stefan Zweig, Franz Werfel, Hugo Von Hofmannsthal
- **painters:** Hans Makart, Anselm Feuerbach

Federal Chancellor Dollfuss, arrested the mayor and dissolved the democratically elected city council. Vienna lost its independent status.

During the following four years, new goals were set. Above all, the social housing programme was immediately stopped. Austrian Fascism led smoothly into the occupation of Austria in March 1938 and Nazi dictatorship. Photographs showing the Heldenplatz in Vienna with Hitler holding a mass meeting of his supporters tended to mean the numerous "others" who resisted developments were forgotten. Many were persecuted for religious or political reasons and imprisoned in concentration camps.

ing – and the end of the Four Power Occupation, in 1955 the Austrian Constitution was renewed and Austria's perpetual neutrality was declared. Since 1955, a major rebuilding programme has been carried out in Vienna, whereby the designers were always at pains to find an appropriate symbiosis between tradition and modernity. Vienna does not want to become an open-air museum, but the entire inner city has been declared a national monument.

Late 20th-century role

Apart from its reputation as a popular venue for congresses, Vienna is the seat of a number of

Despite Nazi plans, Vienna was spared major changes, for lack of time before the outbreak of World War II. The violent extermination of the Jews and the almost total destruction of the synagogues of Vienna in the infamous "Reichskristallnacht" will not be forgotten, nor will those driven into exile or murdered by the Nazis. Vienna suffered considerable bomb damage, most of which could be repaired. The public buildings were rebuilt in their original styles.

After the liberation of Vienna in 1945 – St Stephen's Cathedral caught fire during the fight-

United Nations bodies. The IAEO (International Atomic Energy Organisation), the UNIDO (International Industrial Development Organisation) and a number of other international bodies are in the International Centre, known as UNO City, on the left bank of the Danube.

Since the break-up of the former Soviet Union, Vienna (conscious of its cultural links and associated responsibilities) has acquired a new role in world affairs as a meeting place and bridgehead between East and West. This role was further enhanced when Austrians voted by two to one to join the European Union. After enduring hundreds of years of political turbulence, Vienna at last seemed to have reached calmer waters.

Left: memorial plaque in Karl-Marx-Hof.
Above: "yes" to Europe in the 1994 plebiscite

c der Natur gezeichnet und geätzt von Carl Schütz in Wien 1784.

Haupt Ansicht der Residenzstadt Wien,
und des grösten Theils ihrer Vorstädte, von Belvedere anzusehen.

| Maria Hilf; | St Ulrich. | Kohlkirche. | Augustiner Hofkirche. |
| Pfarkirche auf der Wieden. | Pfarkirche in der Josephstadt. | Pfarkirche in der Alstergasse. | |

*Vüe de la Capitale de Vienne, et d'une
grande partie de ses Fauxbourgs, prise du coté du Belvedere.*

St. Stephan Domkirche.   die Universität.   Salesianerinnen auf dem Rennweg.   Elisabethanerinnen.
die Leopoldstadt.   Oberkirche zu Belvedere.   Augspiner auf der Landstraße.

THE HABSBURGS

Successive Habsburg rulers made personal sacrifices to keep the dynasty going.
Autocrats and eccentrics, they retained power for more than six centuries

The historian Brigitte Hamann has put into words what many locals and tourists think but dare not actually say: "Really, Vienna is far too large a city for such a little country."

How true. Austria is of modest proportions, but it has as its capital one of the most celebrated metropolises in the world. It has few problems coming to terms with this discrepancy. The architectural magnificence was the work of the Habsburg dynasty, whose rise and fall was synonymous with the glory and misery of the house of Austria. *The Habsburgs* would make a good title for a never-ending television series, full of sex and crime, power struggles and romantic dramas, victorious battles and lost domains, madmen with a touch of genius and geniuses declared to be madmen.

Swiss nobility

The Habsburg, the headquarters of the Habsburg clan, was built in about 1020 in the Aargau in Switzerland. The Habsburgs in those days were simple landed gentry, and when on a September night in 1273 Count Rudolf von Habsburg received the news that he had just been elected head of the Holy Roman Empire in France, he thought at first that it must be a joke.

But he soon got used to his new status and laid the foundations of the Habsburg power. His sons inherited the wealthy duchies of Austria, along the Danube, and Styria, which thereafter remained in the family for over 600 years. Rudolf IV paid particular attention to the creation of his capital and residential city, Vienna, where he continued the construction of St Stephen's Cathedral and in 1365 founded the "Alma Mater Rudolfina", one of the oldest universities in the world.

During the 14th and 15th centuries the Habsburgs lost almost all their lands in Switzerland, but extended their domains to include Carinthia and Krain, Tyrol and Trieste. Apart from a few

PRECEDING PAGES: Vienna from the Belvedere, 1784.
LEFT: Emperor Franz Joseph I.
RIGHT: Empress Elisabeth, known as "Sissi"

interruptions, members of the family wore the imperial crown of the Holy Roman Empire until its eclipse in 1806.

Despite the many centuries of Habsburg rule, popular memory is focused less on the dynasty as a whole than on a number of its individual members. Maximilian I, the "Last Knight", who

came to power in 1493, was such a character. To this day, the precipitous "Martinswand" to the north of Innsbruck is a popular excursion destination. Whilst hunting chamois in its rocky crevasses, Emperor Max was trapped in a dangerous position when, in the nick of time, he was rescued by a host of angels (probably a band of sturdy Tyrolean mountain guides, no less). Maximilian was not only an adventurous mountaineer, jouster and archer, but also a talented singer and poet – and a cunning political schemer too.

A skilful marriage policy meant that the Habsburgs gained control of prosperous Burgundy as well as Spain and Naples-Sicily, not to mention the American colonies. Maximilian's grandson, the future Karl V, was thus able to inherit an empire over which "the sun never set".

The rulers of the house of Habsburg were fond of using marriage contracts as a means of power. The family was always highly successful in the delicate marriage market of European royal houses. Marriages were arranged purely for political advantage and took no account of personal feelings.

In her book *The Bartered Habsburg Daughters* the publicist Thea Leitner describes graphi-

ARRANGED MARRIAGES

The children of Habsburg rulers were often forced into unions which strengthened the family's political hand

her as a benevolent mother figure. She herself, however, succeeded in breaking out of her predestined role in order to achieve a degree of power unheard-of for women in her day. When her father, Karl V, died without male issue, it looked as if all the enemies of the Habsburg family had been waiting for just this moment.

In Paris it was claimed that "The house of Habsburg no longer exists", and the troops of Elector Albert of Bavaria marched as far as Sankt Pölten. But Maria Theresa demonstrated that she possessed a

cally how Habsburg princesses in particular were often contracted in marriage whilst they were still babies, to young boys, old men, lunatics and brutal upstarts. *Tu, felix Austria, nube* – Let the others wage war, but you, O blessed Austria, shall marry, was the guiding principle. Neighbouring countries may have mocked Austria over the centuries, but the truth of the motto was proved by the personal misery of countless Habsburg women.

The guardian of virtue

The great Empress Maria Theresa also bartered her children with no apparent second thoughts, despite the fact that her favourite portraits depict

determined fighting spirit. In a dramatic, tear-filled audience in September 1741 she begged the Hungarian estates at Bratislava to come to her assistance. The magnates were deeply impressed and swore loyalty to death to their enchanting young Empress. The Bavarians were driven out of Austria, France sued for peace and Maria Theresa's consort Franz Stephan of Lorraine was elected Emperor of Germany.

Maria Theresa was an energetic woman whose life was largely governed by her love for her husband, despite the fact that she had to keep turning a blind eye to his numerous affairs and gambling debts. When Franz Stephan had overstepped the mark again, the otherwise down-to-earth Empress even had the idea of abolishing vice within her realm.

In 1753 she founded her famous "chastity commission", which was ridiculed throughout the continent. Secret agents were engaged to investigate frivolous behaviour in theatres and ballrooms, travellers' luggage was searched for unsuitable literature and whole carriage-loads of prostitutes were transported from the pleasure-loving capital to the depths of the provinces. The great lover Casanova, who happened to be staying in Vienna, was confronted by these guardians of virtue. In his memoirs he complains bitterly about the "bigotry" of the Empress.

ing to countless hymns of praise and still remaining unattainably distant from his subjects.

Franz Joseph saw himself as an absolute sovereign and adopted a centralised system of government, entering into a close alliance with the Church in order to combat liberalism. His marriage to Empress Elisabeth, the world-famous beauty known as "Sissi", was in reality a marital purgatory, stifled by the chilly pomp of the Viennese Hofburg with its inhuman ceremony.

Death of an empire

Emperor Franz Joseph was buried in 1916. Following the suicide of his only son, Archduke

These stories paint the Habsburgs as benevolent eccentrics. Emperor Franz Joseph, for example, has long since been buried under a mountain of clichés. Initially he was deeply suspicious of liberal trends and innovations, rigorously suppressing the aspirations of the various nationalities and fusing them into a single state. In later years, however, a series of defeats abroad forced him to adopt a more conciliatory attitude. "It was very nice, I enjoyed it very much" – with this standard formula he travelled through Austria-Hungary, pinching children's cheeks and listen-

LEFT: Otto von Habsburg.
ABOVE: funeral of Princess Zita, the last Habsburg ruler

Rudolf, at Mayerling in 1889 and the assassination of Franz Ferdinand in Sarajevo in 1914, Franz Joseph was succeeded by his brother's second son. The latter, however, as Karl I, had no chance of stopping the disintegration of the vast empire. In 1918 he was forced to abdicate, and in 1922 the last Habsburg to sit on the Austrian imperial throne died in exile in Madeira of pneumonia and despair.

Karl's eldest son, Otto Habsburg-Lorraine, renounced his claims to the throne in 1961. Since then he has been allowed to enter Austria, and political thin ice is avoided. The Republic of Austria still indulges occasionally in a hint of Habsburg nostalgia – but a hint is enough.

MUSIC

From wandering minstrels to the Philharmonic Orchestra,
Vienna has always been a city of musical superlatives

Everybody has heard the old saying that music is the lifeblood of Vienna, that here music is the very elixir of life. On a journey to Vienna the sound of music echoes around you at every step, for the treble clef provides the key to many of the city's secrets. You will find that music is played on every imaginable scale here – from the grand State Opera to the pocket-sized Taschenoper – but always with style. Vienna's top notes soar to heights of incomparable brilliance, but the city can also swirl round to the lilting strains of a waltz or nod off complacently to the grumbling sentiment of a Viennese folksong. And yet, Vienna also pricks up its ears whenever a new tune is played. Modern opera or jazz respectlessly crossover or are deeply traditional: the best thing is to keep an open ear yourself.

Soloists, orchestras and choirs

The Babenbergs had hardly had time to establish Vienna as their capital at the height of the Middle Ages before the magnetic attraction of the Viennese court began to lure strolling *Minnesingers*. Very little is known today about the most famous of these wandering minstrels, Walther von der Vogelweide. It seems certain, however, that Duke Leopold V and Friedrich I were both admirers of contemporary lyric poetry, and that it was in Vienna that Walther was initiated into the art of "Singing and Telling" – the secrets of narrating poetry to music – and that he himself greatly enriched the city's musical tradition.

Walther was obliged to leave Vienna eventually, but not before he had laid one of the foundation stones of Vienna as a city of music. To this day, the capital of Austria spares neither effort nor money in its determination to maintain its reputation as a city of musical superlatives. The world-famous names adorning the

PRECEDING PAGES: seeing and being seen in a Burgtheater box; ball in the Hofburg.
LEFT: concert in the Musikverein hall.
RIGHT: Papageno in Mozart's *The Magic Flute*

posters you will see around the city at any season of the year speak for this as eloquently as do the statistics. The latter prove that, every year on 1 January, some 500 million viewers switch on their television to watch the New Year's Concert by the Vienna Philharmonic Orchestra (Wiener Philharmoniker). The concert hall of

the Musikverein, dating from 1870 and elaborately decorated with gold leaf, seats 2,000, yet this represent only a quarter of audience capacity each day in Vienna for fans of serious music. The range of performances on offer extends from the Philharmonic Orchestra in the Musikverein to the typical Viennese songs performed in the traditional wine taverns, the *Heurige*, for in Vienna music is very much an integral part of social life on every level.

In 1498, the Habsburg emperor Maximilian I founded the Court Orchestra, and a succession of famous composers earned their daily bread – often meagre enough, alas – by taking up the conductor's baton at the Hofburg. In the same year, the emperor also summoned twelve boys to his court, thereby establishing the Vienna Boys' Choir (Wiener Sängerknaben), an institution which can look back on 500 years of history. The choir of today comprises some 100 carefully selected boys, whose imperial livery has been replaced by the famous blue-and-white sailor suits. Nonetheless their voices ring out as crystal-clear as ever on Sunday mornings at 9.15 in the chapel of the Hofburg, where they sing Mass, accompanied by members of the orchestra of the Vienna State Opera.

Other emperors too, such as Empress Maria Theresa and Emperor Joseph II, were important

he showed not a scrap of envy but was willing to use his influence on behalf of a youthful genius of somewhat boorish demeanour: Wolfgang Amadeus Mozart.

Born in Salzburg and presented to half of Europe as a child prodigy by his father, Mozart settled in Vienna as a freelance composer at the age of 25. It was in Vienna that he was handed around courtly circles as a charming genius, only to be dropped again when he revealed himself as the free-thinking composer who set Beaumarchais' revolutionary *Figaro* to music. And it was here, too, that he wrote his most important musical compositions and finally

patrons of music, with the result that the lure of Vienna became more and more irresistible for foreign musicians.

Vienna's great composers

Christoph Willibald Gluck, who was Master of the Royal Music under Maria Theresa, does not often appear on the programme of the world's opera houses today, but his opera *Orpheus and Eurydice*, the premiere of which he conducted personally in 1762, paved the way for the achievements of the operatic composers of the Viennese Classical period. He was one of those fortunate musicians whose reputation and material prosperity were so firmly established that

died, obsessed by dark premonitions, whilst still working on his *Requiem*, which had been commissioned by an unknown patron.

Joseph Haydn, a contemporary and admirer of Mozart, had already achieved recognition at

---

MUSICAL EMPERORS

In addition to their patronage of court music, several Habsburg emperors composed music themselves, and some of their works are very creditable indeed. Ferdinand I was the first emperor to try his hand at composing in 1637; his example was followed by Leopold I, Joseph I and Karl VI.

the court of Count Esterházy in Eisenstadt before coming to Vienna. It was he who persuaded Mozart to try his luck in the Viennese capital. It was Haydn, too, who invited a brilliant young pianist from Bonn to Vienna. When Mozart heard the 17-year-old Ludwig van Beethoven play for the first time, he said, "Pay attention to him; people will talk about this man one day." Beethoven did not in fact settle in Vienna until after Mozart's death, nor did he study for much longer under his teacher Haydn

SERIOUS TALENT

Three musical geniuses – Mozart, Haydn and Beethoven – came to Vienna to live and work, and a fourth, Schubert, was born in the city

not only in the realms of opera; and Beethoven overturned the established traditions and gave unique expression to his enlightened ideals of freedom and humanity.

The only one of the great composers who was actually born in Vienna was Franz Schubert. Like Mozart, he died young, and for many years he was dismissed as a superficial Biedermeier artist. By the bicentenary of his birthday, however, the old clichés had been revealed for the untruths they really were. "I was born for

after his arrival; nonetheless, musical history unites the three giants as the "First Viennese School", whose magical music dissolves the boundaries between ponderousness and lightness, between seriousness and gaiety. It was Haydn who developed the string quartet to create what is now known as chamber music; Mozart's compositions opened up new worlds

FAR LEFT: Christoph Willibald Gluck, Court composer under Maria Theresa.
LEFT: a reflective Brahms memorial in the Central Cemetery.
ABOVE LEFT: portrait of Johann Strauss the Younger.
ABOVE RIGHT: Gustav Mahler

no other purpose than to compose", the introverted musician maintained. He only came out of himself when surrounded by his closest friends, who gathered together for the legendary Schubertiades. Schubert wrote more than 600 songs and perfected this particular genre. Towards the end of the 19th century, Hugo Wolf set the poems of Goethe and Mörike to music and set new standards in the sphere of lieder.

Apart from Beethoven, Johannes Brahms and Anton Bruckner were the two most important composers of serious music in Vienna during the 19th century. The city, however, was turning with increasing enthusiasm towards works of a lighter nature. Johann Strauss the Elder and Josef Lanner beat time for the first waltzes, thereby opening the door for one of the most lively periods of Viennese musical history, which was to reach its zenith under Johann Strauss the Younger. The Golden Age of operetta, for which Franz von Suppé and Carl Millöcker are also remembered, finally gave way to the "Silver Age", the era of the Hungarian composers Franz Lehár and Emmerich Kálmán.

The intoxicating lightness could only hide for a short while the fact that the possibilities for artistic expression in tonal music were

Jazz and rock

Hardly a year passes without providing the occasion to honour one of the legends of the Viennese musical tradition by permitting him to call the tune throughout the year in the city's concert and opera programmes. It is no wonder that the "light music" scene tends to remain quietly in the background. This is not for lack of quality – on the contrary, much of its music is for a smaller audience of connoisseurs

Joe Zawinul has earned himself a fine international reputation in the realms of jazz. He has established himself in the U.S. as the congenial partner of Miles Davis, as the leader of

slowly being exhausted and that a revolution was on the way. Arnold Schönberg wrote the first completely atonal piece of music in 1909. Feeling the necessity for a new order and new rules, from 1920 he developed the principle of twelve-tone music. Together with his pupils Alban Berg and Anton Webern, he represents the watershed in the musical world; from now on, increasingly radical approaches were to widen the musical spectrum. The tradition was continued by György Ligeti, Friedrich Cerha and Ernst Krenek. And the young generation of contemporary composers has finally acquired a female protagonist in Olga Neuwirth.

Weather Reports and as an innovative spirit who has influenced a wide range of light music. The jazz guitarists Wolfgang Muthspiel and Karl Ratzer have also made a name for themselves far beyond the city boundaries. Meanwhile, The Vienna Art Orchestra has pursued its own experimental style for more than 20 years.

Kurt Ostbahn is a Viennese rock 'n' roll pin-up; his backing group, the "Chefpartie", draws a fine line between feeling, intellect and convincing humanity. The songs of "Ostbahn Kurti", as he is known, give the listener some idea of the character of the citizens of Vienna and put the clichés of traditional Viennese songs in the shade.

Concert halls and music stages

You can hear original contemporary interpretations of Viennese songs and *Schrammelmusik* in the Metropol (XVII., Hernsaler Hauptstrasse 55; tel: 433 543) or during a session in the Vorstadt-Gasthaus (XVI., Herbststrasse 37; tel: 4 93 17 88).

Apart from the classic Jazzland (I., Franz-Josefs-Kai 29, Tel. 533 2575), Porgy & Bess (I., Spiegelgasse 1, Tel. 512 8438), which is run by Matthias Rüegg, the leader of the Vienna Art Orchestra, has established a reputation as an interesting jazz club. Listening pleasures are also to be gained – often quite by chance – if

tially the object of outspoken criticism. The "House on the Ring" is still the object of attacks to this day, less for artistic reasons than when the city's cultural budget is due for review. It has nothing to do with a lack of popularity.

Vienna's temples of music can also be proud of steadily rising visitor statistics. In the case of the Opera House this is partly due to the official orchestra, the Vienna Philharmonic Orchestra, which plays there daily from September until June (but not in the evenings). Tickets for Philharmonic concerts outside work-time (and the dress rehearsals, which are open to the public) are especially sought-after. They are held on

you attend one of the Jazz brunches which have recently become fashionable in the city, or if you visit one of the many bars offering live music.

The top address for opera fans, with illustrious stars on stage and at the conductor's desk, is undoubtedly the Vienna State Opera House (Staatsoper) (I., Opernring 2; tel: 514 44 2959). The opera house was completed in 1869 as the first of the magnificent buildings bordering the Ring-strasse; like every architectural innovation in Vienna before and since, however, it was ini-

Left: jazz on a Sunday morning, Augarten.
Above : opera in the Rathausplatz

VIENNESE SONGS

The best place to discover traditional Viennese songs (those unique, melodious swan songs extolling inebriation, death and the transitory nature of life) or that other Viennese invention, *Schrammelmusik* (a combination of violin and concertina), is in a *Heuriger*. The legendary Schrammel ensemble, which first performed in 1878 with an original cast of two violins, a guitar and a clarinet (later replaced by the accordion), was formed by the brothers Johann and Josef Schrammel. There is a memorial to the quartet at Elterleinplatz in the 17th district.

The Waltz Kings

Schubert's death in 1827 marked the end of the Classical Era. From this point onwards, musicians in the Austrian capital were increasingly heard playing a new tune, one which was mostly written in 3/4 time. Gently lilting tunes composed in the 18th century were influenced by the Ländler, a country dance from Bohemia; then, during the Congress of Vienna, the new dance suddenly became all the rage. In social circles people began to dance in pairs, succumbing to the sensuous delights of the new rhythms. Waltzes and polkas, and later the operetta, took

gifted musicians. Lanner's oeuvre reached its zenith in his *Schönbrunn Waltz*, whilst Strauss the Elder composed a much-loved evergreen in the *Radetzky March*, which is always played as the final encore at the New Year's Concert in the Musikverein.

The hit of the century, however, was *On the Beautiful Blue Danube*, composed by Strauss the Elder's son. Johann Junior challenged his father's musical success at the age of 19, when he first performed in public with his own orchestra in Heitzing. Less than a decade later, almost 300 musicians played in various ensembles under his direction. Johann Strauss the Younger was perhaps the first entertainer to be drawn into the maelstrom of show busi-

Vienna, the erstwhile world capital of highbrow music, by storm. Serious musicians were aghast and turned their backs on the former cradle of "real" music, complaining that the city had clearly started to pander to the charms of popular taste and had fallen victim to the frivolities of light music.

Johann Strauss the Elder (1804–49) and Josef Lanner (1801–43) were the first orchestral conductors who succeeded in appealing to people of all social classes with their tuneful melodies and sweeping rhythms. Initially they performed together, with Johann Strauss playing the viola, in a string quartet which gradually expanded to become a respectable orchestra. Success, however, resulted in rivalry and disagreements between the two composers, although both of them were inventive and

ness. He dashed from place to place, not only taking up his baton on the conductor's podium, but also playing first violin. For many years, however, he avoided the theatre, and it took a great deal of persuasion to make him change his mind.

Strauss the Younger's third operetta, *Die Fledermaus*, was premièred in 1874. It was a remarkable success and the crowning glory of the Golden Era of Viennese operetta. To this day it is performed every New Year's Eve at the State Opera. The enthusiastic echoes of this intoxicating work are sometimes interpreted as the final brilliance of a dying age. The Waltz King himself did not live to see what the new century would bring: he died on 3 June 1899.

ABOVE: Strauss's music in concert

Sunday mornings in the Musikverein (Association of the Friends of Music) (I., Bösendorferstrasse 12, Tel. 505 8190), but most tickets are reserved for subscribers. At the Musikverein, an endless procession of famous international orchestras, first-class soloists and conductors offers a consolation prize for those who are unable to experience the Vienna Philharmonic Orchestra live in its legendary concert hall.

The second most famous orchestra, the Vienna Symphony Orchestra, has its main concert hall just a few steps away. The Concert House (Konzerthaus) (III., Lothringerstrasse 20, Tel. 712 1211) is the second essential port of call

The object of good-natured ridicule, it was seen to provide shallow, frivolous entertainment in the form of operettas and musicals. Having worked successfully towards a new image, the Folk Opera is starting to assume a more central role.

Chamber operas dating from the 17th, 18th and 20th century are presented on Vienna's third permanent operatic stage, the little Chamber Opera (Kammeroper) at the Fleischmarkt (I., Fleischmarkt 24, Tel. 513 6072). Here, youthful talents first earn their spurs and you will also find one of the city's rare conventional stages.

ABOVE: Capelle and Ballet performing at the Kursalon, Stadtpark

for music fans. It offers a high-quality standard programme and has also come to be regarded as the more dynamic of the two great concert halls following its introduction of unconventional concert cycles which are devoted to avant-garde music as well as old works. It is also famous for its festivals such as "Vienna Modern" or "Film and Music".

There has been movement on the opera scene, too. The Folk Opera (Volksoper) (IX., Währinger Strasse 78, Tel. 514 44 2959) stood for a long time in the shadow of the State Opera.

The Neue Oper Wien (III., Ungarstrasse 17–19, Tel. 712 1487) and the Wiener Taschenoper (V., Straussengasse 14, Tel. 586 5149) are the names of just two of the independent groups which perform exclusively 20th-century opera, from Alban Berg to multimedia operas. They put on some ten performances a year in the most unusual venues; sometimes in the generous space of the museum theatre or the Semperdepot, and sometimes in the more intimate atmosphere of a hotel in the Old City. Their dream of finding their own opera house for contemporary works and dance has already been discussed in official quarters. Whether it will become reality or not remains to be seen.

MUSIC IN VIENNA

The city reverberates with the achievements of past and present-day Viennese composers, musicians and ensembles – all celebrated the world over

Vienna has music in its blood, and music draws people here. Many great composers have lived and worked here, and no other city on any continent can boast two outstanding concert houses with two of the world's top orchestras and the world's most famous boys' choir.

REJECTION OF THE GREATS

But the city has not always been a haven for leading musicians and composers; sometimes they have been cold-shouldered during their lifetimes. Mozart, for example (pictured as a child, above), struggled throughout his short life to achieve recognition and a decent income. Schönberg, Berg and Webern were not even granted the luxury of being ignored: at one performance of Schönberg's chamber symphony in the Musikverein building in 1913, police had to evacuate the elegantly dressed audience when they whistled their disapproval and fights broke out.

The great 19th-century *Lieder* writer Hugo Wolf earned a meagre income from his music; composer Anton Bruckner supplemented his income by moonlighting as an organist and teacher; and Gustav Mahler had to convert from Judaism to Christianity before he could get a job as artistic director of the Vienna Court Opera.

The great cabaret artist and actor Helmut Qualtinger once said: "In Vienna, you have to die before they'll drink a toast to you. But then they'll remember you for a long time." This applies to musicians above all.

△ **MUSIC IN THE AIR**
When the weather's fine, the musicians come out into the open air. One venue for outdoor concerts is among the atmospheric Roman ruins in the gardens of Schönbrunn Palace (XIII, Schönbrunner Schlossstrasse).

▽ **LUDWIG VAN BEETHOVEN, 1815**
Dozens of places commemorate Beethoven, owing to the fact that he was a very difficult tenant who suffered from chronic itchy feet. He moved house some 80 times during the period after 1792 when he settled in Vienna.

◁ **EARLY INSTRUMENT**
This fortepiano, made in 1796, belonged to Joseph Haydn, and propped on it is an original score in the composer's hand. It can be seen at VI, Haydngasse 19.

THE WALTZ KING ▷
Johann Strauss the Younger's waltz music captured the mood of his time. It transported the Viennese to a beautiful dream world.

◁ FULL HOUSE

The Viennese musical year is such a long succession of concerts and festivals that there simply are not enough concert halls to accommodate them all. So the city's many orchestras and choirs perform in other venues too, such as palaces and churches. One such is the Lichtentaler Pfarrkirche (IX, Marktgasse), where the music is of concert quality.

▽ MORE THAN ONE STRING TO HIS BOW

The city has not one, but two internationally renowned orchestras: the Vienna Philharmonic and the Vienna Symphony Orchestra. Both need to keep their instruments in tip-top condition, and Otmar Lang (I, Canovagasse 4) repairs and maintains the Philharmonic's venerable violins, violas, cellos and double basses.

◁ THE MAGIC FLUTE

Mozart's last opera gained a lukewarm reception at its première on 30 September 1791, held in the Freihaustheater, now known as the Theater an der Wien. *The Magic Flute* later became an enormous success, but it was too late for the composer, who died on 5 December of the same year, lonely, exhausted and misunderstood by the music world.

IN THE FOOTSTEPS OF GREAT MEN

The homes of many Viennese composers are now owned by the city of Vienna and are open to the public. They have become museums in their own right, complete with original scores, instruments and other items showing how the great musicians lived and worked.

The most popular of these is the Figarohaus pictured above (I, Domgasse 5), where Mozart lived from 1784 to 1787, the happiest years of his time in Vienna.

The Pasqualatihaus (I, Mölker Bastei 8) is where Beethoven composed *Fidelio* and his violin concerto, amongst other pieces.

Franz Schubert's Biedermeier-style birthplace is at IX, Nussdorfer Strasse 43, and you can also see the room where he died at IV, Kettenbrückengasse 6.

Joseph Haydn's life and work are documented in his house at VI, Haydngasse 19, which also includes a small room devoted to Johannes Brahms.

The last stage in this musical pilgrimage is the house (II, Praterstrasse 54) where Johann Strauss the Younger lived and wrote from 1863 to 1870,

All of these historic buildings are open daily except Mondays, from 9am to 12.15pm and from 1pm to 4.30pm.

CULTURE

The Viennese have excelled in all the arts, from painting to theatre.
Favour swings continually between the conservative and the avant-garde

The climate of Vienna always was changeable, but that has made its ground all the more fertile. At any given time, a sudden cold spell might suddenly engulf the cultural scene, or else there could be a change of wind direction or a spell of invigorating warmth, depending on what interests the ruler of the time pursued. Maria Theresa was one of the first to establish a climate in which art could flourish in her capital. Repressed under Metternich, Vienna's creative genius burst forth once more at the beginning of this century, sowing the seeds of the modern age. The Nazi regime tore out the very roots of this artistic blossoming and left behind it a cultural wasteland. Only slowly did a new awareness start to grow amongst Vienna's artistic spirits. Today, the city's cultural scene is once more refreshingly inventive and encourages the visitor to embark on a series of interesting voyages of exploration.

In focus

Art lovers are bound to find themselves pushed for time whenever they visit Vienna, for the city boasts a Museum of Art History (Kunsthistorisches Museum) with a unique collection of Flemish and Italian paintings, a newly restored gallery of 19th and 20th century art, and two museums dedicated to the vast range of modern and postmodern works, not to mention a lively gallery scene where you will find everything from a watercolour landscape to a video sculpture, from a virtual-reality adventure to a photorealistic world view. *(See pages 242–5.)*

The Old Masters

If you want to make an in-depth study of the art scene in Vienna including the first beginnings of Austrian painting, you should start off with a tour of the sacred buildings in the city centre. The oldest church in Vienna is St Rupert's *(see page 116)*. It houses the city's oldest stained-glass windows, which date from the 13th century. Also dating from Gothic times is the earliest extant altarpiece, today one of the most valuable treasures in the Cathedral Museum and Diocesan *(see page 113)* next door to St Stephen's Cathedral. The portrait of Rudolph IV was painted in about 1365 and is one of the earliest head-and-shoulders portraits in Western

art. The second key work is the altarpiece *The Flight to Egypt* in the Scottish Church (Schottenkirche) *(see page 104)*. Dating from the 15th century, the picture is of interest not only to art historians. Historians and cartographers discovered that the background depicts the earliest known topographical view of the city.

Viennese architecture and painting reached its first climax in the Baroque era. Perfection of form and opulent decoration found expression in sacred buildings as well as in the monuments erected by the Habsburgs. In the capital of an empire which held many peoples under its sway, the universal language was that of power, and it was under the Empress Maria Theresa

---

LEFT: first floor gallery in the Museum of Art History.
ABOVE RIGHT: staircase in the Museum of Modern Art

that Vienna first asserted its status within the European context. Vienna became a magnet for creative artists. Having established his reputation with the monastery church at Melk, Johann Michael Rottmayr completed the dome frescoes of the churches of St Charles Borromeo (Karlskirche) and St Peter's (Peterskirche). The ceiling fresco of St Anne's Church (Annakirche) and the decoration of the Hall of Honour (Prunksaal) of the National Library (Hofbibliothek) are unmis-

A BREATH OF FRESH AIR

The Secessionist motto was: "Art for the age and freedom for art". But buildings designed by Seccessionist architects were derided by the conservative public

nature and slowly moved towards the Impressionist ideal of capturing the essence of a single moment. Ferdinand Georg Waldmüller produced idealised pictures of a rural idyll, and especially his landscape paintings of scenes in the country surrounding Vienna became synonymous with the art of the Biedermeier era. Together with Waldmüller, Rudolf von Alt, Schubert's friend Moritz von Schwind and Peter Fendi were the characteristic artists who influenced

takably the work of Daniel Gran. The finishing touches were added by the undisputed master of the era, Franz Anton Maulpertsch. A selection of Maulpertsch's works, which transcend the summit of High Baroque and point the way towards the art of the 19th century, can be seen in the collection displayed in the Lower Belvedere (*see pages 178–9*).

A new era

As a reaction against the extroverted style of representational painting, the pendulum started to swing back in the other direction with the dawn of the new century. The format of paintings became smaller, subjects were based on

this period of Austrian Realism. For the first time, a woman, Tina Blau, was to be found in the circle of artists surrounding the mood painter Emil Jakob Schindler. Her Prater landscapes made a substantial contribution to the Viennese version of the open-air painting techniques which had been imported from France.

If Waldmüller's name is always mentioned in connection with the first half of the 19th century, then Hans Makart surely belongs to the second half, to the period of Historicism and the construction of the Ringstrasse. Intensive colours, vast canvases and historic themes characterise Makart's style, which recalls the

Baroque era. He himself became a very fashionable artist during the materialistic euphoria which characterised the period of industrial expansion during the 19th century.

At court and in Viennese society, conformity and conservatism were the two most important commandments. Viewing everything new with increasing suspicion, the good citizens of Vienna fought all the more fiercely to preserve the status quo from anything which might cause the slightest irritation. Despite all their efforts, however, nothing could prevent the changes awaiting Vienna at the turn of the 20th century.

erected to house the new association, not in the shadow of the Academy of Fine Arts but rather behind that illustrious edifice's back, the local citizens were vocal in their dismissal of the new masterpiece as a "Forkful of Cabbage". The new association aimed to breathe fresh life into the moribund art scene.

Olbrich, like almost all his important fellow artists, was a disciple of Otto Wagner, the leading figure amongst the Secession architects. Wagner adopted utility as the credo of architectural theory and boldly adopted new building methods and materials. The Post Office Savings Bank (Postsparkassenamt), the restored local

The Secession and the modern era in Vienna

Gustav Klimt, a follower of both Symbolism and Impressionism, was the only Secessionist artist to enjoy at least moderate fame during his lifetime. He was one of the 19 painters, architects and graphic artists who branched away from the conservative Artists' House Association (Künstlerhaus-Vereinigung) dominated by Makart to form the Association of the Secession. When they saw the filigree dome of the Jugendstil building which Joseph Maria Olbrich

LEFT: Golden Chamber, Lower Belvedere.
ABOVE: inscription on the Secession

train station at Karlsplatz, and the Majolica House with its uniquely decorated façade on the Linke Wienzeile, are the principal examples of the master architect's style. Although he enjoyed a large measure of success and numerous public commissions, many of Wagner's projects were never completed.

Adolf Loos, thirty years younger than Wagner, was even more uncompromising in his adoption of the principle of functionality. He attacked the Ringstrasse with its border of pompous buildings in the Historicist style as a sham, and the first house he built became immediately the object of violent criticism and attack. "A monster of a house", the citizens said when they saw the unadorned façade fronting onto the Michaelerplatz opposite the north face of the Baroque Hofburg, and local legend insists that the elderly emperor Franz Joseph henceforth refused to use the Michaelerplatz palace entrance in order to avoid having to look at this eyesore which had apparently been built in blatant disrespect of his person.

The angular, linear nude portraits by Egon Schiele were also regarded as a tasteless provocation when they were first displayed. Schiele was the most talked-about, if not the first, protagonist of Austrian Expressionism. Richard Gerstl before him, who committed suicide at the

age of 25 in 1908, was the first artist to distance himself from academicism as well as the decorative Secessionist style. The third member of the group was Oskar Kokoschka. Born in Pöchlarn and determined to overturn all bourgeois principles, Kokoschka began his career as a theatrical poet as well as an artist, and actually left Vienna in 1916.

After both Klimt and Schiele had died young, Kokoschka remained alone at the centre of the Viennese modern art scene. More than the works of any other artist, his landscapes, portraits and allegories represent the entire range of Austrian painting during this century. In 1933 he returned briefly to Vienna, but was forced to leave in a hurry in view of the turn of political events. Like all forms of avant-garde art, Kokoschka's paintings were stigmatised as "non-art".

Following the trauma of World War I, the only creativity which was able to flourish in Vienna for many years was destroyed by Christian conservatives and right-wing radicals and finally annihilated by the National Socialists. Artists, the one remaining hope of the modern era, many of them of Jewish origin, were expelled or murdered. This brutal break in the artistic creativity of the country continues to affect its cultural life to this day.

After 1945

The first glittering figure to appear on the art scene after World War II was a priest. In 1954, Monsignore Otto Mauer opened the Gallery near St Stephen's, just a stone's throw from his main place of work. It could not provide young artists with a sound financial backing, but at least it offered them a first liberal platform. Above all, however, this unconventional cleric was a respected and eloquent spokesman who did valuable pioneer work in drawing public attention to the work of such luminaries as Arnulf Rainer, Josef Mikl, Markus Prachensky, Maria Lassnig, Ernst Fuchs and Friedensreich Hundertwasser. Today the list of creative young men and women whom Otto Mauer gathered round him reads like a list of the professors of Vienna's academies of art over the past few decades. Their paths may have led in different directions, but they all succeeded in establishing their reputation.

Arnulf Rainer was greatly respected by the international art market for his radical "anti-

SHOCK VALUE

In the 1950s, "painting in order to abandon painting" was a guiding principle. Arnulf Rainer established a radical concept of (self-) destruction which led from his *Self-Portrait as a Dead Man* to his characteristic technique of painting over self-portraits or works by Goya and Rembrandt.

At the beginning of the following decade a group of young artists calling themselves The Viennese Action Artists shocked the conservative establishment by placing human bodies, blood, excrement and dead animals at the centre of their artistic experiments.

portraits". Alfred Hrdlicka, a graphic artist and sculptor as well as a provocative and prophetic man, dismissed the horrors of war and violence in expressive caricatures. Recently, Josef Mikl designed the ceiling painting for the Redoutensaal of the Hofburg, which has been reconstructed after being destroyed by fire in 1992. Maria Lassnig's work is characterised by an interesting cycle of self-portraits.

Apart from such individual artists as Fritz Wotruba, Bruno Gironcoli and Walter Pichler, two schools determined the artistic developments of the postwar decades. They could not have been more different. Today, when Her-

Their art must be seen as a rebellion against the narrow-minded, conservative climate which still dominated the city twenty years after the end of World War II.

The school of Fantastic Realism, by contrast, was exactly what the public wanted to see. Although its appearance was delayed by a few years, it was a reaction to Surrealism. Thanks to the contributions of Ernst Fuchs, Arik Bauer and Rudolf Hausner it represented the first commercially successful genre of the postwar years.

Another artist who refuses to fit into any category is Friedensreich Hundertwasser, perhaps

mann Nitsch announces another of his artistic events, then the public knows that they will be confronted with ritualised action painting in which the artist will probably use the blood of animals in order to realise his idea of a *Gesamtkunstwerk* (synthesis of arts). It is hard to imagine the shock this would have caused at the beginning of the 1960s. The Viennese Action Artists attempted to make a radical break with the traditional methods of painting and sought completely new means of expression.

LEFT: Hundertwasser's KunstHaus Wien art gallery.
ABOVE: painter and architect Friedensreich Hundertwasser

the most popular of all contemporary artists in Vienna. In fact, he is not just an artist, for his greatest success was as the architect of the brightly coloured Hundertwasser-Haus, which within a few years had become a Vienna landmark. Hundertwasser's highly personal concept of a more attractive world, which he realises in the form of churches as well as laybys, has brought him much praise and not a little criticism. Sceptics dismiss him as a shrewd businessman but someone who has stopped developing artistically; on the other hand, his supporters describe him as an indefatigable revolutionary and point out his environment-friendly projects.

A fresh start?

At the beginning of the 1980s, the gallery scene in Vienna was characterless and lacking in impulses. Established artists were omnipresent and left no room for the new arrivals. And then, suddenly, everything changed. Following the success of the "New Wild Man" Siegfried Anzinger, the art market and galleries suddenly began to show signs of life. A new interest in modern art was awakened, and prices rose rapidly. Painters like Hubert Schmalix, Gunther Damisch and Herbert Brandl, the conceptual artist Heimo Zobernig and the light artist Brigitte Kowanz all made interesting contribu-

tions to the boom of the 1980s. In the meantime, things have become quieter once more. Neo-Conceptualism became fashionable. Eva Schlegel's schematic word paintings and the installations by the twin Hohenbüchler sisters are just two examples of young artists' work in Vienna today. Pluralism rules, an interesting network of galleries and a series of modern art platforms provide the necessary structure.

Script and stage

In the Austrian capital, theatrical productions are a talking point not just amongst theatre-goers. From time to time they even steal the

During the first half of the 19th century, the craft of the Vienna Folk Theatre (Volkstheater) blossomed into a Golden Age characterised by the works of playwright-actors Ferdinand Raimund and Johann Nestroy. But in the atmosphere of political and artistic repression under Chancellor Metternich, they were forced to develop new subtleties to outwit the ever-watchful censors.

Raimund tried vainly to succeed as a writer of tragedies, but instead left a legacy of brilliant comedies. His romantic fairy tales – especially

The King of the Alps and *The Misanthropist* – and songs belong to the highlights of Viennese comedy.

Johann Nestroy, who was somewhat younger, chose the apparently harmless genre of dialect comedy in order to avoid the censor's displeasure. He camouflaged his biting satire behind the high comedy of his musical farces – of which he was the ideal interpreter. *The Talisman* and *Lumpazivagabundus* have become classics which are regularly performed by theatres large and small to this day.

limelight as subjects for public discussion. Media of every kind, politicians, intellectuals and onlookers all have plenty to say – before the premiere. At that stage, discussions are the most fun since they are untrammelled by the boring necessity of having to actually see the play oneself.

Vienna's reputation in the theatrical world is unique. Fear of what might be said on stage can lead to a public outcry here as in almost no other city. Here, more than anywhere else, the theatre is still seen to fulfil its role as a discomfiting agent provocateur. To the accompaniment of much media publicity, Claus Peymann has presented on the stage of the Burgtheater the pitiless, glaring visions of Austrian society during recent years as seen through the eyes of Thomas Bernhard, Elfriede Jelinek, Peter Turrini and George Tabori.

However, in the Biedermeier era such unfettered freedom of expression was not possible. Franz Grillparzer, the author of dramas based on Greek legends and Habsburg tragedies, was a perfect example of the dichotomy between the artistic soul and the restricting corset of the bureaucratic state at that time. It was not until the end of the century, however, that tragic drama rose to true greatness as the subconscious began to be explored in both science and art. Arthur Schnitzler was a doctor who wrote down his thoughts on the subject at the same time as Sigmund Freud, the founder of psychoanalysis. Schnitzler, however, preferred the literary, in fact the dramatic, to the scientific form. Schnitzler observed the double standards of Viennese upper-class society and spotlighted the blackest depths of the decadence of the *fin-de-siècle*.

"Young Vienna"

From the 1880s, a group of writers and dramatists known as "Young Vienna" ("Das Junge Wien") finally separated themselves from the naturalistic literary style. One of their most important founders and supporters was Hermann Bahr. Peter Altenberg, who helped to establish the fame of the Viennese coffee house as an ideal place of work for men of letters, became a master of the miniature form. The

focal point of the "Young Vienna" group, however, was a youthful genius who commanded centre stage at poetry readings whilst he was still at grammar school: Hugo von Hofmannsthal.

Hofmannsthal's preferred literary forms were poetry and drama. His play *Everyman*, which revitalises the theme of the medieval mystery play, continues to be an essential item on the programme of the Salzburg Festival every year. In close co-operation with Richard Strauss he also wrote a number of operettas including *Der Rosenkavalier*, which is often performed in the world's great opera houses.

The most eloquent but awkward individual in the group was a political satirist who became the most prominent figure on the intellectual scene in Vienna at the turn of the century. Karl Kraus was the publisher of the monthly journal *Die Fackel* (The Torch). He eloquently and mercilessly attacked the outrages of the age, leaving a voluminous collection of dialogues. *Die letzten Tage der Menschheit* (The Last Days of Humanity) is a shrewd statement of reckoning with those responsible for World War I.

Between the wars

The period between the wars produced a remarkable number of novels. Robert Musil's

---

FAR LEFT: façade of the Burgtheater.
LEFT: statue of Papageno above the entrance to the Theater an der Wien.
ABOVE RIGHT: the controversial writer Arthur Schnitzler

Der Mann ohne Eigenschaften (The Man without Qualities) is still regarded as a work of genius. Other writers often mentioned in the same breath are Stefan Zweig, Josef Roth, Egon Friedell and Franz Werfel. But pride in their remarkable achievements was followed by a harsh and sudden fall. Hitler's march into Austria drove the country's intellectual and artistic elite to suicide or into exile. A few years later, following the destruction resulting from Allied bombing attacks, the cultural centre of the first decades of the century had become a physical as well as a spiritual scene of devastation.

New life on the literary scene

For many years, the cultural life of Vienna remained in the doldrums. Only a few emigrants returned to the city, amongst them Friedrich Torberg. In the 1950s, Heimito von Doderer completed two key postwar novels, *Die Strudelhofstiege* (The Strudelhof Staircase) and *Die Dämonen* (The Demons). The Vienna Group (Wiener Gruppe) which assembled around Ernst Jandl and Friederike Mayröcker developed experimental and absurd themes in the spheres of lyric poetry and drama. Another member of the group, H.C. Artmann, attracted a great deal of attention with his dialect poems *Med ana schwoazn Tintn – Mit schwarzer Tinte* (With Black Ink).

A search for identity, analysis and an embittered attack on the crimes of the past as well as the contradictions in the Austrian soul are the most important themes in the novels and plays of the last few decades. Productions of Thomas Bernhard's brilliantly satirical last play, *Heldenplatz* (Heroes' Square), or *Ritter, Dene, Voss* on the stages of the Burgtheater and the Akademietheater have become classics of the modern theatre which have earned a permanent place in the repertoire.

Curtain up

There is little doubt that the most important theatrical stage in the German-speaking world is the Burgtheater, which has been imbued with new life by current director, Claus Peymann. The main addresses for brand-new, experimental theatre are the Schauspielhaus or one of the other countless stages such as the Theater in der Drachengasse or dietheater Künstlerhaus. The established musical stages are the Theater an der Wien and the Raimundtheater, whilst Vienna's

classical stages include the Theater in der Josefstadt and the Volkstheater. During the summer months, an unusual experience is presented by the Tschauner Stegreifbühne, which performs amusingly down-to-earth humour in the open air and without a precise script.

Culture vultures are well advised to visit Vienna in May and June, for the Vienna Festival (Wiener Festwochen) presents top-notch European drama. During the annual two-month closure of the city's main stages, there is a lively summer scene: the Vienna Jazz Festival, free films of opera performances on the Rathausplatz, dance weeks in the Volkstheater and

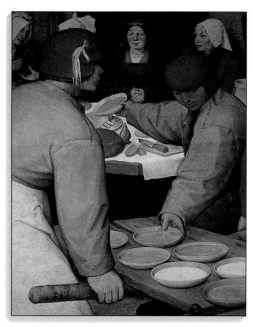

open-air cinema in the Augarten are among the cultural delights on offer.

In the autumn the Viennale, Vienna's film festival, takes place in the second half of October and has attained international acclaim. All the year round, cabaret and farce presented in the Kulisse, the Niedermair and the Spektakel prove that minor art forms too can have major standing.

A mixture of museums

Art treasures and imperial robes, scientific curios and more or less depraved cult objects – in Vienna there is virtually nothing which is not collected, arranged and presented for examination in a suitable setting. From the Hofburg to the Prater, from castle rooms to private apartments, Vienna possesses more than 80 museums which permit the visitor to obtain a detailed picture of the city's multi-faceted countenance.

The gallery of paintings in the Museum of the History of Art (Kunsthistorisches Museum) (I., Maria-Theresia-Platz) contains one of the world's top five collections of Old Masters: Titian and Veronese, courtly portraits by Velásquez and works by Pieter Breughel the

DIARY DATES

May/June: Vienna Festival (arts)
July/August: Musical Summer
late October: Viennale Film Festival

as its counterpart, but it contains, amongst other treasures, the Venus of Willendorf, the small, corpulent limestone statue from the Wachau whose fame lies in the fact that it is the second oldest prehistoric find in Austria. Children, incidentally, particularly like the skeletons of dinosaurs and the creaking wooden floor.

The Albertina (I., Augustinerstrasse 1) is a permanent collection of graphics and drawings. The palais is named after the collector, Duke Albert of Sachsen-Teschen, and it contains the

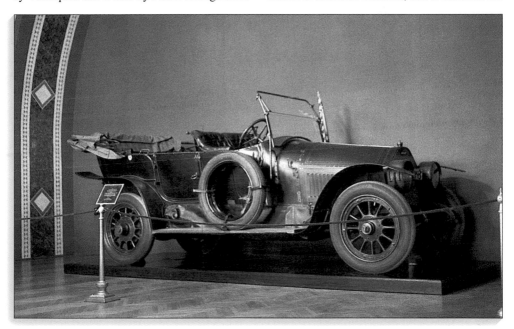

Elder form the crowning glory of the eight departments within the museum. Also worth a separate visit are the Egyptian Collection, the Department of Antiquities and the Collection of Sculptures and Crafts.

The Natural History Museum (Naturhistorisches Museum), housed in the mirror-image building opposite, completes the museum complex which was first opened to the public in 1891. It is not quite as popular amongst visitors

Left: detail of Brueghel's *The Peasant Wedding* in the Museum of Art History.
Above: the car in which Archduke Franz Ferdinand was assassinated in 1914, Museum of Military History

largest graphics collection in the world. The archives are filled to bursting with thousands of drawings and prints, since it is not possible to place everything on display. Pride of place is afforded the works by Albrecht Dürer. Housed in the same building is the Austrian Film Museum, which offers cinema fans a well-chosen selection of masterpieces from the Seventh Art Form.

The Treasury (Schatzkammer) (I., Hofburg, Schweizerhof) displays secular and sacred objects of incalculable worth in particularly attractive surroundings. Beneath the insignia of the Holy Roman Empire of the German Nation stand the orb and sceptre as well as the imperial crown, dating from the 10th century and possibly worn by Otto the Great. Other exhibits include magnificent coronation robes and priests' vestments.

Contemporary art spaces

The exhibitions which provide the link between the Museum of the History of Art and the museums devoted to the 20th century have finally been re-opened after years of renovation: the Lower Belvedere (III., Rennweg 6a) and the Upper Belvedere (III., Prinz-Eugen-Strasse 27) shine once more with renewed lustre. The Austrian Gallery of the 19th and 20th Century

(Österreichische Galerie des 19. und 20. Jahrhunderts), which formerly housed paintings by Klimt, Schiele and Kokoschka, now contains the works of the Classical and Romantic periods as well as the Biedermeier Collection which affords G.F. Waldmüller his rightful place as one of the outstanding personalities of the era.

The lower end of the garden area displays two contrasting themes: the Austrian Museum of Baroque (Österreichisches Barockmuseum) shows paintings and sculptures dating from the 17th and 18th century (Rottmayr, Maulpertsch, Troger, Donner, etc.), while the Museum of Austrian Medieval Art (Museum Mittelalter-

CONTRARY HOUSES OF ART

In 1861, the artists of Vienna joined together to form an association and had the **Künstlerhaus** built as an Artists' House (I., Karlsplatz 5). Today it serves as a cultural centre where major exhibitions are held several times a year. A screening room, theatre and gallery provide the supporting framework. Josef Maria Olbrich's **Secession** (I., Friedrichstrasse 12) was built following a dispute with the Association's traditionalists. Klimt's Beethoven frieze is on permanent display here, and there is a programme of exhibitions devoted to the zeitgeist of modern times.

licher Österreichischer Kunst) exhibits 12th–16th century altarpieces and sculptures.

In the Schweizer Garten, not far from the Upper Belvedere, stands one of the houses devoted exclusively to contemporary art – the Museum of the 20th Century (Museum des 20. Jahrhunderts) (III., Schweizer Garten). The original purpose of the building was to serve as the Austria Pavilion at the World Exhibition in Brussels in 1958. It was then erected in Vienna as a space for temporary exhibitions. The Museum of Modern Art (Museum Moderner Kunst) (IX., Fürstengasse 1) in the Palais Liechtenstein documents in a permanent exhibition the highlights of the present century.

A delight in death

At the same time as the Secessionists were abandoning the traditional rules in art, a nerve doctor was overturning the opinions of traditional medicine. The apartment and consulting rooms in which Sigmund Freud investigated the background of hysteria and the Oedipus complex can be visited today, in the Sigmund Freud Museum (IX., Berggasse 19).

Other museums worth visiting, for those with an interest in Vienna's contribution to medical science, are: the Museum of Medical History (Museum für Geschichte der Medizin) in the Josephinum (IX., Währinger Strasse 25), where

Other museums in Vienna range from the Clock Museum to the Theatre Museum (see listings on *pages 243-5* in the *Travel Tips* section at the back of this book).

New and renewed temples of art

The KunstHaus Wien (III., Untere Weissgerberstrasse 13) opened in 1991 – after being converted to owner Friedensreich Hundertwasser's colourful style – in the building in which the Thonet brothers designed their famous bentwood chairs. Inside, there is a permanent exhibition of Hundertwasser's work and changing restrospectives mostly devoted to famous names.

beautiful wax models imported by Joseph II for for anatomical study in the late 18th century are displayed; and the Museum of Pathological Anatomy, housed in the so-called "Narrenturm" (Fools' Tower) (IX., Spitalgasse 2), where you can see crippled skeletons and foetuses preserved in formalin. The Funeral Museum (Bestattungsmuseum) (IV., Goldeggasse 19) is further proof of the Viennese love for scurrilous and macabre detail.

FAR LEFT: table laid for dinner in Franz Joseph's apartments.
LEFT: anatomical exhibit in the Josefinum.
ABOVE: exhibits in the Clown Museum

Nearby is the Hundertwasser-Haus, the creation for which the painter and architect is best known.

Famous names from the 19th and 20th century and rare treasures from important private collections make the Kunstforum Bank Austria (I., Freyung 8) one of the most attractive exhibition halls. Under the direction of Peter Noever, the Museum of Applied Arts (Museum für angewandte Kunst) (I., Stubenring 5) underwent a highly successful facelift; it was elected Museum of the Year by the Council of Europe in 1996. Further accommodation for modern artistic events was secured at the beginning of the 1990s in the form of a yellow cuboid, the Kunsthalle Wien (IV., Treitlstrasse 2/ Karlsplatz).

THE SECESSIONIST MOVEMENT

Otto Wagner's architecture has made its mark all over Vienna. Others applied the Secessionist philosophy to painting, decorative and functional art

In 1897, a group of 19 young architects, painters and graphic artists declared war on the conservative art establishment dominated by Hans Makart. They dedicated themselves to a different form of art in what they called the Secession: a break with the old-fashioned provincialism which looked back to the great styles of the past rather than to the future. In 1898, Joseph Maria Olbrich built the Secession Building right behind the Academy of Fine Arts, a body which represented everything the Secessionists opposed. The building was a gesture of defiance and a bold statement of a new creed.

SEA CHANGE IN ARCHITECTURE

Also known as *Jugendstil* and Art Nouveau, this new school soon became a legend. Apart from Olbrich, its leading protagonists included Gustav Klimt, Koloman Moser, Josef Hoffmann and Otto Wagner. Wagner, in particular, pioneered a new form of architecture in which functionality and simplicity of ornament were the priority. Many of his buildings, gardens and lamps survive in Vienna, as well as stations for the Stadtbahn, which he was commissioned to design and build in 1894. Among his finest creations are two very different villas in Hüttelbergstrasse and the wonderful Kirche am Steinhof (XIV, Baumgartner Höhe 1). For the Post Office Savings Bank building (I, George-Coch-Platz), built between 1904 and 1906, completely new materials were used, such as glass bricks and aluminium. These combined functionality with beauty, most conspicuously in the 1,700 ornamental aluminium rivets used to hold the marble and granite slabs in place.

△ **A CURTAIN OF FLOWERS**
Inside it's a functional rented house; outside it's a riot of colourful flower motifs. The Majolikahaus – so-called after the weather-proof glaze used on the exterior – was designed by Otto Wagner in 1898 (IV, Linke Wienzeile 40).

ART ABOVE THE ROOFTOPS ▷
The Ankerhaus (I, Graben 10), which Otto Wagner designed in 1893, has a glass roof structure which he used as his studio; today, this is where Friedensreich Hundertwasser paints his colourful pictures.

◁ PAVILIONS FOR THE UNDERGROUND SYSTEM

Otto Wagner's two wonderfully ornamental stations for the Stadtbahn on Karlsplatz date from 1894. He combined a green iron framework with marble slabs and golden sunflower decoration to give a brightly coloured appearance to buildings which would have a pedestrian purpose. They now serve as a café, exhibition hall and museum of Wagner's life and work.

ARTS AND CRAFTS FOR ALL

The Secessionist movement rejected the traditional hierarchical divide between the artist who designed an object and the craftsperson who made it. The distinction between the aesthetic and the functional also became blurred, and people were called upon to fill their lives with objects of beauty. As a result, small-scale crafts enjoyed a major revival, and the Wiener Werkstätte (Viennese Workshop) was founded in 1903 by Josef Hoffmann, Koloman Moser and Fritz Waerndorfer. They used simple forms and geometric designs in items such as glasses, lamps, furniture and tableware.

The work of the Wiener Werkstätte is on display in the Museum of Applied Arts (I, Stubenring 5). You can also buy crafts in the Secessionist style, some made to the original designs of Josef Hoffmann and Adolf Loos, in several shops in Vienna.

▽ TIME FLIES

Otto Wagner believed in designing his buildings right down to the last detail. This clock is inside the Stadtbahn station on Karlsplatz, which has been converted into a café.

◁ WAGNER'S SUMMER RESIDENCE

The large "Wagner-Villa I" (XIV, Hüttelbergstrasse 26) is dominated by a triaxial Ionic colonnade with a coffered ceiling. The figure in the central niche is the work of its current owner, the academic painter Ernst Fuchs.

▽ "THE CABBAGE"

This was the disrespectful nickname given to the Secession Building by the unimpressed people of Vienna, probably partly because of its proximity to the food market (I, Friedrichstrasse 12).

◁ ORNATE GOLD DECORATION

No. 38 Linke Wienzeile, designed by Otto Wagner, represents the apex of the style he developed. As with his other "Wagner Apartment" in this street, the Majolikahaus, the inside is fairly plain, but the outside is extravagantly decorated with women's heads in gilded stucco (detail right) by Kolo Moser.

DER ZEIT IHRE KVNST
DER KVNST IHRE FREIHEIT

THE VIENNESE

Journalist Jutta Kohout provides an insider's view of the city's people and suggests some definitions of the "typical Viennese"

Viennese humour and Viennese grumpiness, Viennese *Gemütlichkeit* and the Viennese heart of gold – does any of it exist? Or is it just an illusion, like the little angels, who spend their holidays – where else? – in Vienna, at least according to a popular song. Dream and reality, caricature and original, the Viennese zigzag between these poles, constantly in danger of falling into sugarsweet pretence. Usually it's left to the last moment before they snap out of it and wink with self-directed irony: "It's all not true." If you believe it, it's your own fault.

Cliché city

Clichés are carefully guarded and polished up before each new surge of tourists arrives. "If we're not feeling cheerful, well then we're just a bit grumpy, if you please, your humble servant". Complaining in the style of the former film legend Hans Moser is part of the repertoire of every self-appointed one-man show between Grinzing and Kagran.

And the Viennese undeniably like complaining about their city. But woe betide the "outsider" who dares to criticize us. Then we stick together like *The Third Man*. After all, we've nothing to be ashamed of, certainly not a few Nazi smears on our spotless past. The world's an ungrateful place, is a sigh often heard in Vienna. After what we've done for the world: Maria Theresa and Bruno Kreisky, Johnny Strauss and Falco, *Wiener* sausages and *Sachertorte*.

Tirelessly the Vienna Boys' Choir and the Lipizzaner horses travel the globe as special ambassadors of good will; in the New Year concert, the Philharmonic fiddles away on satellite TV, showing the world from Greenland to Timbuktu what culture is all about.

Major decisions in world politics may be made elsewhere today, but we only have to pop into the Capuchins' Crypt where the Habsburgs are buried to remind ourselves that we are great.

Or at least, we were once great. After all, we still live quite happily on the interest paid by the past. "Good day, Your Honours, would the longer city tour please you? From Schönbrunn to Mayerling, war and love, all included in the price."

The world has simply painted its own picture of Vienna and the Viennese, and we sigh and try

to fit in. We're not interested in the invasion of the culture seekers. We'd rather invade our local round the corner and calmly watch events from a distance, through clouds of steam from the roast with dumplings. Live and let live is our motto.

Roast beef and dumplings

People eat well in Vienna. For once that's no cliché but the obvious truth. "You're looking well" is one of the highest possible compliments among Viennese, and means that the person addressed is heavily overweight. The current ideal of beauty would probably make any figure-conscious American woman go on a strict diet.

PRECEDING PAGES: a Renaissance courtyard.
LEFT: a *Fiaker*.
ABOVE RIGHT: cheese stall at the Bauermarkt auf der Freyung

Instead of slimming, a few seams are let out, it's that simple. Warning voices calling for restraint in this Land of Cockaigne are "not even ignored", which is why choles-terol levels are on the rise nationally. The so-called "Vien-nese cuisine" is rich and heavy. Nouvelle cuisine and healthy fibre is for ascetic eccentrics.

The home-grown cuisine can claim to be a melting pot unique in the world. There may be no specific Paris, Berlin or London cuisine, but the collection of recipes and snacks innocently titled "Viennese

> ### EATING FOR AUSTRIA
> Vienna must be the only Western capital in which a large fashion house has enjoyed success with the slogan "Plump is Beautiful"

wife and cook considers a personal insult. At any rate, historical discoveries in the State Archives do show that Field Marshal Radetzky, returning from Italy in the year of revolution, 1848, not only reported to the Imperial govern-ment in Vienna on the defeat of the rebels but also mentioned a certain "*costoletto alla Milan-ese*" and gave the recipe to the Imperial kitchens – in the strictest confidence, of course.

The undeniable Viennese peculiarity, howev-er, is the cult of beef. Beef dishes have their

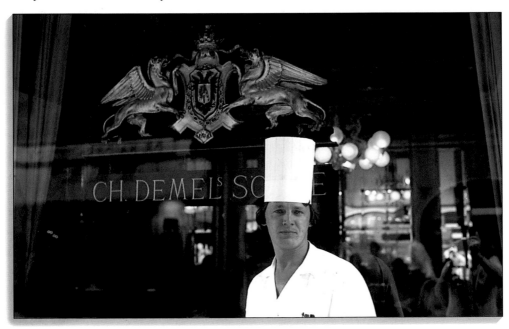

cuisine" definitely exists. It's a giant plagiarism of the most varied dishes of the multi-cultural Empire; Hungarian, Bohemian, Italian, Serbian, Croatian, Slovenian, Friaulian and Dalmatian national dishes, adapted to the Viennese palate.

The basic ingredient of most dishes is still the famous (or infamous) *einbrenn*, a sauce made from butter and flour. From soup to vegetables to the paprika-flavoured stew à la goulash it's used in everything to "refine" it, thus neutraliz-ing the taste. Meat is usually eaten *paniert*, i.e. rolled in flour, egg and breadcrumbs and then fried swimming in lard or oil. It's claimed that the world famous *Wiener Schnitzel* was actually invented in Milan, a rumour which every house-

fixed place on every menu, from the small pubs to the expensive restaurants. The dish of *Tafel-spitz* isn't eaten, it's celebrated. In his novel, *Radetzkymarsch,* the author Joseph Roth describes the traditional Sunday meal of *Tafel-spitz* in the family of a civil servant, Trotta. The meal acts as a symbol for the fading, quaintly pedantic Imperial world: "After the soup, the garnished *Tafelspitz* was brought in, the old man's Sunday dinner for many years. His satis-fied inspection of this dish took up more time than half the meal. At first his eye caressed the delicate border of fat which surrounded the col-ossal piece of meat, then the individual little plates, on which the vegetables were served, the violet sheen of the beetroot, the rich green of the first spinach, the cheerful pale lettuce, the plain white of horseradish, the faultless ovals of the new potatoes, swimming in melting butter, which reminded him of dainty little toys... A fortunate fate allowed Trotta to unite the satisfaction of his appetite with the demands of his duty. His was a Spartan nature. But he was an Austrian."

A famous restaurant in the Graben, Meissl & Schadn, which no longer exists, had 26 different kinds of boiled beef on its menu, from *Tellerfleisch* (a stew of cheaper cuts) to joint-sized *Kruspelspitz*. On 26 October 1916, after dining on one of these dishes, young Friedrich

menu thinking they're in Bielefeld or Omaha. Apricots instead of *Marillen* and Hawaiian style roast pork – it's enough to give you the horrors. Flight to the *Konditorei* (pastry shop) is a must.

Powidltatschlkerln, Guglhupf, Wuchteln, Millirahmstrudel, Palatschinken, Mohnbeugerl, Golatschn – Viennese cakes defy translation and description. The highest praise for a piece of the Viennese pastrycook's art is to say it's "like a poem".

Translations are often unintentionally comic. *Besoffene Kapuziner*, little cakes soaked in alcohol, turn into "drunk monks", *Topfengolatschn* become "puff pastry cottage cheese buns". So

Adler, son of the legendary founder of the Austrian Social Democrats, Viktor Adler, carefully wiped his lips on his napkin, walked over to Graf Sturgkh, who was dining at the next table, introduced himself with a well-mannered bow – and shot the unloved Prime Minister dead. The world ends in style, at least it does in Vienna.

Today there isn't much in the way of shooting in Viennese restaurants, but the service tries too hard to please – particularly at tourist times. Then, the astonished Viennese sit staring at the

if you are faced with *Gebackene Mäuse* (literally: baked mice), don't panic. These are merely a form of *Krapfen*, a crispier, lighter relative of the doughnut.

The original Sachertorte

Sachertorte – or *Sacher Torte*, depending which *Konditorei* you patronise – is the best-known Viennese cake. The original *Sachertorte*, a rich chocolate cake iced with more chocolate, was invented in the kitchens of the Hotel Sacher about 100 years ago. Several other *Konditoreien* also serve almost identical cakes – but the Hotel Sacher even went to court to establish its exclusive right to the name.

LEFT: outside the Café Demel.
ABOVE: at the sausage stall

The original *Sachertorte* is spelled as one word (as sold in the Hotel Sacher); *Sacher Torte* (two words, as sold everywhere else) is the copy. The Konditorei Demel objects, however, and claims to possess the true original *Sachertorte* – its argument is based on the fact that the chef who invented it left the Sacher and came to work at the Demel, bringing the recipe with him.

Eating in Vienna is always combined with communication. If you want to test this for yourself, go to one of the two hundred or so *Würstelstände* (sausage stalls), which are found throughout Vienna in a strategically planned network. While eating a *Burenwurst* (order *einmal*

Heyday of the coffee house

"Not at home and not out in the fresh air", that's a motto followed for centuries by the lovers of what is probably the most famous Viennese institution, the coffee house. In 1683, Franz Georg Kolschitzky received from the Emperor, as a reward for his services as a spy during the Turkish siege, permission to open a public coffee brewing house. It's claimed that he also baked the first Viennese *Kipferl*, a cake made of flaky pastry inspired by the Turkish crescent, which people like to dip furtively into their coffee. If it's not true, at least it's a good story.

If you go to a coffee house just to drink cof-

Heisse mit Senf – a hot one with mustard) people reflect upon religion, politics and football. "The meat content of the 'hot one' hardly bothers the Viennese. After all, they are world champions in repressing the unpleasant, an attitude that probably forced the development of psychoanalysis. They trust in the anti-toxic properties of the garnish, the hottest possible peppers". This is the ironic comment of the "alternative" guide to Vienna *Dieses Wien – Klischee und Wirklicheit* (Vienna – Cliché and Reality).

At any rate, the Viennese are rightly pleased that a branch of a famous American hamburger chain had to close for lack of customers. Serves them right too.

fee, that's your own fault. You go to a coffee house to read, to write, to play chess or cards, to daydream, to flirt, to argue... It's a "place for people who want to be alone and need company to do so", the poet Alfred Polgar once wrote. Up until the time between the wars, the literary life of Vienna was mostly lived on red velour sofas at marble tables.

When the legendary Café Griensteidl was knocked down at the turn of the century, the era of the Café Central began. As well as the famous names *(see box on page 74)*, scroungers were part of the decor in every coffee house of repute. They moved from the Central to the Herrenhof or the Museum Café and provided the

The Jewish Community

In the late 19th century and during the 1920s and 1930s, Jews were much stronger and more visible in Vienna than in other western European capitals. Ten percent of the population were Jews, from the assimilated members of the upper middle class to the small traders who had come from the "Stetl" of Galicia and Bukovina. The progressive Emperor Joseph II had granted the Jews of the Empire substantial rights in his Edict of Tolerance in 1781. In

174 editorial posts in the Viennese daily papers, 123 were held by Jews.

Sigmund Freud had his practice in the Berggasse, District 9. Opposite, at No. 6, Theodor Herzl worked on his book *The Jewish State*, which detailed his vision of an exodus to Palestine. Anti-Semitism was put on the back burner, it was simply bad manners. As a corporal and failed artist, Hitler said: "In my eyes this city is a pearl! I will give it a setting worthy of such a pearl." In 1938, he put his threat into action, incorporating Austria into the German Reich. In the Viennese Kristallnacht on 9 November 1938 the windows of Jewish shops were smashed, and nearly all the synagogues were burned down.

District 2, in Leopoldstadt, the "Mazzesinsel" (orthodox community) grew up with Torah schools, synagogues and kosher shops.

The author Arthur Schnitzler (1862–1931) described another Jewish world in his novels and plays, that of the enlightened bourgeoisie. His works evoke moods and detached, melancholic humour. Psychological analysis drives them, whilst the corrupt last years of the Habsburg empire provide a recurring background theme. *Der Weg ins Freie* (The Road to the Open) is specifically about Jews in Austria.

Jewish intellectuals shaped the development of art and science, literature and journalism. Of the

LEFT: Café Griensteidl, 1896.
ABOVE: Sigmund Freud's couch

Before the Holocaust, more than 200,000 Jews lived in Vienna. Today the number is barely 7,000. The "Nazi-hunter" Simon Wiesenthal has set up his documentation centre in the former Jewish textile quarter. The Jewish Welcome Service tries to keep in contact with emigrants all over the world.

Recently, political developments have encouraged a cautious Renaissance of Jewish culture in Vienna. In the premises of the Israeli Cultural Association, there is a Jewish Museum documenting the role played by Vienna's Jews in the intellectual and cultural arena. The Synagogue in the Seitenstettengasse has rising attendance figures. But the wounds have not healed and, as a young Viennese Jew puts it: "You never know when you'll have to pack again."

regulars with news and gossip – whose turn it was to be devastated by Karl Kraus' acidulous pen, for instance – and helped to start intrigues or smooth out misunderstandings. In between they quickly ate a small goulash on the house, and all of them nursed their daydreams of rising from the level of extras to the Olympian heights of the poets. The coffee-house writer, Anton Kuh, gave these uncounted wasted lives a memorial in one sentence: "Only a few people know that not writing is also the fruit of a long and difficult struggle."

Loss of a generation

The Viennese coffee house has never really recovered from the intellectual bloodletting of World War II. The regulars emigrated – Sigmund Freud, aged 82, had to go into exile in London – or ended up in concentration camps. With wit and dignity a whole generation of the Jewish intelligentsia went to their deaths. Shortly before his murder in Buchenwald, the Viennese cabaret artist Fritz Grünbaum asked for a piece of soap. He was told it was too expensive. Grünbaum calmly replied: "If you haven't got the money, you shouldn't run a concentration camp."

In the postwar years, coffee houses rich in tradition were converted to banks or even had to accept the humiliating demotion to Espresso with gleaming Italian chrome coffee machines. It's only in the last few years that a Renaissance of these old Viennese institutions has begun.

Students and yuppies have rediscovered them as oases in times of stress. The tourists sit amazed among the splendours of the renovated Central and are instructed by the "Herr Ober"

in the complicated art of drinking coffee. The vast variety on offer is legendary *(see page 239)* You can sit for hours in the warm coffee house with a small *Brauner* (white coffee) for 20 Schilling, chat, read the paper, observe other guests: "Aha, there's the editor with the Minister's secretary, well, well, well." You're in the know.

Wine, women and song

Only warm summer evenings can temporarily lure coffee house devotees away from their regular table by the window, right next to the cake counter. They swap it for a hard wooden bench,

REFUGES FOR POETS AND REVOLUTIONARIES

The guest list of the **Café Central** in the Herrengasse reads like a *Who's Who* of European intellectual history. Theodor Herzl and Viktor Adler, Peter Altenberg and Egon Friedell, Rainer Maria Rilke and Egon Erwin Kisch, Hugo Hofmannsthal and Arthur Schnitzler, Sigmund Freud and Alfred Adler all frequented this legendary coffee house.

Colleagues, friends or bitter enemies, they quarrelled or ignored each other. Many a chess player was thoroughly underestimated by his contemporaries. "Who's going to start a revolution in Russia? Herr Bronstein from the Café Central,

perhaps?", Graf Berchthold, the last foreign minister of the Empire, wrote in the margin of a despatch in 1917. "Herr Bronstein", alias Leon Trotsky, was well on his way home to the collapsing empire of the Tzars.

The talented chronicler of his times, Karl Kraus, sat in the **Café Imperial**. For 37 years he published the magazine *Die Fackel* (The Torch) and he wrote the monumental work *The Last Days of Mankind*. In the **Café Museum**, designed by Adolf Loos, tables were reserved for famous artists. Alban Berg and Oscar Straus came here, as did Klimt, Schiele and Kokoschka.

which should preferably be standing in a cool, shady courtyard in the area of Sievering, Nussdorf, Kahlenbergerdorf, Stammersdorf or Strebersdorf. Outside the gates a green bush is hanging on a long pole, a signal to the dehydrated traveller that the vintner's wine is ready to drink.

Here they sit, as they do every year, at the *Heuriger* to drink the *Heuriger*, the new wine, or as they commonly say in Vienna, to "bite" it. This may all seem a bit complicated to foreigners, but after drinking several quarter litres, a comfortable comprehension is usually assured.

During the reign of Leopold I, a priestly gentleman complained of the impious habits of the city: " On Sundays and holidays you hear a continual fiddling, lute playing, leaping and dancing in all the inns and drinking houses, from the afternoons till late at night." In the 19th century, the suburb of Neulerchenfeld was even described as "the largest inn in the Holy Roman Empire, where on a single fine Sunday 16,000 people sought refreshment."

Those in search of refreshment guard the address of their favourite *Heuriger*, now as then. Secret recommendations are passed on unofficially to a select few. A good *Heuriger* isn't

Vienna and wine, a combination famed in song, can look back on a thousand years of history. Discoveries of grape seeds prove that the Celts were already using the mild climate of the region to grow vines. The legionaries of the little garrison town of Vindobona didn't despise the grape, either. They're commemorated by the Probusgasse, named after a Roman emperor, in Heiligenstadt. The art of viticulture was passed on and refined from generation to generation, as was the art of drinking and "biting" the wine.

LEFT: the Viennese actress Julia Stemberger.
ABOVE: monks in the Graben shopping precinct.
ABOVE RIGHT: waitress, KrahKrah restaurant

crowded. Shuddering, the Viennese give the tourist traps of Grinzing – where the guests are served their roast chicken as if on a conveyor belt, while the next coachload is waiting outside – a wide berth. They prefer to drive out to Nussdorf or Sievering and turn into one of the twisting alleys, where they seem to be swallowed up without trace by the cobblestones. There you sit at a rough wooden table and fetch yourself a piece of bread and dripping with onion rings from the buffet, along with a few *Brezeln*. If you prefer to take the leftovers of Sunday's roast pork with you, you'll be given a plate and cutlery without any difficulty. With that you drink a litre of white wine, for starters, in a wide-

MELANCHOLIC MOOD

The Viennese *Heuriger* mood is a bit sad and a bit sentimental, *Weltschmerz* (world-weary) in the knowledge of the passing of the pleasures of the hour

bellied glass carafe. You might have a Grüner Veltliner or a Müller-Thurgau, a Neuburger or a Riesling. The wine should be fruity and dry, pleasantly acid. You can sit contented like this hour after hour, swapping salt and pepper and a few profound pearls of wisdom with your neighbours, slapping in vain at the gnats.

Class and social barriers are torn down as twilight falls, a classless society toasts its members with big, beermug-style glasses: "*Servus, du.*" The company director pats his secretary's knee. Next morning nobody remembers anything anyway. But "Whooping, cheerful, high-spirited and comfortable – that's merely the stereotype of the Viennese", some argue; in their heart of hearts, the Viennese are melancholy. They may not manage tragedy, but philosophy is another matter. The Viennese song begins and ends in a minor key.

"The noblest nation of all the nations is resignation", said the talented but sharp-tongued 19th-century satirical playwright, Johann Nestroy. In Viennese song, the responsibility for personal failure is often attributed to supernatural powers: "If God doesn't will it so, it's all in vain". Visitors can hum along with these songs, but they'll hardly understand a thing, even if they speak German. These original Viennese texts are hard to understand for those who live outside Semmering. For example: "A *Hallodri* (womaniser) has yet another *Gspusi* (affair), for once we're *fidel* (happy), but only till the next *Pallawatsch* (catastrophe), as long as we don't indulge in *Spompanadeln* (daft ideas)."

The language is a cosmopolitan mixture of Czech and Hungarian, Italian and French, plus the Yiddish that is such an important element of Viennese dialect. You're usually preserved at the last moment from descent into deep depression after a lengthy *Heuriger* session by the classic Viennese diminutive, the syllable "*erl*". For example: "That really was quite a *Räuscherl* (I was really drunk) yesterday evening, but don't be cross, *Schatzerl* (darling), I'll give you a *Buschketterl* (kiss)."

Schrammel music and death

A very specialised branch of Viennese song is the *Schrammelmusik*. The very first band was founded at the end of the last century by the brothers Johann and Joseph Schrammel. They played in the *Heuriger* on a concertina and a bass guitar – the combination produces an addictive sound, its followers claim. Good *Schrammel* music is never sweet or schmaltzy, but a bit on the bitter side, for some ears, a bit coarse.

Like folk music everywhere, the *Heuriger* songs are in danger today of degenerating into inoffensive tootling and sing-songs. One musi-

cian who is trying to keep up the true Viennese musical tradition is Roland Neuwirth with his "Extremschrammeln". He loathes the fake Viennese cosiness, and prefers to offer his enthusiastic audiences numbers like *Delirium-Tanz* or Every Rat loves its Sewer. In his song *Ein echtes Wienerlied* (A Genuine Viennese Song) sixteen different expressions for dying are introduced with feeling: "He made an exit, he stretched out his slippers, he laid himself down, he studied the potatoes from underneath, he put on wooden pyjamas...".

The Viennese don't find such a text tasteless or shocking. After all, Roland Neuwirth is only continuing an old and honourable tradition – the unafraid and easy-going attitude to death. Sometimes it seems as if it actually lives, personified, in this city. "Death must be a Viennese", the late Alfred Polgar discovered – and the Viennese are good friends with one of their own, it's an intimate relationship. Old grannies, silent drinkers, failed poets see the visit of the Grim Reaper as the last, possibly the only high point in an uneventful life. When they die, there ought to be a "lovely funeral", which should be something to talk about. They want to be seen off with organ

DEATH IN VIENNA

In the 1970s an elderly emigrant came back to Vienna to die. But he was frustrated twice and had to leave again, only achieving his end at the third attempt

association, *Die Flamme* (The Flame), with 160,000 members. "A proletarian life, a proletarian death and a cremation that accords with culture and progress" was the rather heretical slogan.

Children learn in school about "*lieber Augustin*", a singer and bagpipe player, who in the 17th century fell, totally drunk, into a plague pit, woke up and went on singing cheerfully among the stinking corpses. Right among the shoppers in the high-class pedestrian precinct, Graben in the 1st District, is the splendid Baroque

music and a child choir, candles and wreaths, tears and pious fibs.

In Vienna people save up for such a spectacle, and the *Sterbevereine* (funeral associations) are highly respected institutions. All your life you can pay in little stages for the grand finale. Nothing upsets the true Viennese more than the prospect of being buried one day "like a dog", with only four *Pompfüneberern* (pallbearers, from *pompes funèbres*).

Even the progressive social democrats in power between the wars had their own funeral

LEFT: Café Landtmann.
ABOVE: a stallholder at the Naschmarkt

Plague Column (Pestsäule), a reminder of the "merciful removal of the divine chastisement of plague richly deserved by this city". All around the skilfully portrayed horrors, children are playing, *Maronibrater* (chestnut sellers) pour their hot wares into homemade paper bags, organ grinders turn their handles. Death and the joys of life are not mutually exclusive in this city. Even if those who suffer in and from Vienna are driven out to the furthest ends of the earth – to die in a foreign land, that really is a dreadful prospect, God preserve us.

André Heller once called the Viennese cemeteries "stations of farewell". Yet they are much more. They are not only, as in other cities, places of grief to be avoided if possible. In Viennese cemeteries, you can take a walk, chat a bit, get some fresh air, feed the squirrels and the sparrows, decode inscriptions on weathered tombstones. They're particularly lovely in autumn, when colourful leaves cover the narrow gravel paths, the last rays of the sun light up the statues and eternal flame lanterns on the graves. Near the exit, you can buy a sausage and hot tea.

The biggest cemetery in the city, the Central Cemetery, is four-fifths of a 2 sq. km (sq. mile) in size. The giant park has its own bus service, and every autumn there's a hare hunt among the

graves. "Long live the Zentralfriedhof, and all its dead," sang the Liedermacher Wolfgang Ambros, and his song became a hit in the Austrian charts. The magnificent state tombs provided by the city are all too often witnesses to a bitter truth: only once you're dead can you really make it in Vienna. Wolfgang Amadeus Mozart has his official last resting place here, a memorial stone in the state tombs, group 32a, No. 55. The life-loving composer was buried in 1791, quite impoverished, in a mass grave which can no longer be located in St Mark's Cemetery.

Children may be firmly shooed off the lawns, but the city has a big heart for the dead and for small animals. On the banks of the Danube, to the east of Vienna, lies the Cemetery of the Nameless (Friedhof der Namenlosen). Unknown corpses swept ashore by the river here found their last rest under simple wrought iron crosses. But dachshunds, pussycats and hamsters, much-loved companions in loneliness in Vienna, have for the last few years escaped compulsory delivery to the glue and fertilizer factories. Vienna's first mobile crematorium for pets will give dear "Waldi" dignified last rites. An employee of the company says a few deeply felt words, the mourners noisily blow their noses, and Waldi's soul rises up to heaven. A little heap of white ash remains, which can be put in a dainty little urn and kept on the mantel shelf at home. God have mercy on him!

Curious characters

Strangers may shake their heads over customs like these, but in Vienna the times – and the hearts – are a bit different. Strange and wonderful characters thrive here. Eccentrics are lovingly cared for. The so-called "genuine Viennese" are threatened with extinction. These are the characters, bad-tempered, devious, loyal and charming, commemorated by the unforgettable cabaret artist, author and actor Helmut Qualtinger in his play *Der Herr Karl* (Mr Karl). The whole of Vienna was outraged at the exposure – I beg your pardon, the première.

In enclaves you can still find them: in the markets of Vienna, for instance, in the Brunnenmarkt in the suburb of Ottakring, the Viktor-Adler-Markt in the working class district Favoriten, or in the Naschmarkt, which stretches across the regulated river Wien starting at the Karlsplatz, flanked by gold-decorated Otto Wagner houses. Here the stallholders run their well-regulated businesses, usually rather well-built women with aprons and headscarves who stand out in all weathers praising their "*Kronprinz*" (a type of apple), potatoes and *kohlrabi*.

The Ringstrasse coachman

A very picture of the "genuine" Viennese warm heart and kindly nature is presented by the *Fiaker* waiting for customers at the Stephansplatz. Well, it's one way of getting a tip. Their name comes from the Rue Saint Fiacre, in which the Parisian cabbies used to park their traps. With whips and bowler hats, a good grip on the reins of their well-groomed horses, they drive *"Amis"* (Americans) and *"Itaka"* (Italians) round the Ring, giving a short embroidered account of Austrian history. The first coach hire licence was awarded by Leopold I in 1693 and the best time for the *Fiaker* was the economic upsurge of the so-called "Gründerjahre" in the second half of the 19th century. There were *Fiaker* balls, in which the guests danced waltzes and polkas till they dropped in the grey dawn. And one of the most beautiful Viennese songs is about the melancholy farewell of a *Fiaker* driver leaving his *Zeugl* (team).

Today the number of traps driving in Vienna is greatly reduced, but of course they still leave behind certain traces, the so-called *Rossknödel* (horse dumplings). The perfectly serious suggestion made by the city administration in 1979, that given the fouling of the streets the horses should wear "diapers", aroused the vigorous protest of the coachmen. The cunning counter-argument, "then you'd have to put panties on the pigeons," put the bureaucrats in the Town Hall on the defensive and in the end they had to give in. After that, peace descended once more, and even the first female *Fiaker* in Vienna, a cheeky young lady, was stoically accepted by her male colleagues.

The Viennese of course never ride in a *Fiaker* (except in moon-in-June operettas), but in the tram. But visitors from all over the world love our trams: like the terrorists who, in December 1975, attacked the conference of OPEC ministers meeting in a building on the Ring – and like good little commuters they took the tram to get there.

There are 35 routes altogether travelling on nearly 250 km (156 miles) of track, moving about 250 million passengers a year. Vienna can boast the biggest tram network in the western world. The loved and hated *Schaffner* (conductors) turn every trip into an adventure. Their insignia are official caps and clippers, their domain is the coach, their word is law. "Come along there, move up, no pushing, ladies and gentlemen." Today, all routes have been converted to driver-only trams. A tram ride is only half as much fun, and Vienna is a little bit poorer.

LEFT: monument in the Central Cemetery.
RIGHT: a *Fiaker* with his trusty horse

The new Viennese

Although it is less noticeable here than in Paris or New York, and although the city has no predominantly foreign districts as London has, Vienna is a multi-ethnic city. For centuries, immigrants have left their mark on its countenance, bringing with them their customs, traditions and tastes. They join the community and a couple of generations later will even be regarded as "typically Viennese".

The city's magnetic attraction was particularly in evidence at the end of the 19th century. Vienna seemed for many to be a glittering mirage, the dream of so many Czechs and Hun-

garians, Slavs and Jews eking out a colourless existence in their little provincial towns on the fringes of the empire. In 1900 the city's population had just passed 1 million, and Czechs represented 25 percent of the total. Even today there are countless pages in the Vienna telephone directory which look as if they would be more at home in Prague, although most of these

LAST OF THE *FIAKERS*

Bowler-hatted coachmen used to be as much a Vienna institution as their horse-drawn traps, but only about 30 *Fiakers* still ply their trade with the tourists descendants of the original immigrants cannot even speak their native language.

The caretakers

During the 1970s, Vienna saw a vast influx of immigrants from what was then still Yugoslavia, and from Turkey. These "guest workers" were responsible for fuelling the economic boom of the time as they sent for their families and gradually took over entire sections of everyday life. For example, the occupation of *Hausbesorgerin*, a sort of equivalent of the French concierge, used to be the prerogative of Czech immigrants but has long since been

taken over by resolute Croatian or Turkish women. The markets have changed, too. At the Naschmarkt or the Brunnenmarkt, some of the snack stands now serve hot *Langos* – hot bread with lashings of garlic – instead of sausages with mustard and horseradish. Some Viennese observe this development with distrust and grumble at the way their city is changing, but it's difficult to moan about "foreigners" if your name is Pavkovic.

By mid-1992, some 15 percent of the residents of Vienna were foreigners. They range from the Egyptian newspaper boys to students from South Tyrol, from German company directors to the officials from overseas who

occupy the UNO district on the other side of the Danube. Added to these is the growing tide of refugees and others seeking asylum, especially from the neighbouring states to the east whose history is linked to that of Austria. Many of these new – like those who have fled from Bosnia – arrivals hope to be able to return to their own country one day. Emergency accommodation has been provided for them in schools and warehouses, in church halls and the homes of volunteers.

The new tourists

After the fall of the Iron Curtain, increasing numbers of visitors came to Vienna from the north-east. The dusty buses from the Czech Republic or Hungary became a familiar sight, although their breathtaking exhaust fumes met with little enthusiasm. Most of these tourists were less interested in Schönbrunn or the Hofburg than in the streets surrounding Mariahilferstrasse in the 6th District. A maze of shops sprang up selling coveted video recorders and deep freezers, apple-perfumed shampoo and alarm clocks with Micky Mouse ears.

There are still a lot of visitors from Eastern European countries but this fact now draws less attention and they no longer base their visits on shopping frenzies. Many of them would like to remain and make a new life here. Like the other countries of Western Europe, however, Austria recognises a right to asylum only on political and not on economic grounds.

The great Chancellor Metternich once ironically observed that the Balkans begin in Vienna. The city has always distinguished itself from its elegant sisters further to the west. Despite all the magnificence it was a little shabbier, more chaotic and heterogeneous... Today, things remain much the same, and it is to be hoped that in this respect, at least, nothing will change. The students from Bratislava and Bolzano in the attic, the Counsellor with the Hungarian grandmother and the Polish uncle on the first floor, and on the ground floor the caretaker from a little village near Laibach who can swear so picturesquely in dialect. It's a typical house somewhere between the Ringstrasse and the Gürtel, and it's home for a colourful collection of people. Typically Viennese.

Above Left: meeting in a splendid Vienna doorway.
Right: Leopold Hawelka in front of his café

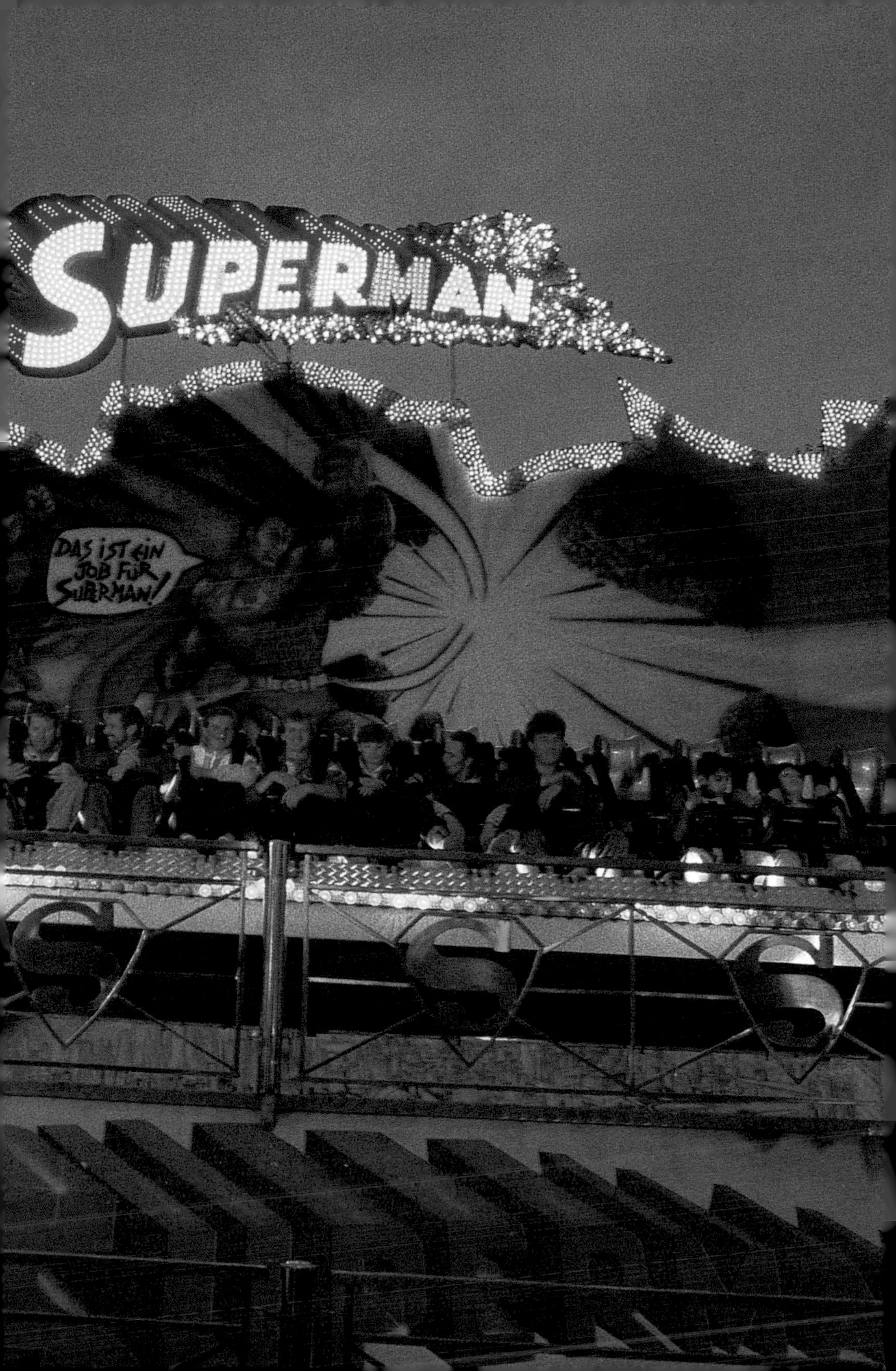
SUPERMAN
DAS IST EIN JOB FÜR SUPERMAN!

PLACES

Insight Guides' numbered maps will help you find your way around the beautiful and historic Austrian capital

Vienna is a city for pedestrians, for strollers and promenaders, for thinkers and dreamers. You don't need a car to see Vienna at its most beautiful. The heart of the city lies in the district inside the Ringstrasse, in the "Innere Stadt".

You should take plenty of time to view Vienna, to let the city work on you like a piece of music, to rediscover the magic of the past: in the delicate, romantic charm of St Rupert's Church, in the wide vaults of the Gothic nave of St Stephen's Cathedral, in the twisting medieval alleys of the old city, in the aristocratic palaces around the Herrengasse, in the Imperial state rooms of the Hofburg and the upper-middle-class apartments on the Ringstrasse.

The following pages show several routes through the city centre. The first leads from the Opera crossroads (Opernkreuzung), the middle of present-day Vienna, through the pedestrian precincts of the Kärntner Strasse and the Graben to the medieval squares of Am Hof and Freyung. From there, follow the Herrengasse to the Imperial Vienna of the Hofburg and back to the Opera House.

The second tour begins and ends at St Stephen's Cathedral. It leads into old Vienna, the Vienna of narrow alleys, in which the medieval buildings of the once walled city have survived.

The Ringstrasse is different. A keener wind blows here. The city walls had been demolished, and at last the middle class could and would show what they could do: in the Viennese style, of course, imitating the best buildings of the past. A necklace of impressive buildings surrounds the city centre. Here, too, there are two routes leading from the Opera crossroads to help you discover the splendours of the 19th century.

After the second siege by the Turks, the city threatened to burst at the seams. The court and the aristocracy built their pleasure palaces outside the city. Today, they are favourite destinations for Viennese outings. But you can find jewels of Baroque architecture even further out: the guide to the suburbs and surrounding countryside will point them out as you travel through the Wachau and the Burgenland to the forests and hills to the south of the city.

One thing you shouldn't forget when walking through Vienna: the architectural scenery is only the background against which the life of the delightful Vienna of today is lived, in which visitors very quickly find their way about and feel at home.

PRECEDING PAGES: St Stephen's Cathedral in winter; Art Nouveau relief; Superman ride at the Prater. **LEFT:** another Viennese landmark: a highly polished *Fiaker* lamp

90

Frankgasse
Votivkirche **42**
Sigmund-Freud-Park
Roosevelt platz
Schotten tor
Polizei-präsidium
Börse (Stock Exchange) **43**
Börse-platz
Werdertor-gasse
Henrichsgasse
Rudolfs-platz
Goldsdorfgasse
Josefs-

Universitätsstraße
Universität **41**
Grillparzer-straße
Schottenring
Reichsratsstraße
Liebiggasse
Schottenbastei gasse
Schottenstorfer gasse
Rockhgasse
Wipplingerstraße
Straße
Concordia-platz
Salz-
Maria am Gestade **19**
Passauer-platz
Sterngasse
Marc-Aurel-Straße
St. Rupre

Felderstraße
Rathaus-
Neues Rathaus (Town Hall) **39**
Rathaus-platz
Lichtenfelsgasse
park
Stadion-
Reichsratsstraße
Bartenstein-
Burgtheater (National Theatre) **40**
Schreyvogel-
Oppolzer
Teinfaltstraße
Schottenstift Schottenkirche (Scots Church) **8**
Freyung
Renn-
Künstler-forum
Feuer-wehrmuseum
Puppen- und Spielzeug-museum
Juden-platz
Bezirks-amt
Altes Rathaus (Old Town Hall)
Hoher Markt **18**
Seitenstett gas
Synagoge

INNERE STADT
Am Hof **7**
9 Chöre der Engel
Graben
St. Peter **6**
Dom- u. Diözesanmuse (Cathedral Mus **17**

Kaiserin-Elisabeth-Denkmal
Volks-
garten
Parlament **38**
Pallas-Athene-Brunnen
Minoriten-kirche **9**
Minoritenplatz
Herrengasse
Bundesministerium f. Inneres
Bundeskanzler-amt
Schaufler gasse
Theseus-tempel
Ballhaus-platz
Kaiser-appartements (State Apartments)
Schatzkammer (Treasury) Alte Burg **10**
Michaeler-platz
St. Michael **13**
Pestsäule
Café Hawelka
Haas-Haus
Stephans-platz
St. Stephan **4**
Figaro-haus
Deutsch-ordenskirche
Schatzkammer des Dt. Ordens (Treasury of Teutonic Order) **29**
Franzisk kirc

Volkstheater
Naturhistorisches Museum (Natural History Museum) **34**
Maria-Theresien-Platz
Maria-Theresia-Denkmal
Heldenplatz **35**
Erzherzog-Karl-Denkmal
Prinz-Eugen-Denkmal
Burgtor (Heldentor)
Neue Burg
Völkerkunde-museum (Ethnological Museum) **36**
Spanische Hofreitschule (Spanish Riding School) **14**
Stallburg (Stables)
Jüdisches Museum
Hofburg-Kapelle **11**
Hofburg
Josefs-platz
National-bibliothek
Augustiner-kirche
Dorotheum **5**
Kapuziner-kirche
Kaiser-gruft **2**
Stadtpalais des Prinzen Eugen (City Palace of Prince Eugene) **3**
Malteser-kirche
St. Anna
St. Ursula
Finanz-ministerium

Volkstheater
Burggasse
Messe-palast
Schweighoferstraße
Stiftskaserne
Stiftskirche
Bellariastraße
Museumstraße
Volksgartenstr.
Dr. K.-Renner-Ring
Burg ring
Kunsthistorisches Museum (Museum of Fine Arts) **33**
Babenberger str.
Babenberger Straße
Robert-Stolz-Platz
Opern-
Burg-garten **32**
Inst. der Universität
Albertina **16**
Albertina Platz
Philharmoniker-str.
Staatsoper (State Opera House) **1**
Hotel Sacher
Hotel Bristol
Mayseder g.
Krugerstr.
Walfisch-
gasse
Schwarzenbergstr.

Getreidemarkt
Gauermanng.
Akademie d. bildenden Künste (Academy of Fine Arts) **31**
Schiller-platz
Secession **30**
Café Museum
Karlsplatz
Handels-akademie (Academy of Trade) **44**
Künstler-haus **45**
Kärntner Ring
Bösen-
Akademie str.

St.-Josef
Mariahilferstraße
Theo-bald-
Königsklostergasse
Technische Universität
Papageno-gasse
Millöckerg.
Theater an der Wien
Wienzeile
Naschmarkt
Linke bräckengasse
Ketten-brückengasse
Technische Universität
Karlsplatz
Resselpark
Historisches Museum der Stadt Wien (Historical Museum) **46**
Karls-kirche **47**
Brucknerstr.

Alfred-Grünwald-Park
Kühn-platz
Rilke-Frankenberg-platz
Technische Universität
Panigl-
Gußhaus-

Central Vienna

0 — 500 m
0 — 500 yds

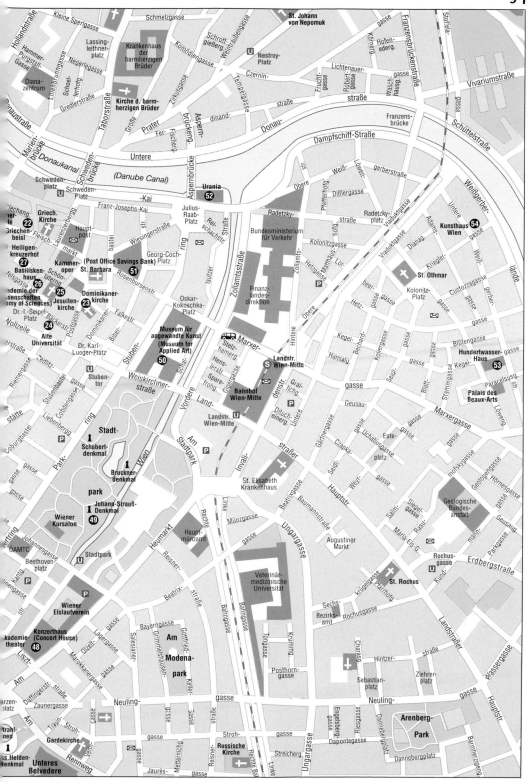

SPLENDOURS OF VIENNA

The historic centre is crammed with sacred and secular architectural gems from all periods. Highlights are St Stephen's 14th-century cathedral and imperial era nobles' palaces

Map, page 90

To get to the starting point of your walk, go to the Opernkreuzung – the crossroads of the Ringstrasse and the Kärntner Strasse at the State Opera House – which is an historically interesting point in the city centre. The Kärntner Strasse leads to St Stephen's Square (Stephansplatz). Where the street narrows, medieval Vienna begins.

Near the Opera crossroads there once stood the fortified Carinthian Tower (Kärntner Turm), which was fought over fiercely during the first siege by the Turks in 1529. The surrounding wall, dating from the end of the 12th century, was replaced by Renaissance fortifications with huge bastions, surrounded by a *glacis* free of buildings. The fortifications were demolished in 1857, leaving insignificant remnants. The State Opera House stands on the site of one of the projecting bastions. The Ringstrasse zone stretching out on both sides is built on the site of the former *glacis*. Looking out of town, you can see the oldest suburb, the Wieden, today the 4th district. The first major building on the Ringstrasse was the **State Opera House** (Staatsoper) ❶, 1861–9, which was designed by August von Siccardsburg and Eduard van der Nüll in the Historicist style and decorated by famous artists.

The sculptor Julius Hähnel created the bronze statues in the loggia and the Pegasus statues above; Moritz von Schwind painted the loggia and the foyer. These were almost the only parts that survived the devastating bomb attacks in March 1945. The fountains on either side of the building display allegorical figures by Hans Gasser. The Opera House was restored in the original style (only the auditorium was modernised), and when the occupying forces left in 1955 it was re-opened with a performance of Beethoven's *Fidelio*.

The State Opera is the leading opera house in Austria and the company is of international standing. It has always been able to attract the best conductors and singers and has made a considerable contribution to establishing Vienna's reputation as a musical city. Its orchestra is the Vienna Philharmonic. The annual Opera Ball is a world-famous social event. The area around the Opera House was the first section of the Ringstrasse to be built during the 1860s.

Vienna's main shopping street

In the **Kärntner Strasse**, before you reach the pedestrian precinct, you can see to your right the elaborately decorated façade of the Palais Todesco (No. 51), built in the Renaissance style by Theophil Hansen and Ludwig Förster. In the 19th century, the salon of the banker Eduard Todesco was a popular meeting place for VIPs from the world of politics and theatre. If you look into the Walfischgasse, just past the Palais (to your right), you

LEFT: the Spanish Riding School.
BELOW: fountain in front of the State Opera House

Map,
page 90

The knights who founded the Maltese Church were given the island of Malta by Karl V in 1530.

BELOW: looking for international custom

can still see the line of the old city wall where the houses pass the Moulin Rouge bend toward the city. To the left, in Philharmonikerstrasse, is the famous **Hotel Sacher**; part of the site used to be occupied by the Kärntnertortheater, which was demolished once the Opera House was completed. The Kärntner Strasse has fundamentally changed its appearance several times. In the 18th century, Gothic buildings were replaced by Baroque. In the second half of the 19th century, most of these fell victim to the widening of the street. In 1944–5 many 18th-century houses were destroyed by bombs and fire. Since 1974 the street has been a pedestrian precinct. Among the few historically important buildings left are the Baroque Palais Esterházy and the Church of the Knights of Malta . The Palais Esterházy (No. 41) dates from the middle of the 17th century – one of the few surviving Viennese palaces from before the second Turkish siege (1683). Today it houses Fred Adlmüller's *haute-couture* salon and the casino.

In the **Annagasse**, which leads off just past the Palais, a few steps will take you to **St Anne's Church** (Annakirche), No. 3b. It was built as a Gothic hall church in the 14th century, but altered in Renaissance times and finally given a Baroque interior by the Jesuits in the 18th century. St Anne and the Holy Family preside above the entrance (a notable 17th-century sculpture) and over the altar (a wooden carving circa 1510). Around the church a number of other interesting old buildings have survived.

The **Maltese Church** (Malteserkirche) (Kärntner Strasse 37) has a façade in the neo-classical style of Louis de Montoyer (1806–08), but is Gothic within. The Knights of Malta who founded the church were invited to Vienna in 1200. On the left inside is an 1806 memorial to Grand Master Jean de la Valette, who defended Malta's capital against the Turks.

The Ball of Balls

Everybody dance the waltz! When this clichéd imperative is shouted out on the last Thursday during Fasching (Viennese pre-Lenten carnival), the elegant restraint of permed ladies and well-dressed gentlemen turns to crazy chaos. It's a magnificent fairground, a display of human vanities: the annual Opera Ball!

Throughout the carnival season, many balls are held in Vienna – and if you don't know the steps, you can attend waltz classes in one of the dance schools in preparation. Venues include the Hofburg, the Neues Rathaus and the Musikverein. However, the Opera Ball is by far the grandest. On one night only, the normal rules of the Opera are laid aside, everyone scrambles to see and be seen, and TV teams hunt for extravagantly dressed VIPs. The King and Queen of Spain, the British consort Prince Philip and star tenor Luciano Pavarotti have all been to this ball of balls.

The evening begins with a performance by the Opera House ballet company. Then jazz and waltz orchestras play in seven dance halls. Gaming tables round off the non-stop entertainment.

The Opera Ball is the successor to the Court Opera balls which delighted Imperial Vienna from 1877. These ended when Austria became a republic; the Opera Ball was revived in 1935, only to be put on hold again when the Opera House was bombed during World War II. The Ball was finally brought back in 1965. It has been held every year since, but it is very expensive.

The 150 boxes, from which you can watch *jeunesse dorée* making an entrance into the adult world, cost vastly more than an ordinary ticket, but it's undeniable that the opening ceremony can be seen most comfortably while drinking champagne above the fray. Every year about 1,000 hopeful couples apply to the organiser to be one of the 80 couples taking part in the opening dance. For most of them, it remains a dream.

BELOW: stepping out in the extravagant white dresses traditionally worn at the Opera Ball

TIP

Tickets for Sunday
mass sung by the
Vienna Boys' Choir
(except in summer) in
the Hofburg's
Burgkapelle have to be
booked at least eight
weeks in advance.
They must be collected
and paid for half an
hour before the service
begins.

The **Johannesgasse** is on the right and, close by is No. 5, Palais Questenberg-Kaunitz, probably built around 1701 according to plans by Johann Lukas von Hildebrandt. No. 6a is the **Archive of the Court Chamberlain** (Hofkammer-archiv), built 1843–6, with a room commemorating the poet Franz Grillparzer, director of the court archives 1832–6. Continue along the Marco-d'Aviano-Gasse opposite the Johannesgasse to the **New Market** (Neuer Markt).

The Habsburg tombs

You are now in front of the **Church of the Capuchins** (Kapuzinerkirche) ❷ (open daily 9.30am–4pm), famous for its **Imperial Vault** (Kaisergruft), also known as the Capuchins' Crypt (Kapuzinergruft). In 1619, Emperor Matthias had it built as a tomb for the Habsburg family, underneath the monastery which his wife, Anna, had founded. Over the centuries the crypt was extended. In the centre of the building, open to the public, is the famous Rococo double sarcophagus made for Maria Theresa and her husband Franz Stephan (designed by Balthasar Moll, 1753). Once the Capuchins' Crypt became well known and mentioned in literary works, it was indivisibly linked to the Habsburgs. The façade of the church was rebuilt in 1933–6 according to old drawings. Inside is a single barrel-vaulted nave. The high altar, decorated with inlay work, dates from the early 18th century. On the left is the **Imperial Chapel** (Kaiserkapelle).

Continuing towards the city, on the same side as the church (past the Planken-gasse), some Baroque houses have survived (Nos. 13–16) which suggest the original appearance of the square. On the site of the Ambassador Hotel once stood the *Mehlgrube*, one of the city's most famous pleasure houses in Baroque times. In the middle of the square is the **Providence Fountain** (Providentiabrunnen) –

BELOW: Donner's
Fountain

the famous Baroque sculptor Georg Raphael Donner created the models (1737–9). This is the first fountain the city administration built simply to decorate a square. In the middle of the basin is the figure of Providentia (Providence); the sculptures around the edge symbolise tributaries of the Danube. These are copies in bronze, as the original lead figures are in the Baroque museum in the Lower Belvedere. Maria Theresa had them removed because of their "inadequate" clothing, but the sculptor Messerschmidt rescued them.

Looking from the fountain across into the Plankengasse, you can see the tower of the Protestant Church (built in 1783–4). The Emperor Joseph II's Edict of Tolerance (1782) allowed non-Catholics to build churches. Take a look at the Herrnhuterhaus (No. 17, built 1900–1) which has been connected with the textile industry since the late 18th century. Now go back to the Kärntner Strasse via the Kupferschmiedgasse. In the **Himmelpfortgasse** opposite (No. 8) pay a visit to the former **Winter Palace of Prince Eugene** (Stadtpalais des Prinzen Eugen) ❸. This Baroque palace, begun in 1695–8 by Johann Bernhard Fischer von Erlach and completed by Hildebrandt in 1702–9, has a superbly crafted façade and a fascinating interior. It now houses the Ministry of Finance. Pass the Kärntner Durchgang (with the famous Art-Nouveau style American bar created by Adolf Loos in 1907) and the Weihburggasse (with the house by Kornhäusel, No. 3, "Zur Kaiserin Elisabeth"). Past the bend is the Franziskanerplatz with the **Franciscan Church** (Franziskanerkirche); you then arrive at the **Stock-im-Eisen-Platz**.

The heart of the city

The name comes from the "Stock in Eisen" (club in iron) on the corner of the Kärntner Strasse. This is a tree trunk studded with nails, mentioned in 1533 and

Map, page 90

ABOVE: relief from the portal of Prince Eugene's Winter Palace.

BELOW: the Franciscan Church

Master craftsman Anton Pilgrim designed an intricate pulpit for St Stephen's Cathedral. This self-portrait under the organ loft depicts him with the tools of his trade.

BELOW: the roof of St Stephen's Cathedral

the subject of a local legend. Demolition in the 19th century means this square leads into St Stephen's Square and the Graben (to the left), and offers an unobstructed view of the cathedral tower. The square would have sat outside the Roman walls which marked the limits of the city centre in 1137, as would Vienna's oldest church — St Stephen's.

St Stephen's Cathedral (Stephansdom) ❹ (open daily 6am–11pm; guided catacombs tours (also in English) daily 10–11.30am and 2–4.30pm; climbing St Stephen's Tower daily 9am–5.30pm) should be seen from both outside and inside. It is mainly Gothic. The Romanesque basilica, one of the last to be built in a Germanic country, remains on the west front. The two **Towers of the Pagans** (Heidentürme), 65 metres (213 feet) tall, mark the breadth of the cathedral at that time. The high roof with its glazed tiles (renewed after the fire of 1945) dominates the appearance of the cathedral and harmoniously combines various architectural styles. In the centre of the west front is the **Giant's Doorway** (Riesentor), a late Romanesque (circa 1230–40) portal richly adorned with sculptures.

Around 1500, the cathedral got its projecting pointed arch. Late Gothic doors lead into the cathedral on both sides. On the north side is the **Bishop's Door** (Bischofstor, 1380–90). This was opposite the Bishop's Palace (Bischofshof), today the Archbishop's palace (Rotenturmstrasse 2). On the south side is the **Singer's Door** (Singertor) by Hans Puchsbaum (1440–50). You can also enter at the foot of the Gothic towers (the northern one was never completed). Notice the statues of worldly (Habsburg) founders in some of the doorways – this was a rarity in the Middle Ages.

On entering, you will see a Gothic three-aisled nave of impressive dimensions: the central aisle is 28 metres (92 feet) tall, and the nave is 36 metres (118

feet) wide. The fan vaulting rests on pillars almost 3 metres (9 feet) thick, each with six niches for statues. The triple-aisled choir, the oldest part of the Gothic cathedral (1304–40), has cruciform vaulting. Here the Gothic statues on the pillars were incomplete until the end of the 19th century. The landmark of the cathedral (and Vienna) is the **South Tower**. Dating from the high Gothic period, it is almost 137 metres/450 feet tall and is the highest in central Europe after Ulm and Cologne. Begun in the reign of Duke Rudolf IV in 1359, it was completed by Hans Prachatitz. The northern or **Eagle Tower** (Adlerturm) was begun in 1467, but building stopped in 1511. Kaspar and Hans Saphoy built an octagonal top for the tower 1556–78.

Inside, it is a good idea for a first visit to limit yourself to the most important works of art. The high altar is adorned with Tobias Pock's *Stoning of St Stephen*; behind, in the choir, are remains of Gothic stained glass (circa 1340–60). In the left aisle of the choir is a Gothic altar with triptych (Wiener Neustädter Altar, 1447), with 72 saints painted on the gold background of the panels. To the left of the altar is the (empty) tomb of Rudolf IV and his wife with reclining figures (Rudolf began the building of the naves and the tower). In the right aisle of the choir is the tomb of Emperor Frederick III (1452–93), designed by Niclaes Gerhaert van Leyden (1467–1513) as a sarcophagus of red marble with reclining figure and intricate carving. In the central aisle notice the late Gothic pulpit by Anton Pilgram (circa 1500), the most notable artwork in the nave. A self-portrait of the artist at the pulpit's foot *(Fenstergucker)* shows Pilgram looking out of a window. In front of the pulpit is the *Dienstbotenmadonna* (Madonna of the Servants, 1340); in the left aisle, near the exit to the tower, is the late Gothic organ base with a portrait bust of Pilgram (1513).

Map, page 90

TIP

Need help or advice? At the top of Kärntner Strasse (No. 38) you'll find a tourist office. They can give you tips, information, brochures and all kinds of good ideas for your stay in Vienna.

BELOW LEFT: the spire of St Stephen's Cathedral.
BELOW RIGHT: the high altar

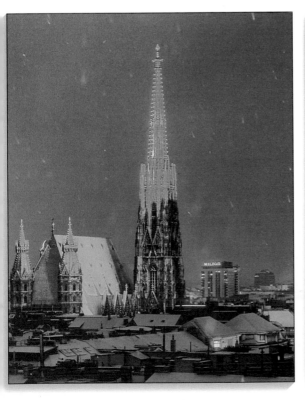

The chapels on the outside of the Romanesque towers can be reached from the aisles: to the left stands the **Chapel of the Cross** (Kreuzkapelle), with the tomb of Prince Eugene and a 15th-century crucifix, plus the tomb of the humanist Johannes Cuspinian. To the right is the **Duke's Chapel** (Herzogskapelle) with a late-Gothic carved triptych altar and a stone statue of the Virgin carved around the middle of the 14th century.

Clockwise tour round the cathedral

On the left façade of the main body is a relief of the Mount of Olives (circa 1440). North of the Eagle Tower is a Renaissance epitaph for the humanist Conrad Celtis (1459–1508). On the wall of the choir is an epitaph with a sandstone relief of *The Judgment*. Next to it stands the chapel in which the funeral of Mozart was held in 1791, and the pulpit (circa 1430) from which the Franciscan monk called the citizens to join the *John Capistrano* crusade against the Turks in 1451. This is surmounted by a Baroque group showing St Capistran with a banner above a fallen Turk, after a design by François de Roettiers. Then go past six late Gothic frescoes of *The Passion* (circa 1500) to the right of the Singer's Door to view *The Man of Sorrows* (circa 1435). Immediately to the right of the Giant's Door you can see a scratched "05", a symbol of the Austrian resistance in World War II. A separate tour will take you on a visit of the important buildings surrounding the square (*see page 113*).

A busker plays to Graben shoppers.

On **St Stephen's Square** (Stephansplatz), by the cathedral, the site of the Chapel of St Mary Magdalene is outlined in red stones – it burned down in 1782. The house Zur Weltkugel (No. 2), had its façade restored around 1900 by the Sparkasse savings bank, which had its headquarters in the house. You then return to the **Stock-im-Eisen-Platz**. Here is the richly ornamented Equitable House (No. 3), typical of the 19th century, built in 1890–1 for a New York insurance company (note the US eagle on the roof). The bronze doors were the work of Rudolf Weyr; the reliefs illustrate the Stock-im-Eisen legend.

BELOW: the Plague Column on the Graben

The **Graben** gets its name from the ditch surrounding the Roman camp, which was levelled around 1200. At the entrance to the Graben stands the modern **Haas House**, with its once controversial futuristic glass façade. The local citizens have become accustomed to it, especially as the café on the upper floor offers the best view of the cathedral.

In the Middle Ages the Graben was an important market, in the 18th century a popular meeting place for high society, and today it's a busy pedestrianised shopping centre. Until the middle of the 19th century both ends were bounded by houses. Of the Baroque houses from these times, only the **Palais Bartolotti-Partenfeld** (No. 11) survives. It may have been built by Hildebrandt (circa 1720). Today, the neo-classical Sparkasse building (No. 21) is surrounded by Historicist or Secessionist façades. In the middle of the road is the **Trinity Column** (Dreifältigkeitssäule), better known as the **Plague Column** (Pestsäule). It was commissioned by Emperor Leopold I in 1679 to commemorate an outbreak of plague. It is an excellent example of Viennese high-Baroque architectural sculpture, designed by

Johann Bernhard Fischer von Erlach and Ludovico Burnacini, who with Paul Strudel created the pyramid of clouds. It is crowned by a group portraying the Trinity. The fountains at either end of the Graben originally stood in front of the houses bounding the square. They bear statues of St Leopold and St Joseph by Johann Martin Fischer (1804). Near the fountain in front of No. 21 is a special attraction – an Art Nouveau-style underground toilet.

The district as far as the Stallburg is a centre of the Viennese antique trade. The auction house **Dorotheum** ❺ can be found here, too (on Dorotheergasse 17, open Mon–Fri 10am–6pm, Sat 8.30am–noon). Between Graben Nos. 25 and 21 you can see Hildebrandt's Baroque **St Peter's Church** (Peterskirche) ❻. For centuries a Romanesque church stood on this site. The church, built in 1702–33, has a portal by Andrea Altomonte, 1751–3, and is characterised by its diagonally placed towers (1730–3) and the cupola. The cylindrical central space is raised above an elliptical ground plan. The fresco in the cupola, *The Assumption of the Virgin Mary*, was painted by Johann Michael Rottmayr (1713–14). The interior boasts a very high altar by Antonio Galli-Bibena, with an altar panel by Martino Altomonte. The pulpit is by Matthias Steinl (circa 1716), and the gilded carving opposite depicts the *Fall of St John Nepomuk into the Vltava* by Lorenzo Mattielli (circa 1729). Mattielli also carved the statues on the outside of the choir. The aisles are decorated with paintings by famous artists.

In the Middle Ages, the **Kohlmarkt** connected with the start of the western trade route (now Mariahilfer Strasse). The name derives from *Holzkohle* (charcoal), which was sold here. From the 14th century onwards, the Kohlmarkt gained status from the nearby Hofburg and developed into an expensive shopping street. In the Middle Ages, the **Tuchlauben** were homes to wealthy cloth

Map, page 90

BELOW: the Haas House on St Stephen's Square

Modern statues stand in front of imposing 19th-century buildings in the Freyung.

BELOW: Baroque façades on the elegant Am Hof

merchants. In the pedestrian precinct you can see a remarkable Baroque building, the Hochholzerhof (No. 5). Built in 1719, its impressive, rich façade follows the curve of the street. The pharmacy Zum Weissen Storch has been at No. 9 since the 17th century. In No. 19, a medieval house with a Baroque façade (1716), Vienna's oldest secular frescoes were discovered. They date from circa 1400 and illustrate subjects from Neidhart poetry. On the **Steindlgasse**, No. 4, Zum Goldenen Drachen, dates from the 16th and 17th centuries. Note the house sign and the late Gothic Madonna. The Steindlgasse offers a good view of the Gothic choir of the church, Am Hof and the Seitzergasse and brings you to the **Bognergasse**. No. 9, the pharmacy Zum Weissen Engel, has an Art Nouveau façade. Take the **Naglergasse**. On your left is a well-preserved line of burghers' houses dating from the late Middle Ages and early Renaissance, which lay along the Roman camp wall (later the city wall). At Haarhof you can still see the dip of the ditch, and the curve of the walls can be followed as far as Heidenschuss.

Leave the Naglergasse via the Irisgasse (to the right) and move on into the square **Am Hof**. Here Heinrich II Jasomirgott built his castle in 1155. Today the older buildings on the square are Baroque. You have already seen from the outside the Gothic choir of the church **Nine Choirs of Angels** (Zu den neun Chören der Engel) ❼. Its early Baroque façade dominates the square. From its balcony Pope Pius VI gave his blessing *urbi et orbi* in 1782. It bears a strong resemblance to its models in Rome. The keep of the castle once stood here, then the Carmelites built a Gothic hall church in 1386–1403. In the early 17th century, the Jesuits gave it a Baroque appearance. The side chapels and the white stucco hide all Gothic traces. The most famous preachers in Vienna delivered sermons in the neo-classical pulpit. It is the oldest Jesuit church in Vienna, and the only one

styled as Jesuit churches in Rome. It marks the climax of the early Baroque period. The **Palais Collalto** (No. 13), connected to the church by an arch, received its Baroque façade in 1720 (note the portal and the wrought-iron balcony railings). This was where Mozart first appeared in public in 1762, aged six. During the French occupation of Vienna in 1809, Napoleon's General Lefèbvre lived in the Palais. The **Urbani House** (No. 12) next door was given its Baroque façade in the style of Hildebrandt around 1730. The relief of the Virgin dates from the 16th century, the Urbanikeller inn sign from the 18th.

Also in Am Hof is the former **City Arsenal** (Bürgerliches Zeughaus), No. 10), now housing the Fire Brigade. The fine gabled façade was created by Anton Ospel after French and Spanish models (1731–2). The sculptures (allegories symbolising an election slogan of Charles VI and bearing a globe) are by Mattielli. The Arsenal played an important part in the two Turkish sieges, and also during the 1848 revolution. The Minister of War at the time, Latour, was murdered by the enraged crowd in Am Hof.

Until the 19th century, No. 9 was the home of the Mayor (at first floor height, an angel holds a shield with the Viennese double eagle and imperial crown). No. 7, one of the most beautiful Baroque houses in the centre, was built in 1727–30 by Hildebrandt. The proportions of the façade are similar to those of palaces of the nobility dating from this period, but the ground floor has been altered. The garage doors for the Fire Brigade have replaced the portal. In the middle of the square is the **Column of the Virgin** (Mariensäule), erected in 1664–7 by Balthasar Heroldi. It replaces an older column erected by Ferdinand III in 1644 to mark the removal of the threat of the Swedish army in the Thirty Years' War. Head for the Freyung, leaving behind you the hollow marking Roman and medieval Vienna, but before doing so look at the curve in the Naglergasse (on the left) that echoes the camp boundary.

The **Freyung** is surrounded by impressive buildings, but is dominated by the Scottish Church (Schottenkirche) – though its monks were Irish. Immediately left of the square is the **Palais Hardegg** (No. 1), a palatial apartment block in the Romantic Historicist style, built by Romano and Schwendenwein in 1847. Next door (No. 2) is the **Palais Ferstel**, built 1856–60 by Heinrich Ferstel (designer of the University) in Historicist style for the Austro-Hungarian Bank. A lane through to the Herrengasse widens into a square holding the **Fountain of the Danube Nymphs** (Donaunixen-Brunnen).

By Fernkorn (No. 3) is the **Palais Harrach**, built at the end of the 17th century but whose main façade dates from 1845. In the extension of the Herrengasse is a jewel among Vienna's Baroque palaces – the **Palais Daun-Kinsky** (No. 4), built 1713–16 by Hildebrandt for Reichsgraf Daun, father of Maria Theresa's victorious general. In 1784, the Palais passed to the Kinsky family – the salon of Rosa Kinsky was famous. The well-proportioned portal, the statues and the splendid staircase testify to the decorative gifts of the architect. Next to the Scottish Church is the neo-classical **Schottenhof** (No. 6), one of the earliest big apartment houses in Vienna, built in 1826–32 by Joseph

 Map, page 90

BELOW: doorway of the Kinksy Palace

Kornhäusel, the great architect of the Biedermeier period. The composer Franz Liszt lived here 1869–96. In the gallery of the monastery is the famous Altar of the Scottish Master (circa 1470), showing two of the oldest views of Vienna.

In the monastery's grammar school, the **Schottengymnasium**, many famous men studied, among them Nobel Prize winner Julius Wagner von Jauregg, Johann Nestroy, Johann Strauss and Victor Adler. The **Schottenkirche** was founded by the Babenberg Henry II Jasomirgott in 1155, outside the walls of the 12th-century city. Today it appears as a Baroque church (1638–48), with towers that rise only slightly above the central portion of the building. We know its architects included members of the Carlone and d'Allio families. The interior was altered by Ferstel in 1883–9 (especially the high altar, pulpit and painted ceiling). Seventeenth-century paintings survive on partially renovated side altars, and Vienna's oldest statue of the Virgin (c. 1250) sits above the tabernacle of the altar in the left transept.

The Café Central, on the historic Herren-gasse, was visited in its heyday by Viennese opinion-makers such as Freud and Hofmannsthal.

BELOW: entrance to the Minorite Church

Aristocratic palaces

The route from the Freyung to the Hofburg follows the **Herrengasse** – the line of the old Roman road along the *limes* and boundary of the Roman empire. Many nobles built palaces here in the 16th century, close to the Hofburg, generating the name "Herrengasse" (Lords' Street). Surviving palaces date from the 16th to the early 19th centuries. The first of these is the **Palais Porcia** (No. 23), with its mostly original Italian-style façade (mid-16th century), followed by the mid-17th century **Palais Trauttmansdorff** (No. 21) and the early 18th century Palais **Batthyány** (No. 19, on the corner of the Bankgasse – note the interesting portal). On the other side of the Herrengasse you can see the backs of the Palais Har-rach and the Palais Ferstel.

More palaces can be seen in the **Bankgasse**; No. 3 is the Austro-Hungarian Bank building, built in 1873–5 by Friedrich Schmidt, designer of the Town Hall. On the corner of the Strauchgasse is the legendary **Café Central**, meeting place for Viennese intellectuals until 1938 (now re-opened). Its rival was the Café Herren-hof. Opposite the junction with the Strauchgasse is the **Landhaus** (No. 13), former seat of the government of Lower Austria. A free-standing, late neo-Classical block of buildings with an impressive row of pillars, parts of the interior date from Renaissance and Baroque times. In the 1848 revolution, dramatic scenes played in front of the Landhaus.

Walk around the Landhaus and you enter the **Minoritenplatz**, a square surrounded by impressive palaces. Particularly notable are the **Palais Dietrich-stein** (No. 3) with its delicately proportioned Rococo façade; the **Stadtpalais Liechtenstein** (No. 4) with its impressive portal; Bankgasse (No. 9) with another note-worthy portal on the Minoritenplatz (sculptures by Giu-liani); and the **Palais Starhemberg** (No. 5) which dominates part of the square and was built around 1650 by an unknown architect.

In the middle of the square is the **Minorite Church of St Mary of the Snows** (Minoritenkirche Maria Schnee) 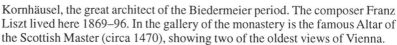, the Italian national church in Vienna. The Minorite order was invited to Vienna in 1224, and the church and monastery were built from 1340–1400. You enter the triple-aisled church through the impressive central portal (c. 1350) with a three-part relief on the tympanum that shows French influence. The triple-naved interior is 18th century. In the centre of the left-hand wall is a remarkable mosaic copy of da Vinci's *Last Supper*, commissioned by Napoleon in 1806. The monastery was demolished in the early 20th century to make room for No. 1 – the Household, Court and State Archives (Haus-, Hof- und Staatsarchiv). Next door is the Federal Chancellery (Bundeskanzleramt) on the Ballhausplatz.

Go back to the Herrengasse and turn right towards the Michaelerplatz. You'll see the **Palais Mollard Clary** (No. 9, Lower Austrian State Museum); its present appearance dates from 1760. The neo-classical façades of the **Palais Modena** (No. 7) conceal parts dating from the 16th century. Nearby is the **Palais Wilczek** (No. 5) with a façade dating from the post-1719 period. The poets Grillparzer and Eichendorff lived here for a time. The **Palais Herberstein** (Nos. 1–3) was built by Carl König in 1897 as part of a programme of alterations to the Michaelerplatz.

The Hofburg

The **Michaelertrakt** is the most recent part of the Hofburg, built in 1889–93 by Ferdinand Kirschner according to plans by Joseph Emanuel Fischer von Erlach. The characteristic concave wall with its portals forms an impressive front onto the **Michaelerplatz** and the city centre. On both sides of the main portal there are four statues of Hercules, and at the side are two monumental wall fountains: to the left *Power on the Seas* by Rudolf Weyr, 1895; to the right *Power on Land* by Edmund Hellmer, 1897. The area in front of the Reichskanzlei (officials'

Map, page 90

BELOW LEFT: façade of the Michaelertrakt. **BELOW RIGHT:** cradle of Napoleon's son in the Hofburg Imperial Treasury

The Imperial Cross, circa 1024, is one of the valuable items in the Hofburg Imperial Treasury.

BELOW: public rooms in the Hofburg

quarters) remained undeveloped for a time because the old Hofburgtheater could not be demolished until the new theatre on the Ring was opened in 1888. Behind the left part of the Michaelertrakt lies the Winter Riding School, which was connected to the old Burgtheater.

Passing through a magnificent wrought-iron gate, you enter a circular hall, surmounted by a huge dome with statues symbolizing mottos of the Habsburgs. To the left is the entrance to the **State Apartments** (Kaiserappartements) ➓ (open Mon–Sat 8.30am–noon, 12.30–4pm, Sun 8.30am–12.30pm). The next gate leads to the **Platz in der Burg** and a memorial to Emperor Franz I of Austria (1792–1835) by Pompeo Marchesi (1842–46).

The history of the Hofburg's construction can be read like a book. To your left is the oldest part, the **Schweizerhof**, Gothic in origin and begun in the late 13th century. The **Imperial Chapel** (Hofburgkapelle) ➓ was first mentioned in 1296; it was rebuilt in 1447–49 and the interior redesigned in the Baroque style in the 17th and 18th centuries. You enter the courtyard through the splendid Renaissance **Swiss Gate** (Schweizertor). Here are the entrances to the Imperial Chapel (you can see the Gothic choir from a neighbouring courtyard) and the world-famous **Imperial Treasury** (Geistliche und Weltliche Schatzkammer) ➓ (open daily 10am–6pm, closed Tues) with the imperial crown jewels. To the right the Platz in der Burg is bordered by the **Amalienburg**, originally a separate building. Built 1575–7, its present appearance dates from 1600–11.

The connecting building is the **Leopold Wing** (Leopoldinischer Trakt), built in 1660–6 in Early Baroque style according to plans by Philiberto Lucchese. Today it is the official seat of the Federal President. The six sets of 16th-century windows to the left mark the residence of Archduke Ferdinand. The fourth side

of the square is the High Baroque **Imperial Chancellery Wing** (Reichskanzleitrakt) by Joseph Emanuel Fischer von Erlach (1723–30). Until 1806, when the Habsburgs relinquished the crown of the Holy Roman Empire, this was the home of the imperial government. Three portals form the focal points of the façade, and Mattielli's sculptures at the side again refer to the Hercules myth. Go through the living apartments of Ferdinand to the Heldenplatz with its neoclassical Ceremonial Hall (Zeremoniensaal) to the left, built 1802–6 by Louis de Montoyer, and the Neue Hofburg (1881–1913).

If you leave the Platz in der Burg between the Leopoldinische Trakt and the Amalienburg, you come to the **Ballhausplatz**. Sticking out to your left is the Leopoldinische Trakt, further over is the Volksgarten, and straight ahead the **Federal Chancellery** (Bundeskanzleramt). This was built to plans by Hildebrandt in 1717–19, as was the **Court Privy Chancellery** (Geheime Hofskanzlei), altered by Nikolaus Pacassi in 1766 and extended into the Löwelstrasse in 1881–2. The main façade still follows Hildebrandt's design. The building, in which the Congress of Vienna met in 1814–15, is the seat of the Federal Chancellor and Government. In a National Socialist coup in 1934 the Federal Chancellor, Dr Dollfuss, was shot here.

Return via the Schauflergasse (right) to the Michaelerplatz. The building at the start of the **Schauflergasse** (left) is modern, with an Historicist-style façade. In the 16th century a building for ball games stood here, hence the name Ballhausplatz. The first **Church of St Michael** (Michaelerkirche) ⑬ was built around 1100. Towards the end of the 12th century it was included in the Babenbergs' expansion of the city and at the end of the 13th century it was improved during the building of the Hofburg (Schweizerhof section). The oldest parts of

Map, page 90

BELOW LEFT: the Swiss Gate, built in 1552.
BELOW RIGHT: statue of Franz I in an inner courtyard of the Hofburg

Among the crown jewels in the Imperial Treasury is a 10th-century crown set with enamel plaques and cabochons.

the present church date from the second quarter of the 13th century (choir and transept); the nave followed during the third quarter. You can still see Romanesque carved arches and Gothic elements in the choir if you go into the Habsburgergasse. In the porch, a sandstone sculpture *Fall of the Angels* by Mattielli is still Baroque (1724–5), although the façade is neo-classical (1792). Inside is a three-naved pillared basilica with cruciform vaulting. The Baroque high altar, set forward like a stage, contrasts with the central nave with its late Romanesque arches and capitals. The wall painting (*Last Judgement*) on the triumphal arch is 14th century; the stucco relief *Fall of the Angels* on the choir wall above the high altar is by Karl Georg Melville (1782).

Looking around the Michaelerplatz, which has recently undergone major renovation, you will see a variety of building styles. The Grosses Michaelerhaus (No. 4, corner of Kohlmarkt 11) was built in 1720, the Kleines Michaelerhaus (No. 6) in 1735. In a passage along the outer wall of the church there is a massive relief of the Mount of Olives, framed in colour (1494). If you take a look into the Reitschulgasse, you will see the **Stallburg**, an important Renaissance building. The **Riding School Wing** (Reitschultrakt) of the Hofburg opposite is Baroque, the Michaelertrakt Historicist. The most recent building (No. 3) was built in 1910–11 by Adolf Loos, and the unaccustomed simplicity of its Secessionist façade caused considerable excitement and also criticism at the time.

The Lipizzaner stables

BELOW RIGHT: ceiling of the Great Hall in the National Library

An arcaded passage leads through the Stallburg, part of the Hofburg that was built from 1558–65 as a residence for Archduke Maximilian, later Emperor Maximilian II (1564–76). The four-winged building with its almost square

THE SPANISH RIDING SCHOOL

This world-famous equestrian spectacle has its origins in the foundation in 1572 of an Imperial school of horsemanship. A stud was set up in Lipizza near Trieste (now in Slovenia), hence the name "Lipizzaner stables". Originally an Arab, Berber and Spanish cross, the horses were imported from Spain and bred for their qualities of grace and stamina. The dressage steps of the trained horses look highly artificial but actually derive from Renaissance battle manoeuvres. These include the "Capriole" – a leap into the air with the hind legs kicking out; the "Levade" – a rear up with the hocks of the hind legs almost touching the ground; and the "Croupade" – a leap into the air with all four legs tucked under the belly.

design was once an independent complex and is now joined on to the **Winter Riding School** (Winter-Reitschule). The magnificent three-storeyed arcaded courtyard is the most important Renaissance building in Vienna. The Stallburg contains the **Stables of the Spanish Riding School** ⓮ (with the Lipizzaner horses) and the **Old Court Pharmacy** (Alte Hofapotheke).

The performances by the Spanish Riding School take place in the Winter Riding School, commissioned by the Emperor Karl VI and built from 1729–35 by Joseph Emanuel Fischer von Erlach.

Map, page 90

A treasury of books

Leaving the arcaded passage you come to the **Josefsplatz** ⓯, architecturally the most uniform square in the city centre. In the middle is the **National Library** (Hofbibliothek), begun by Johann Bernhard Fischer von Erlach in 1723 and completed by his son in 1726. The main façade of the Baroque building is dominated by the central section with its cupola-like mansard roof, behind which is the world-famous **Grand Hall** (Prunksaal) with its oval cupola space, decorated with a grandiose painted ceiling (1730) by Daniel Gran. The architectural shape of the square was finalised in 1767–73, when the two side buildings went up with façades that were stylistically in keeping with the library building.

To the right are the two **Redoutensäle**, which were damaged by fire in 1992. The left-hand building was erected in front of the façade of the Church of the Augustinians, whose Gothic style can now only be seen from the side of the church on the Augustinerstrasse. Opposite the library are two aristocratic buildings: the **Palais Pallavicini** (No. 5), with a neo-classical façade, built after the demolition of the Queen's Monastery (Königinkloster) in 1783–4 by Johann

BELOW: the grandiose National Library

TIP

If you haven't booked months in advance to see the Spanish Riding School (Hofburg, A-1010 Wien), far cheaper tickets for the morning performances can still be ordered at the entrance on Burggraben/Innere Burg (Tues–Fri 10am–noon; often closed!).

BELOW: Emperor Joseph II's memorial

Ferdinand Hetzendorf von Hohenberg, and the **Palais Palffy** (No. 6), built in a plain style by an unknown architect in 1575 (but note the neo-classical portal).

In the centre of the square is the **Monument to the Emperor Joseph II** (1780–90) by Franz Anton Zauner (1795–1807). The bronze equestrian statue, portraying the Emperor as a Roman general, is modelled on the statue of Marcus Aurelius in Rome. Joseph II, son of Maria Theresa, was one of the most important imperial reformers of the House of Habsburg.

The **Church of the Augustinians** (Augustinerkirche) was built from 1330–9 by Dietrich Ladtner of Pirn, a Bavarian. It stood beside an Augustinian monastery founded in 1327 by Frederick the Fair. In 1630, influenced by the Counter-Reformation, Frederick II transferred the monastery to a stricter branch of the barefoot Augustinian order, and raised the church to Court Church status. The tower was not built until 1652. Alterations to the Josefsplatz robbed the church of its façade, but the Gothic side façade and interior, which has three aisles, very long and high with slender pillars, remained. In 1784–5, the interior of the church was given a new "Gothic" appearance by Hetzendorf von Hohenberg. In the right-hand aisle of the church is the neo-classical tomb of Marie-Christine, daughter of Maria Theresa and wife of Albert von Saxe-Teschen, by Antonio Canova. Here you will also find the Loretto Chapel and the Chapel of St George, and behind them lies the **"Heart Vault"** (Herzgruft) with the urns containing the hearts of the Imperial family from 1637 to 1878.

In 1683, Jan Sobieski's Service of Thanksgiving for the liberation of Vienna from the Turks was held in the Church of the Augustinians. In 1810 the wedding of Napoleon and Marie Thérèse was held here, and in 1854 that of Franz Joseph to Elisabeth of Bavaria.

Map, page 90

From the Augustinerstrasse, you can take a further look in the Dorotheergasse with its two Protestant churches and the auction house "Dorotheum"; then, passing the **Lobkowitz Palais**, turn towards the **Albertina** ⑯ (open Mon, Tues and Thurs 10am–4pm, Wed 10am–6pm, Fri 10am–2pm, Sat and Sun 10am–1pm; closed July and August). You will follow a ramp leading up to a surviving part of the city fortifications, at the foot of which is the sculpture *Reclining Youth* by Fritz Wotruba, arriving at the palace of Duke Albert of Saxe-Teschen. In 1801–4 he had sections of the Palais Taroucca (1742–5) rebuilt by Louis de Montoyer, incorporating parts of the Augustinian monastery.

The interior was re-designed in the neo-classical style by Joseph Körnhausel. Duke Albert was the founder of the Graphische Sammlung Albertina, the largest collection of graphic works, drawings and woodcuts in the world. In front of the Palais is the equestrian statue of Archduke Albrecht, victor of Custozza (1866), by Caspar Zumbusch (1899). Albrecht was the son of Archduke Carl, who was the first to defeat Napoleon in 1809 at Aspern.

You can look back at the Palais Lobkowitz from the platform of the **Augustinerbastei**. Its façade is in the style of palaces predating the second Turkish siege, although it was not built until 1685–7, probably by Giovanni Pietro Tencala. Johann Bernhard Fischer von Erlach gave the façade its present form. Ludwig van Beethoven's *Eroica* was first heard in 1803 during a private concert in the palace.

The **Danube Fountain** (Danubiusbrunnen), 1869, decorates the fortifications at the Albertinaplatz. It was designed by Moritz Lohr and the sculptures are by Johann Meixner. In the triangular place in front of the Albertina stands Alfred Hrdlicka's monument commemorating the victims of Fascism.

BELOW LEFT: nave of the Augustinian Church.
BELOW: "Warning against Fascism and war", Albertinaplatz

OLD VIENNA

*This second city-centre tour takes you to some of the
oldest districts, including the sites and remains of
Roman settlements and Vienna's oldest square*

Map,
page 90

St Stephen's Square (Stephansplatz) did not begin to assume its present
appearance until the end of the 18th century. In 1732 the graveyard surrounding the cathedral building was closed down; in 1792 the row of
houses in front of the Giants' Gateway was demolished, and in 1803 the link to
Stock-im-Eisen-Platz was established. In April 1945 many of the surrounding
houses also went up in flames during the air raid which damaged the cathedral.

If you walk round the cathedral in an anti-clockwise direction, you will first
come to the **Haus zur Kugel** (No. 2), onto which the 18th-century **Churhaus**
(No. 3) is directly joined. In the corner lies part of the **House of the Teutonic
Order** (Deutschordenshaus) (No. 4). You will return here at the end of the tour.
At No. 5, stands the **Cathedral Chapter House** (Domherrenhof) (1837–42).

Continuing along the northern side of the square you will pass the **Zwettler
Hof** (No. 6) (open Tues–Sat 10am–5pm), built in 1844 and now housing the
valuable collections of the **Cathedral and Diocesan Museum** (Dom und Diöze-
san museum) **⑰** and the **Archbishop's Palace**, the main façade of which lies
on Rotenturmstrasse. On St Stephen's Square the chapel juts forward from the
façade (1638). The palace was built in 1632–41 by Giovanno Coccapani and
has been the seat of the Archbishop of Vienna since 1732.

The route continues to the Lichtensteg. You will
return later to the Sonnenfelsgasse and the Bäckerstrasse, both of which contain some well-preserved
buildings. Turning left, you will soon arrive at the
Hoher Markt ⑱, the oldest square in Vienna.

LEFT: Church of the
Dominican Order
BELOW: Art Nouveau
"Anchor Clock"

Medieval Vienna

The history of the market begins at the time of the
Roman military camp Vindobona, when it was the site
of the camp commandant's palace. Access to the Roman
Ruins will be found at No. 3. During the Middle Ages
the Hoher Markt was the centre of the historic town,
with its market, court building, guild houses and aristocratic palaces.

Several houses survived the ravages of World War II:
No. 5, built in 1855, and Nos. 10–11, the "**Anchor
House**", built 1913–14. The most interesting feature is
the Anchor Clock (Ankeruhr), built by Franz Matsch
and mounted on an archway linking the two houses. An
animated figure from Austrian history appears from the
Art Nouveau jacquemart timepiece every hour. A crowd
usually gathers at noon to see the parade of all the characters. The **Fountain of the Virgin's Wedding** (Ver-
mählungsbrunnen) is also known as Joseph's Fountain,
and is the work of Joseph Emanuel Fischer von Erlach.
It was completed in 1729–32. When Archduke Joseph
laid siege to the fortress at Landau in 1702, his father,
Leopold I, vowed to commission a column. He duly did

so, but it was later replaced by the present masterpiece. The marriage group by Antonio Corradini, depicting the Virgin Mary, Joseph and the High Priest, stands on a huge pedestal. The bronze baldachin is surmounted by the Holy Trinity.

Leaving the Hoher Markt via the Wipplingerstrasse, the route continues past two important buildings at the narrowest point in the street. On the left is the former **Bohemian Chancellery** (No. 7), designed by Johann Bernard Fischer von Erlach (1708–14). The building was extended by Matthias Gerl in 1751–4, but it is almost impossible to see where the old building ends and the newer one begins.

Opposite, at No. 8, stands the **Old Town Hall** (Altes Rathaus). Part of the building, in the Salvatorgasse, dates back to the 14th century, as does the **Redeemer's Chapel** (Salvatorkapelle). The Town Hall has been extended several times. In about 1700 the Town Council ordered the construction of a Baroque façade whose two magnificent portals were both elaborately ornamented with great skill. The sculptures on the eastern doorway, on the side nearer the Hoher Markt, were added in 1781, by Johann Martin Fischer. The Council Chamber on the first floor is decorated with the coats of arms of all the members of the council in 1713–14. The Old Town Hall also houses the **Archives of the Austrian Resistance**. A fountain by Georg Raphael Donner, depicting the Greek mythic figures Perseus and Andromeda, is set into the wall of the Town Hall.

Gothic churches

A narrow alley, the **Stoss im Himmel**, links the Wipplingerstrasse with the Salvatorgasse. On the corner stands a Gothic angel bearing the coats of arms of Austria and Vienna. Bearing left, you will shortly arrive at one of the city's

Fischer von Erlach's Bohemian Chancellery (below) *is the first example of Palladian style (blended with French and Italian High Baroque features) in Austria.*

Gothic masterpieces, the **Church of Our Lady of the River Bank** (Kirche Maria am Gestade) . As long ago as the 12th century, a Romanesque church stood here on the street which is now known as Salzgries, on a steep bank overlooking a main branch of the Danube.

The main door has sculpted reliefs dating from 1410. The side door dates from about 1500, and the pierced dome is one of the loveliest examples of Gothic art in Vienna. Inside, the organ loft (1515) appears to be hovering above the angels and corbels. The elegant tracery of the balustrade is worthy of note, and there is an Angel of the Annunciation (1380) on the sixth pillar on the left. The interior furnishings mostly date from the 19th century. The exceptions are four 14th/15th-century windows in the choir, the Renaissance altar in the left-hand choir chapel with carvings of the Virgin, St John the Baptist and St Nicolas, the Gothic and Baroque statues surmounted by baldachins and the Baroque crucifix (1730) on the high altar. The choir windows contain Gothic stained-glass panels.

Returning to the Salvatorgasse and continuing past the rear façade of the Old Town Hall, you will arrive in front of the Renaissance portal of **St Saviour's Church** (Salvatorkirche) (No 5). Originally the private chapel of a nobleman's house and subsequently of the Town Hall, the church was enlarged in 1520.

Turning down the Fischerstiege on the opposite side of the street, you will reach the Sterngasse on the right. No. 3 is now the Wiener Neustädter Hof, which has an interesting façade and a pretty inner courtyard (1735–7). The "Turkish Bullet" set into the wall dates from 1683. Crossing **Marc-Aurel-Strasse** with its statue of the Roman emperor and philosopher in front of No. 6, you find yourself in the district where the first civilian settlement grew up after the Roman armies had withdrawn. The stone blocks found nearby were originally part of the Roman baths.

> Map, page 90

Our Lady of the River Bank was partly built above the town's original Roman fortifications, and a Roman temple dedicated to the goddess of fertility may originally have stood on this site.

BELOW LEFT: St Rupert's Church. **BELOW:** Church of Our Lady of the River Bank

Vienna is famous for its calorific desserts such as Palatschinken *(pancakes).*

If you look towards the left at the end of the Sterngasse you will see the **Ruprechtsplatz** and the Church of St Rupert, whilst to the right lies the **Judengasse** (Jews' Alley). House Nos. 7, 9, 11 and 16 all date from 1796–1838.

St Rupert's Church (Ruprechtskirche) ⑳ (open Mon–Fri 10am–1pm) was supposedly founded in 740, but many experts believe that the nave and tower of the present building date from the 11th century. It is a simple Romanesque hall church with some elements (tower windows) in this style, as well as Gothic details (main doorway). The central window of the choir, from the late 13th century, is the oldest stained-glass window in the city. A statue of St Rupert with a barrel of salt stands in front of the church. In Roman times a small harbour on the Danube lay beneath the present-day stairway. During the Middle Ages this harbour was important for the salt trade.

The former ghetto

A few paces into the Seitenstettengasse stands the headquarters of the **Israeli Cultural Association** (No. 2). It was built in 1824–6 by Joseph Kornhäusel. Its courtyard houses the oldest **synagogue** (Stadttempel) ㉑ (1825–6) to be built in the city centre since the expulsion of the Jews in 1421. It was the only synagogue to survive the notorious Reichskristallnacht in 1938, when the Nazis burned all the others to the ground. It was saved by its location in the midst of a densely built-up area.

At No. 5 is the **Seitenstetter Hof**, with ornamental reliefs on the façade by Kornhäusel. Continuing past the **Kornhäusel Tower** (No. 2) on the corner of Judengasse and Fleischmarkt – built by the famous Biedermeier architect in 1825–7 as his own residence – you will finally arrive at the Fleischmarkt. The **Fleischmarkt** is first mentioned in records as early as 1220 and was where the butchers had their shops. Its first stretch is dominated by Art Nouveau houses (Nos. 1–7 and 14). No. 9, from the 15th and 16th centuries, has a crooked façade with a Gothic bay window, a relief of the Virgin Mary and a row of arcades in the courtyard. It is linked to No. 11 by a wide archway spanning the Griechengasse. The building today houses the **Griechenbeisl** ㉒, whose name (Greeks' bistro) refers to the Greeks who settled here in the 18th century. It enjoyed great popularity during the 19th century, and was a regular haunt of Wagner, Strauss and Brahms.

The Greek district is one of Vienna's oldest and is closely linked with Augustin, a popular musician and hero of the song *O, Du lieber Augustin* – the German version of *Ring a Ring o' Roses*. During the plague of 1679, he was out one evening decidedly the worse for alcohol. He stumbled and fell down on the street, too drunk to get up. The plague runners, who removed the corpses of the dead before dawn every day, carted away his apparently lifeless body to one of the mass graves outside the city walls. When Augustin woke the next morning, he clambered out of the pit, started playing his bagpipes again and sang the song which guaranteed his immortality: "*O, du lieber Augustin, s'Geld ist hin, s'Mensch ist hin, O, du lieber Augustin, alles ist hin!*" (O, poor Augustin, your money has gone, the people have gone, everything has gone).

BELOW: organ grinder

The late 17th century was a time of affliction in Vienna, and the emotions of fear and claustrophobia characterising the era can still be sensed in the narrow streets of the city centre. The economic stagnation which followed the Thirty Years' War (1618–48) had not been overcome when the bubonic plague arrived. The preacher Abraham a Santa Clara described it as God's punishment and called upon the citizens to pray and do penance. The strict hygiene advocated by Dr Paul de Sorbait, however, seemed to offer greater hope of success. Houses and entire streets were placed under strict quarantine for 40 days. Even pieces of paper on which the interned citizens wrote their requirements were not allowed to be touched. Nevertheless the illness followed its fearful course. Entire streets were deserted, either because the inhabitants had fled (thus contributing to the spread of the plague) or because they had all fallen victim.

At least a third of the population of the city perished, and it was not until the summer of 1680 that the survivors were able to celebrate the end of the pestilence. Emperor Leopold I had a wooden plague column erected, from the pedestal of which Abraham a Santa Clara delivered one of his famous sermons. In 1687, it was replaced by the stone Trinity Column.

However, no sooner had the Viennese recovered from the plague years, than the Turks appeared at the city gates, and the same generation was confronted with the horrors of war. The city did not begin to prosper once more until the Turkish threat had also been banished. Most of the buildings in the old city date from this period of Baroque renewal.

In the **Griechengasse** you will notice kerbstones along the house fronts. They were intended to prevent damage by passing coaches. In the courtyard of No. 9 a Gothic tower has been preserved.

Map, page 90

Whether Augustin really existed is doubtful, but he is a symbol for the irrepressible optimism of the Viennese, just like the Stehaufmanderl, *a wooden toy acrobat which always bounces back onto its feet.*

BELOW: the plague in Vienna (1679)

Near the Griechenbeisl, at No. 13, stands the **Greek Church** (Griechische Kirche), built in 1782–7 by Peter Mollner and extended in 1858–61 by a Byzantine-style porch by Theophil Hansen. No. 18 bears an inscription on the third floor recalling the Edict of Tolerance of Joseph II guaranteeing the right of free religious practice.

The **birthplace of Moritz von Schwind** (No. 15) has a richly decorated Baroque façade dating from the early 18th century. Continuing along the Postgasse, you will pass the former **main tollhouse** (No. 8). Built in 1773, its façade dates from 1852. Turning to the right, the street widens out to form a sort of square flanked by Kornhäusel's Library Wing of the Old University (1827–9). On the left is the **Church of St Barbara** (Barbarakirche) (No. 10), the city's second Greek church.

Also on the left-hand side stands the **Church of the Dominicans** (Dominikanerkirche) 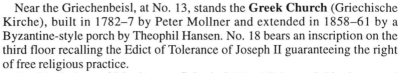 from 1631–4. The interior has elaborate stucco decorations (1666–75) and ceiling frescoes by Matthias Rauchmiller (nave) and Carpoforo Tencala (choir). Opposite stand the buildings of the **Old University** (Alte Universität) ❷. The oldest of them date from 1385, although the university had been founded by Duke Rudolf IV in 1365.

Following a passageway at the end of the building, you will next arrive at **Dr Ignaz-Seipel-Platz**, an attractive square. In front of you stands the former Assembly Hall of the university, and on your right the **Jesuit Church** (Jesuitenkirche) ❷, built in 1623–7. Its present appearance dates from 1703–7, when Andrea Pozzo added the two massive High Baroque lanterns atop the towers. The sculptures decorating the façade depict Saints Barbara, Leopold, Joseph and Catherine (the patroness of knowledge). The lower row portrays the Jesuit saints Saints Francis Xavier (right) and Ignatius Loyola (left). Worthy of examination are Andrea Pozzo's ceiling frescoes, with a *trompe l'oeil* dome and the *Assumption of the Virgin* adorning the high altar.

The **University Assembly Hall** (Universitätsaula) is the only Rococo monumental building in Vienna. It was built in 1753–5 by Jean Nicolas Jadot de Ville-Issey and was based on French models. Today it serves as the headquarters of the Austrian Academy of Sciences (Akademie der Wissenschaften). The gables on the side projections are adorned with allegorical figures personifying the faculties of medicine and jurisprudence. The vestibule and main hall are both lavishly decorated.

BELOW: painting in the Jesuit Church

Fine old houses

Take the **Sonnenfelsgasse** which runs between the assembly hall and the church. No. 19 is the **Pedell House**, dating from the 17th century, and No. 17 also dates from the same period and has bay windows on all floors. No. 15 has a Renaissance gateway. Turning right into **Schönlaterngasse**, there is a good view from the place where the street bends across one of the oldest districts in town. No. 7 is known as the **Basilisk House** (Basiliskenhaus) ❷ after the mythical creature – a cross between a cock and a toad – whose poisonous breath is said to have threatened the local citizens as they attempted to dig a well. A baker's apprentice is said to have climbed down and held a mirror in front of the creature, whereupon it was overcome with fear at its own ugliness and was instantly turned to stone – a lump of sandstone, bearing a certain resemblance to an animal, serves as the house's sign. The foundations date from the 13th century, but the present façade was added in 1740.

Map, page 90

Opposite, at No. 6, stands the **House of the Beautiful Lantern**; its façade, from about 1680, still reveals the plaster sections typical of the period. No. 4, next door, was built in the second half of the 17th century and is characteristic of the time. Passing through a gateway, you will enter the **Heiligenkreuzer Hof ㉗**. The Heiligenkreuz Abbey started to build the complex during the 13th century; by the 16th it had reached considerable dimensions, and by the mid-18th century its Viennese *dépendance* looked more or less as it does today. The **Chapel of St Bernard** in the courtyard was built in about 1730. Despite its unassuming exterior it has an interior of great artistic merit, including the ceiling frescoes by Antonio Tassi and a high altar painting of *The Manifestation of the Virgin* by Martino Altomonte. The painter died in the courtyard in 1745 whilst working for the monks. The garden wall with its sculptures from the atelier of Giovanni Giuliani dates from 1729.

The mythical creature after which Basilisk House is named is depicted in a carving on the façade.

It is a tranquil, atmospheric place. If you cross to the far side before leaving the complex, you will find yourself in the **Köllnerhofgasse**. No. 2 is the **Köllner Hof** itself, built in 1792–3 with a Classical façade by Peter Mollner. From here you should return to the **Sonnenfelsgasse**. Looking down the alley to the left you will see a row of old houses, some of which have retained their Baroque façades. The most noteworthy examples are on the left-hand side of the street; No. 3 is the **Hildebrandt House**, built in 1721. It has an elaborate façade in the style of Johann Lukas von Hildebrandt, but with various early Rococo elements.

BELOW LEFT: ceiling in the Academy of Sciences building. **BELOW RIGHT:** plaque outside the Academy of Sciences

No. 12 Bäckerstrasse has a 16th-century fresco on the façade depicting a cow and a wolf, the symbols for Protestants and Catholics.

BELOW: Bruno Magli's shoe shop in Singerstrasse

No. 5 is in the neo-classical style and No. 11 has a Baroque portal dating from about 1710. The houses on the right-hand side extend as far as the Bäckerstrasse, into which you should turn.

Crossing **Lugeck Square**, with a number of old buildings, pause to look at No. 7, on the corner of Rotenturmstrasse. Known as the "**Grosser Federlhof**", it was built in 1846–7. No. 5 has an early 19th-century façade.

Between Sonnenfelsgasse and Bäckerstrasse stands the former Orendi department store (1897). In medieval times the site was occupied by the inn of the Regensburg merchants where even Emperor Frederick III spent the night. There is a commemorative statue of him on the Bäckerstrasse façade. The Cologne merchants had their headquarters nearby, in the **Köllnerhofgasse** (hence the name). For centuries, the area between Sonnenfelsgasse and Bäckerstrasse was occupied by a village green, the centre of a trading suburb called "Outside the Hungarian Gate", which grew up between Fleischmarkt and Wollzeile.

On the **Bäckerstrasse** there are a large number of exceptionally fine old houses. In one of the few 16th-century examples to survive (No. 7, built before 1587), you can see the only remaining example of a Renaissance courtyard in the entire city. The wrought-ironwork in the courtyard comes from the collection of the Biedermeier artist Friedrich Amerling. No. 12 is a residence dating from the 15–16th centuries with an 18th-century façade and Renaissance bay window.

Following the Essiggasse between No. 8 and No. 10, you will reach the **Wollzeile**. The street formerly led to the Stubentor, one of the city gates, and still contains some fine old houses.

Passing along the Strobelgasse you will soon come to the **Schulerstrasse**, which owes its name to the Law School (1389) or perhaps even to St Stephen's

grammar school (1237). You will go by the **Mädelspergerhof** (No. 7), which continues as far as the Wollzeile, and the house **Zum König von Ungarn** (No. 10, with an 18th-century façade). The latter is one of the oldest inns in Vienna, and is a hotel today. You will also pass the rear façades of the houses in the **Domgasse** (in this case, No. 6 and No. 8).

Map, page 90

Where Mozart composed

The Domgasse is world-famous as the location of the **Figaro House** (Figarohaus) ㉓ (No. 5) (open daily 9am–12.15pm, 1–4.30pm, closed Mon), so named because Wolfgang Amadeus Mozart lived here from 1784 to 1787 and wrote, amongst other compositions, his opera *The Marriage of Figaro*. From his study he had a view of the Schulerstrasse. It is the only Mozart residence in the city still in existence, and has been turned into a museum. No. 4 is the **Trienter Hof**, built in 1755 by the bishopric of Trient. No. 6 dates from 1761 and is noteworthy for its characteristic façade design and the prominent house sign, a picture of the Virgin Mary in a Rococo framework.

To complete this tour of the old city you should now walk along the **Blutgasse**. First mentioned in the 14th century, it lies in one of the oldest districts of Vienna. The main façades of some of the most important buildings face onto other streets: No. 1, the **Trienter Hof**, looks onto the Domgasse; No. 2, the **Chapter House**, overlooks St Stephen's Square; and No. 4, the House of the Teutonic Order, onto Singerstrasse. However, if you turn into No. 5e, the **Fähnrichhof**, you can wander through a succession of charming courtyards which give a fine impression of the lifestyle of the citizens of Vienna during the 17th and 18th centuries. The complex is considered to be a good example of the restoration and renovation of historic buildings whilst retaining the original fabric. Leaving the complex on the Singerstrasse side, you will pass, at No. 7e, the **House of the Teutonic Order** – a medieval complex linked together during the 17th century and grouped around two inner courtyards. Mozart stayed here in 1781. The house contains the **Treasury of the Teutonic Order** (Schatzkammer des Deutschen Ordens) ㉙ (open May–Oct: Mon, Thur, Sun 10am–noon; Wed, Fri, Sat 3–5pm; Nov–Apr: Mon, Thur, Sat 10am–noon, 3–5pm; Wed, Fri 3–5pm). The order was summoned to Vienna in about 1200 and made its headquarters here.

Next door stands the **Church of the Teutonic Order** (Deutschordenskirche), built on the site of the 13th-century chapel in 1720–2 and rebuilt in 1864–8 to create its present neo-Gothic appearance. The south wall of the church is incorporated into the main façade of the house. Inside the church, the main altar is surmounted by a Dutch winged altar (about 1520) from St Mary's Church in Gdansk and an altar picture by Tobias Pock (1668). The walls are decorated with the coats of arms of the Knights of the Teutonic Order (from around 1720) and the Renaissance epitaph for the humanist Johannes Cuspinian. The church is the most important example of early 18th century Baroque (post-Gothic) architecture in Austria.

From here you can return to the starting point of the walk, St Stephen's Cathedral.

BELOW: in front of Mozart's house in the Domgasse

THE RINGSTRASSE

The Ringstrasse is a magnificent showpiece of late 19th-century town planning. Here we tour its west and east sides, each time starting from the State Opera House

A fter the Emperor Franz Joseph I had ordered the Renaissance fortifications, the so-called *Basteien*, to be demolished and houses to be built on the woodland surrounding the town, an international competition was established in 1858 to redesign the Ringstrasse. Eighty-five architects from all over Europe entered the competition. The emperor demanded the capital be "made bigger and more beautiful". A jury chose the winning design, which was approved by the monarch in 1859. The first public and representative building to go up was the Opera House (Hofoper).

The first phase of building of the Ringstrasse is referred to as the "Ringstrassenära" ("Ringstrasse Era"), whose almost mythically nostalgic fascination still remains. It coincides with the Classical and late Historicist periods. Only at Stubenring, where barracks were left standing after the revolution in 1848, were the buildings not erected until the 20th century. Here you will find the only Ringstrasse buildings representing the style of the "Secession" artists *(see page 64)*. This new Ringstrasse soon became the domain of the upper classes and the aristocracy, intent on imprinting their stamp forever on this part of town. The court was represented by several official buildings; the church, however, was not.

It was a happy coincidence that the greatest skills in the fields of art and architecture were combined to present to the world such an impressive example of artistic virtuosity. Today, this "complete work of art" has no parallel in the town planning of late 19th-century Europe. This magnificent boulevard is about 4 km (2½ miles) long and 57 metres (62 yards) wide. It was officially opened on 1 May 1865, although it was not completed until just before World War I.

National Opera to the Stock Exchange

Once again, the tour starts at the State Opera House *(see page 93)*, built in 1861–9 and based on a design by August von Siccardsburg and Eduard van der Nüll. Walking along Operngasse (leaving town), you come to the building of the **Secession** ❸⓿ (open Tues–Fri 10am–6pm, Sat and Sun 10am–4pm) which Otto Wagner's disciple, Joseph Maria Olbrich, built in 1897–8 for those artists who shunned the company of their conservative contemporaries, and admirers of the acclaimed painter, Hans Makart. Recognisable from afar by its dome formed from gilded iron laurel twigs, it is appropriately, if disrespectfully, known by the local citizens as the "Cabbage Top" (Krauthappel).

At the **Opernring Square**, there is a row of dignified houses (Nos. 7–23), almost wholly representative of the early days (1861–3) of the construction of Ringstrasse. On the right, between the Palais Schey (No. 10) and the Burggarten, is the **Goethe Memorial** by Edmund Hellmer (1895–1900).

Opposite the Goethe Memorial, facing Robert-Stolz-Platz (with a monument commemorating the famous composer who lived nearby), on Schillerplatz, is the **Academy of Fine Arts** (Akademie der bildenden Künste) ❸❶ (open Tues, Thur, Fri 10am–4pm; Mon 10am–1pm, 3–6pm; Sat 9am–1pm). It was built by

Map, page 90

At No. 23 Opernring Square is the house in which the famous operetta composer, Franz von Suppé, passed away.

BELOW LEFT: entrance to the Academy of Fine Arts.
BELOW: sculpture on the façade, Academy of Fine Arts

Map, page 90

Theophil Hansen in 1872–6 in the Italian Renaissance style. The massive main entrance is impressive. The 24 figures carved into the niches between the windows are copies of original antique terracotta sculptures. Inside, the painting on the ceiling – *The Fall of the Titans* (Titanensturz) - by Anselm Feuerbach is of great importance, as is the collection of paintings which includes German, Dutch, Italian and Spanish masters. In the park is a fine collection of statues of writers.

By the Goethe Memorial you can enter the **Burggarten** ❷ which provides a beautiful view of the garden front, Neue Burg. In it are fine sculptures and odd buildings, including (at the back, on the right) a Jugendstil conservatory by Friedrich Ohmann (1901–5). Leave the park at the **Mozart Memorial** and proceed to the outer gate of the castle, passing by the neo-classical "Corps-de-Logis" wing, which was built in 1821–4 by Luigi Cagnola and Pietro Nobile.

Here is the centre of a complex designed by Gottfried Semper, which was never completed. His idea was to design a "forum for the Emperor" which was to consist of two new wings of a new Hofburg, only one of which was built. His design also included the middle section of the Leopoldian Wing of the old Hofburg and some gigantic triumphal arches which were to span the Ringstrasse, extending from the wings of the castle to the castle museums. What was completed, however, is still impressive, and the unfinished work leaves unimpaired the view from Heldenplatz to the Parliament Building, Town Hall, University and Burgtheater.

Carl Hasenauer was commissioned in 1866 to design the **Museum of the History of Art** (Kunsthistorisches Museum) ❸ (Burgring 5) (open daily 10am–6pm, closed Mon) and the **Natural History Museum** (Naturhistorisches

BELOW: the Natural History Museum

Emperor Franz Joseph and the Ringstrasse

In 1916, the Emperor Franz Joseph's funeral procession bore the monarch from the Hofburg across the Ringstrasse before following the Franz-Josephs-Kai to the city centre and St Stephen's Cathedral. This Ringstrasse had been Franz Joseph's very own project; in 1857, he had given instructions for it to be built in the oft quoted document "Es ist Mein Wille..." (It is Our will...). In 1859, he approved the plans, and in 1865 he performed the official opening ceremony. The procession coincided with his silver wedding anniversary.

The glories of the Ringstrasse often led people to forget that the Emperor hindered Vienna more often than he helped the city. Architects from the whole of Europe answered

the monarch's call and came to Vienna to take part in planning and building the Ringstrasse area. Theophil Hansen came from Athens, the South German Schmid from Milan, the North German Semper from Zurich. Together with the Viennese Hasenauer, Ferstel and many others, they didn't want to miss out on the opportunity to prove themselves in the design of a whole district close to the city centre yet on land free of existing buildings.

The early French Renaissance-style State Opera House was the first building to be completed. Other notable buildings are the Natural History Museum, the History of Art Museum, the neo-Gothic Town Hall, the University, the Burgtheater, the Parliament, the Stock Exchange and the Central Law Courts. Although many historical styles, fitting in with 19th-century taste, were used, the Ringstrasse did develop as a whole, a series of buildings protected as part of Vienna's heritage and unique in Europe: more so as most of the World War II damage was reparable. The impressive buildings of the Ringstrasse area have kept their attraction.

BELOW: Franz Joseph, who reigned for 68 years

The Museum of the History of Art houses the fourth largest art collection in the world including magnificent works by Brueghel, and this image of Summer by Arcimboldo (above).

BELOW: *Theseus Vanquishes the Centaur* (Museum of Art History)

Museum) ❸ (No. 7) (open daily 9am–6pm, closed Tues). The façades were later redesigned by Gottfried Semper, but most of the interior design has remained as Hasenauer intended. The two four-storey buildings (1872–81) are symmetrically juxtaposed and include features inspired by the Italian Renaissance.

In the middle stand octagonal domes with four side domes attached to each. At the main entrances on Maria-Theresien-Platz, you pass allegorical seated figures by the most important sculptors of the time (Hellmer, Kundmann, Tilgner, Zumbusch). Inside, the spaciousness of the design of the hall and the staircase is apparent, with the paintings *The Apotheosis of Art* (Apotheose der Kunst) by Michael Munkáczy, and *The Cycle of Life* (Kreislauf des Lebens) by Hans Canon, on the ceiling. On the landing of the main staircase in the Museum of the History of Art stands the marble sculpture, *Theseus Vanquishes the Centaur* by Antonio Canova, and in the Natural History Museum hangs the painting, *Emperor Franz I surrounded by his governors* (1760). The art collections in both (now nationalised) museums are among Europe's largest and finest.

The monument to **Maria Theresa** was created by Caspar Zumbusch (1874–88). It covers an area of about 604 sq. metres (756 sq. yards) and is nearly 20 metres (66 feet) high. Four equestrian statues of her advisers (Laudon, Daun, Khevenhüller and Abensberg-Traun) are grouped around the base, while the centre is occupied by the statues of four diplomats (Kaunitz, Haugwitz, Liechtenstein and van Swieten). The arches depict 16 famous people (including the composers Mozart, Haydn and Gluck).

The former Imperial Stables (at Messeplatz, at the other end of the street) were built in 1719–23 by Johann Bernhard and Joseph Emanuel Fischer von Erlach. They were until recently the home of the **Vienna International Trade Fair**.

Leaving by the **Outer Gate** (Äussere Burgtor) you enter the **Heldenplatz** ㉟, where the Burgbastei (bastion) once stood. It was heavily besieged in 1683. After Napoleon had it blown up in 1809, the ground was levelled and a park (Volksgarten) built.

In 1933–4, the main gate of the castle, the "Burgtor", was redesigned as a cenotaph. In March 1938, Hitler, standing on the balcony of the Neue Burg, accepted the ovations of a large crowd of followers. However, after World War II, a memorial for the victims among the Austrian freedom fighters was erected. It commemorates the 35,000 Austrian members of the Resistance who were condemned to death or died in Nazi prisons and concentration camps, and also more than 65,000 Jews killed by the Nazis. Another 100,000 Austrians were imprisoned for political reasons.

On the south-east side of Heldenplatz stands the **Neue Burg** ㊱, which was designed by Semper and Hasenauer. Building began in 1881 and was finished in 1913. Emil Förster, Friedrich Ohmann and Ludwig Baumann (in that order), who made some alterations to the garden façade, supervised the building during those years. Towards Heldenplatz, the building curves inwards, and the middle is dominated by the balcony. The Neue Burg is home to the National Library and the **Museum of Mankind** (Museum für Völkerkunde) (open daily 10am–4pm, closed Tues).

Walking through the **Volksgarten** ㊲ (built 1819–23), which is famous for its rose gardens and its coffee house (originally, the famous Corti'sche Kaffeehaus, built by Pietro Nobile, where Strauss and Lanner used to give concerts), you come, at the other end, to the **Temple of Theseus** (by Nobile, 1820–3, based on the original in Athens), and then to the monument commemorating **Franz**

Map, page 90

In Heldenplatz, there are two monuments (both by Anton Dominik Fernkorn) to great generals: Prince Eugene (near the Neue Burg), who conquered the Turks and was a great patron of the arts; and Archduke Carl, who defeated Napoleon at Aspern in 1809.

BELOW: the Neue Burg

Busts of the three founders of the Austrian Republic – Jakob Reumann, Viktor Adler and Ferdinand Hanusch – were erected outside the Palace of Justice in 1928.

BELOW: Pallas Athene beside the Parliament Building

Grillparzer, who died in 1872 and was one of Austria's most important dramatists. If you continue walking you will arrive at the memorial of the **Empress Elisabeth** by Ohmann and Bitterlich (1907). The sculpture on the fountain, *The Satyr and the Nymph* (Faun und Nymphe), is by Tilgner, while the fountain is by Fernkorn.

You will now find yourself back on the Ringstrasse, with the **Palais Epstein** directly opposite (occupied now by the Education Authority). This was designed in the style of the Italian Renaissance by Theophil Hansen in 1870–3 for the banker Gustav Ritter von Epstein. The main entrance is given an air of importance by the pillared portico with four caryatids by Vinzenz Pilz. A plaque is dedicated to the Social Democrat Otto Glöckel, who successfully fought for revolutionary school reforms in the years following World War I. From 1945 to 1955, the Soviet military leadership took up residence in the Palais Epstein.

Further on towards the parliament is the **Memorial to the Republic** (Denkmal der Republik), erected in 1928 with bronze busts of Dr Viktor Adler, the founder of the united Social Democratic Party (by Anton Hanak), Jakob Reumann, the first Social Democratic mayor of Vienna (by Franz Seifert) and Ferdinand Hanusch, the founder of modern social policies (by Mario Petrucci).

Looking across Schmerlingplatz behind the memorial, you can see the **Palace of Justice** (Justizpalast), a monumental building built in 1875–81 in Italian Renaissance-style by Alexander Wielemans. The main façade is dominated by a massive portico with pillars, a ramp and a staircase. The main hall is more than 20 metres (66 feet) high, with a glass ceiling and a staircase with the statue of justice on the landing (by Emanuel Pendl). The ensemble is very impressive indeed. In 1927, rioting workers set the building on fire, and between 1945 and 1955 it served as the headquarters of the Soviet military leadership. Towards the end of World War II, this area had become the centre of the military Austrian Resistance movement "05", which had its headquarters in the nearby Palais Auersperg.

Symbolic architecture

Walk along **Dr Karl-Renner-Ring** towards the Burgtheater on the right to be confronted by another group of impressive buildings, including the Parliament Building, Town Hall, University and Burgtheater. This part of the Ringstrasse owes its existence to the mayor Dr Cajetan Felder (1868–78), who convinced Emperor Franz Joseph that even in this part of the boulevard, reserved for military parades, houses should be built.

Each architect involved in the construction of this particular ensemble of buildings had his own reasons for his design and the style favoured. Friedrich Schmidt, formerly master-builder at the cathedral of St Stephen, chose neo-Gothic for the Town Hall to remind people of the golden days of the bourgeoisie in the Gothic period. Theophil Hansen, the Dane from Athens, chose the Hellenic style for the home of the Imperial Council (seat of the Austrian parliament since 1918) to establish a connection between the Ancient Greek city-state and the constitutional monarchy. Heinrich Ferstel preferred the style of the Italian Renaissance because that period stood for the golden age of European universities.

The **Parliament Building** (Parlament) ❸, today the seat of the National Assembly and the Federal Council, was built between 1872 and 1883. It is two storeys high with two side wings and four pavilion-like protruding canopies. A monumental ramp leads up to the entrance, accentuated by an eight-column portico with an allegorical relief on the pediment, and in the middle is a representation of the "Investiture of the Constitution by Emperor Franz Joseph". The ramp is lined by seated marble figures representing ancient historians (the Greeks on the left, Romans on the right) with two bronze horse-breakers at the bottom. There are also eight bronze quadriga and 60 marble figures of famous Greeks and Romans.

In front of the parliament, the **Pallas-Athene-Brunnen** was erected in 1898–1902 after a design by Hansen in 1870. The Goddess of Wisdom on top of the fountain (by Kundmann) is surrounded by allegorical figures representing the rivers, as well as various female figures symbolising the executive and legislative powers. The **Town Hall** (Rathaus) ❸, built in 1872–83 by Friedrich Schmidt, should originally have stood opposite the Stadtpark. The massive front is dominated by the main tower, over 90 metres (300 feet) high (with the *Rathausmann* statue on top, a copy of which can be more closely inspected in the park), flanked by two side towers, almost 60 metres (200 feet) high. The arcaded courtyard (Arkadenhof) is open to the public, and is used for concerts in summer. Guided tours (Mon–Fri 1pm) start in the Schmidthalle, where there is also an information centre at the rear of the building. The ornaments on the building itself are lavish. There are also various statues representing the white-collar professions. The **Rathauskeller** is one of Vienna's most popular inns.

Walking through the **Rathauspark**, you arrive at the Burgtheater. The park, designed and landscaped by Rudolf Sieböck (director of the municipal parks)

Map, page 90

TIP

The main representative rooms are on the first floor of the Town Hall. The banqueting hall and committee rooms for the national and municipal councils are all open to the public.

BELOW: beneath the columns of the Parliament Building

Map, page 90

Vienna is home to the oldest German-language university.

BELOW: the Town Hall at Christmas

in 1872–3, is one of Vienna's most beautiful parks. It is divided into two parts, the borders marked by four statues of famous personalities. Vienna's "Christmas fair" (Christkindlmarkt) is held here. There are two fountains and many monuments: to the chancellor Dr Renner on the Ringstrasse near the Parliament Building (by Alfred Hrdlicka), to the mayors Seitz (1923–4) and Körner (1945–51) opposite the Burgtheater, plus the Strauss-Lanner memorial in the southern corner and the Waldmüller memorial in the northern corner.

The **Burgtheater** ⓴, Austria's National Theatre, was built in 1874–88 in Italian Renaissance style, based on designs by Semper (exterior) and Hasenauer (interior). It replaced the old Burgtheater at Michaelerplatz, which had been given the status of "Nationaltheater" by the Emperor Joseph II in 1776. Its most impressive feature is the arched, protruding front with its almost 18-metre (60-ft) relief, *Worshippers of Bacchus* (Bacchantenzug), by Rudolf Weyr. Above the relief is the massive statue, *Apollo and the Muses Melpomene and Thalia* (Apollo mit den Musen Melpomene und Thalia). Perched above the windows on the first floor are busts by Tilgner of famous playwrights, each allocated a character from one of his plays right beneath him (by Weyr). The grand staircases in the foyer have the original ceiling paintings, some by Gustav and Ernst Klimt. The Burgtheater is one of the most important stages in the German-speaking world. The list of the actresses, actors and directors who have worked here reads like an historical *Who's Who*.

The **University** (Universität) ⓶, founded in 1365 by Duke Rudolf IV, was redesigned by Heinrich Ferstel in 1873–83. An outside staircase and a ramp lead up to a portico with a balcony crowned by a pediment. Another striking feature of the building is the 38 statues representing important men of letters who greatly

The Burg

"No illegitimate children are allowed on the stage, and kings must always be good", the intellectuals sneered in 1845, when censors tried to emasculate the plays written for the "National Theatre beside the Burg".

Censorship is no longer a problem. But kings, even if not good, must at least be well played. The most important ingredient of a good play for the Viennese is the cast; the quality of the acting is paramount. This is where top stars in the past celebrated the high dramatic art. Cast lists are still filled with famous actors: Klaus Maria Brandauer, Gert Voss and Erika Pluhar *et al*.

"Burg" is short for one of the oldest theatres in the world. The first lady of the "Burg" was Empress Maria Theresa. In 1741, she granted the use of an empty ballroom in the Hofburg for the "Theater nächst der Burg". Her son Joseph II actually took charge of the the-

atre himself for a short time. His Majesty the director promoted the theatre to "Nationaltheater" in 1776 and gave the actors the rank of court official. He also forbade curtain calls, a prohibition which is still respected today.

In the theatre on the Michaelerplatz "well-crafted translations" and "German originals" were performed, while a new theatre was being built on the Ring to designs by Karl Hasenauer and Gottfried Semper. Ernst and Gustav Klimt painted part of the ceiling in an opulent Renaissance style.

On 14 October 1888, Vienna's elite, led by Emperor Franz Joseph, attended the opening, a performance of *Esther* by the Austrian classic playwright Grillparzer. The first reactions to the Burg were negative: "In Parliament you can't hear anything, in the Town Hall you can't see anything and in the Burgtheater you can't hear or see anything." Ten years later the auditorium was adapted to improve the poor acoustics. The "Burg" was seriously damaged during World War II and was restored in the early 1950s. Artistic quality wasn't damaged this time.

BELOW: the Burgtheater (National Theatre)

influenced Western culture. The rear of the building (the library in Reichsrats-strasse) is decorated with *sgraffito*. The buildings surround a courtyard, with arcades housing statues of former directors and professors of the university. The Guardian of the Spring fountain (Kastaliabrunnen) was built by Edmund Hellmer in 1904.

Opposite the University are the ruins of the Mölkerbastei bastion, dating back to the 17th century. It was demolished in 1861–72. At No. 8 is the **Pasqualati-haus** (museum open Tues–Sat 9am–12.15pm, 1–4.30pm), where Beethoven lodged several times between 1804 and 1815.

Continuing to Schreyvogelgasse 10, you reach the so-called **Dreimäderlhaus** (House of the Three Girls), its late Josephine façade a typical feature of Viennese architecture. (The story that connects Franz Schubert with this building is fic-titious.) Walking past the **Ephrussipalais** (Dr-Karl-Lueger-Ring 14), built by Theophil Hansen (1872–3) and easily recognisable because of its yellow-red front, you will arrive at the **Schottentor**. The old city gate into Schottengasse gave this gate its name.

Schottengasse is a very narrow street, like so many in this part of the town, and famous for its monasteries. On the left is **Schottenhof**, built by Joseph Korn-häusel (1826–32), while on the right stands **Melker Hof**, which dates back to the 15th century and was rebuilt by Josef Gerl in 1770–4. The cellars under-neath these cloisters have been converted into restaurants.

A short distance from the Ringstrasse is the imposing neo-Gothic **Votive Church** (Votivkirche) 🖲 with two spires 99 metres (33 feet) high. It was built by Heinrich Ferstel in 1856–79 before the demolition of the fortifications, and opened for the silver wedding jubilee of Emperor Franz Joseph and Elisabeth. It

While living in the Pasqualatihaus, Beethoven composed the opera Fidelio *(1805), his fourth piano concerto, the Seventh Symphony and the violin concerto in D major.*

BELOW: café society outside the Landtmann

is also a reminder of the abortive assassination attempt on the emperor's life in 1853. The only building of importance between Schottenring and Franz-Josefs-Kai is the **Stock Exchange** (Börse) ⓭, built in 1874–77 and designed by Hansen. You can now walk back through the bustling old city to the Opera, where your next round trip is about to begin.

The tour of the city continues from the National Opera towards the Schwarzenbergplatz. During the decades preceding World War I this was the section of the Ringstrasse along which the famous Ringstrasse Parade (Ringstrassenkorso) was held by the city's Top Ten Thousand. People came here to stroll, flirt, make conversation and above all to see and be seen. It was considered fashionable to repair afterwards to Demel at the Kohlmarkt or Gerstner in the Kärntner Strasse or one of the other famous cafés, or maybe to dine at the Hotel Sacher or Bristol.

Karlsplatz to KunstHaus Wien

Walking along the Kärntner Strasse away from the city centre, you will shortly arrive at the **Karlsplatz**, for many years the favourite guinea-pig of the city's planners. The slanting alignment of the Baroque Church of St Charles with the river Wien, which until the turn of the century flowed openly across the site towards the Danube Canal, has proved highly problematic. The square lies on the edge of the Ringstrasse zone and is surrounded by notable buildings. On the left stands the **Academy of Trade** (Handelsakademie) ⓴, built in 1860–2 by Ferdinand Fellner the Elder. In front of its neo-Gothic façade are statues of Christopher Columbus and Adam Smith, the economist.

The side of the Karlsplatz nearest to the city centre is flanked by the Künstlerhaus, the "House of Art" built to house exhibitions, and the Association of Music (Musikverein). On the square itself are two restored underground stations designed by Otto Wagner. (The "Stadtbahn", called the U4, was built in 1894–1900.) On the "suburban" side of the square, which today lies in the 4th District, are the Historical Museum of the City of Vienna, St Charles' Church, the Technical University, the Protestant School and the new wing of the library of the Technical University.

The **Künstlerhaus** ⓯ was built in 1865–8 in the Italian Renaissance style by August Weber to a design by a team of architects. It served as a meeting place and exhibition hall for the Association of Viennese Artists.

The **Music Association Building** (Musikvereinsgebäude) (Dumbarstrasse 3) was built by Theophil Hansen in 1867–9 for the "Association of the Friends of Music", which had been founded in 1812. As in his later design for the Parliament Building, the Danish architect chose Greek-inspired forms, freely incorporating ancient and modern elements. The Association of the Friends of Music plays a vital role in the musical life of the city. The façade of the building faces the Künstlerhaus. The "Golden Hall" in the middle section is magnificently ornamented, with 16 gilt caryatids down each of the long sides and a ceiling fresco by August Eisenmenger depicting Apollo and the nine Muses.

On the Ringstrasse side, the building stands next to the former palace of Duke Philip of Württemberg (Kärtner

Map, page 90

In recent years the Künstlerhaus has achieved fame throughout Europe for its major exhibitions organised by the Historical Museum.

BELOW: exterior detail on the Music Association Building

Ring 16). It was built in 1862–5 by Arnold Zanetti and Heinrich Adam. In 1872–3, on the occasion of the World Exhibition in Vienna, it was transformed into a hotel. As the **Hotel Imperial** it has accommodated countless statesmen and prominent visitors from all over the world. In 1875–6 Richard Wagner stayed here for several months whilst supervising rehearsals for his operas *Tannhäuser* and *Lohengrin* at what was then the Court Opera.

The **Historical Museum of the City of Vienna** (Historisches Museum der Stadt Wien) **46** (open Tues–Sat 9am–4.30pm), designed by Oswald Haerdtl (1954–9), houses a chronological exhibition describing the most important events in the city's history.

Baroque with an oriental flair

Not far from the museum stands the imposing bulk of **St Charles' Church** (Karlskirche) **47**, one of the most important Baroque buildings in Vienna. It was built to fulfil a vow made by Karl VI during the plague in 1713. Building progressed from 1716 to 1723 under the supervision of Johann Bernhard Fischer von Erlach, and was completed by his son, Joseph Emanuel from 1723–37.

St Charles' Church contains sumptuous altar paintings and frescoes.

The church is dedicated to St Charles Borromeo, the patron saint of plagues. At the time of construction the church stood beyond the meadows bordering the River Wien, on the edge of vineyards. Its façade was designed to present an imposing silhouette from afar. The church's position opposite the optical extension of the Augustinerstrasse later presented serious problems in the design of the Karlsplatz.

BELOW: outside St Charles' Church

The bell-towers which mark the right- and left-hand corners reveal oriental influences. The sculptures adorning the façade were the work of the leading sculptors of the day. Above the gable can be seen, from left to right, statues of Charles, Religion, Mercy, Repentance and Piety, all by Lorenzo Mattielli. The pillared portico has a relief by Giovanni Stanetti in the tympanum, representing the vanquishing of the plague. Underneath is a Latin inscription: "I fulfil my vow in the face of those who fear God" (Psalm 21). In front of the portico are two statues of angels, one bearing the Cross, and the other a cross and a brazen serpent, symbols of the Old and New Testaments. On the triumphal columns are bas-reliefs of scenes from the life of St Charles Borromeo by Johann Christoph Mader.

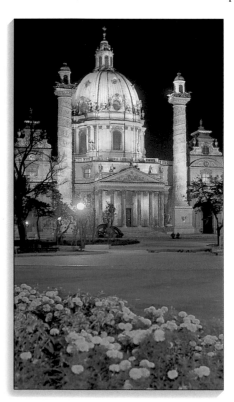

The interior is oval and is dominated by Johann Michael Rottmayr's dome fresco *Upon the Intercession of St Charles Borromeo, the Virgin Mary Implores the Holy Trinity to Save the City from the Plague*, flanked by groups representing the three heavenly virtues of Faith, Hope and Love. To the left under the group portraying Faith are Martin Luther and an angel; the angel is holding a torch with which he is burning Luther's Bible. The altar paintings are by Daniel Gran (right transept) and Martino Altomonte (oval chapel to the right of the entrance), amongst others. The fresco above the magnificent organ loft represents St Cecilia, the patroness of music, and is also by Rottmayr. Fischer von Erlach's design combines the Classical architecture of Rome, Athens and Constantinople in a brilliant synthesis of creative adaptation. The church is intended to provide the visitor with a visual reminder of the universal supremacy of the Church and Empire. In the centre of the pond in front of the church stands the sculpture *Hill Arches* by Henry Moore, a gift from the artist to the city of Vienna.

The **Technical University** (Technische Universität) (No. 13) was built in 1816–18 in the late neo-classical style to house Johann Joseph Prechtl's "Polytechnical Institute". The Ionic columns and high mansard roof of the main building face the Resselpark; on columns in front of the façade are eight busts of famous professors.

In the park itself there are **monuments** to **Siegfried Marcus**, the Austrian inventor of the petrol-driven car, **Josef Madersperger**, who invented the sewing machine, and **Joseph Ressel**, the inventor of the ship's propeller. There is also a monument by Rudolf Weyr to the composer **Johannes Brahms**, who brought the Viennese classical music era to its apotheosis. Brahms came to Vienna from Hamburg in 1862 and died in 1897 not far from here at Karlsgasse 4. The Tilgner fountain is a memorial to the sculptor **Viktor Tilgner**.

At the corner of Wiedner Hauptstrasse stands the **Protestant School**, built by Theophil Hansen in 1860–2. Of interest are the statues of the Evangelists on the columns, by Vinzenz Pilz.

The most remarkable feature of the **Schwarzenbergplatz** is its architectural unity of form. It was thus designed at the express wish of Julius Hähnel, who was anxious that his Schwarzenberg Memorial (1867) should be placed in a harmonious setting. Field-Marshal Prince Karl Philipp Schwarzenberg commanded the allied armies against Napoleon in the "Battle of Nations" at Leipzig in 1813.

On the town side, the square is dominated by corner buildings, between which the central buildings are set further back. Directly on the Ringstrasse stand the former **palace of Archduke Ludwig Viktor** (No. 1), built in 1886–9 in the Italian Renaissance style by Ferstel, and the former Palais Wertheim (No. 17), also built by Ferstel in similar idiom in 1864–9.

On the opposite side are two massive neo-Baroque edifices facing each other; No. 4 is the **House of Industry**, built in 1907–9 by Carl König, which housed the headquarters of the Allied Commission from 1945–55 and in which the preliminary talks leading up to the Austrian National Treaty (1955) were held. No. 14 is the "**House of Trade**" (1905).

On the side furthest from the city, the boundary of the square is marked by the **Fountain**, completed in 1873 to mark the installation of the first water supply system. Behind the fountain stands the **Red Army Liberation Monument** (Russ Helden Denkmal) (1945). Continuing in this direction you would arrive shortly in front of another architectural ensemble consisting of the Belvedere, the Schwarzenberg Palace, the Guard Chapel and the Church of the Nuns of the Visitation (Salesianerinnenkirche).

The route, however, continues along the Äussere Ringstrasse (here known as the **Lothringerstrasse**) to the Concert House, the Academy of Music and Drama and the Academy Theatre, a harmonious ensemble of buildings built in 1910–13 by the theatre architects Fellner and Helmer in partnership with Ludwig Baumann.

Map, page 90

TIP

The Historical Museum has several interesting alternating exhibitions on its ground floor — and the catalogue is excellent.

BELOW: Karlsplatz Pavilions doorway, designed as an Underground exit.

Schindler is one of figures in the arts commemorated with a statue in the Stadtpark.

BELOW: a favourite pastime of young and old

The **Concert House** (Konzerthaus) **48** is the second most important concert hall in Vienna. Continue across Beethovenplatz; the neo-Gothic brick building is the **Academic Grammar School**, designed in 1863–6 by Friedrich Schmidt. Its severe lines are softened by the elaborately decorated centre section. The **Beethoven Memorial** is by Caspar Zumbusch (1880). Now return to the Ringstrasse once more, to the section named after the great Viennese composer Franz Schubert.

Between the Schwarzenbergplatz and the Wollzeile, the main architectural features of the Ringstrasse are the noblemen's palaces and apartment houses designed for the well-to-do middle classes. Striking examples along the Parkring section, which flanks the municipal park, are the **Palais Leitenberger** (No. 16, 1871), the **Palais Henckel** von Donnersmarck (No. 14, 1871–2, today transformed into a hotel), the former **palace of Archduke William** (No. 8, the so-called "Deutschmeister Palace", built by Theophil Hansen in 1864–7) and the **Palais Dumba**. On the city side the road is bordered by various modern buildings, between which you will notice the neo-classical garden façade and massive row of columns facing the Ringstrasse of the **Coburg Palace**. It stands on the site of the Braunbastei, which once formed part of the city fortifications, and was built in 1843–7, about 10 years before the demolition of the old city walls.

The **Stadtpark** (Municipal Park) is the largest historic public garden in the Ringstrasse area. Like the park by the Town Hall, it was laid out in 1862 by Rudolf Sieböck, the Director of Public Gardens at the time. The design sketches were the work of landscape painter Josef Selleny.

The site now occupied by the Stadtpark was filled in Biedermeier times by a mineral-water pavilion. At the request of the town council, in 1865–7 Johann

Garben added a Pump Room (Kursalon). Designed in Italian Renaissance style, the building provided an elegant setting for balls, concerts and other social events. Many famous orchestras played in its music pavilion, in particular that of Eduard Strauss.

Continuing towards the River Wien, you will reach the **Wien River Gate** (Wienflussportal), an important example of Art Nouveau architecture designed by Friedrich Ohmann and Josef Hackhofer in 1903–6. The entire complex forms a harmonious group consisting of pavilions, staircases and decorated river-bank promenades. It was designed to mark the completion of the regulation of the River Wien (1895–1903) and stands at the point where the river resurfaces from its underground channel.

The Stadtpark, whose groups of ancient trees are interspersed with picturesque lakes and ponds, is full of **monuments to composers** (Bruckner, Schubert, Lehár, Stolz), **painters** (Amerling, Canon, Makart) and **writers** (Schindler). There is also a memorial to Andreas Zelinka, the mayor during whose term of office the park was constructed. The most famous and popular of all the monuments, however, is that to **Johann Strauss the Younger** ❹ (1921), designed by Edmund Hellmer.

Leaving the Stadtpark via the Weiskirchnerstrasse exit, you will glimpse on the town side the monument to another mayor, **Dr Karl Lueger** (1897–1910), the chief representative of the Christian Socialist era *(see page 30)*. Karl Lueger remains a popular personality in the city's long history, and one who is often quoted.

The last section of the Ringstrasse is the **Stubenring**, which leads from the Wollzeile to the Danube Canal. The origins of the name are cloaked in mystery.

Map,
page 90

BELOW : busts and Art Nouveau pavilion in the Stadtpark

As long ago as the 12th century the district was known as "Stuben" ("Rooms"), probably because there were drinking rooms (i.e. taverns) and public baths in the area. The old name was revived by the designers of the Ringstrasse.

The imposing buildings dominating this section of the road provide no clues to the impoverished history of this part of town. The far (right-hand) side of the Ringstrasse was the first to be built up. Of interest are the College and Museum for Applied Arts and Government Building. Until 1900, the sister establishment of the Rossauer Barracks, the Emperor Franz Joseph Barracks, stood on the town (left-hand) side. Today the site is occupied by a group of Secessionist buildings, in particular the Post Office Savings Bank (Postsparkassenamt).

The **Museum for Applied Arts** (Museum für angewandte Kunst) **50** (open Tues–Sat 10am–6pm, Thur until 9pm) was built in 1866–71 by Heinrich Ferstel in the Italian Renaissance style. In 1906–8 it was extended by Ludwig Baumann, taking advantage of the land which had become available thanks to the regulation of the River Wien. The pleasing brick façade is elaborately decorated with reliefs, *sgraffito* and artistic medallions. The museum contains a rich variety of collections, especially furniture, china, carpets, glass, ceramics and textiles. Between the museum and the college (No. 3) is a wall with a fountain of Minerva, above which can be seen a mosaic portrait of Pallas Athene against a gold background, by Ferdinand Laufberger (1873).

The **Post Office Savings Bank** (Postsparkassenamt) **51** by Otto Wagner (1904–6) is one of Vienna's most important Secessionist buildings. Characteristic are the exterior's functionality and cubist architectural form, and the interior's strict functionalism. The banking hall in particular is of great architectural interest. The riveting of the façade adds an unusual note. Near the Savings Bank are a number of other buildings with Historicist and Secessionist façades from the same period.

Opposite the Savings Bank stands the **Government Building**, which houses five ministerial departments. It was built to a design by Ludwig Baumann in 1909–13 as the Imperial War Ministry of the Austro-Hungarian monarchy. The building is decorated with typical military themes and a double eagle weighing 40 tonnes. In front of the building stands the equestrian statue of Field-Marshal Radetzky, bearing the motto "In your camp is Austria".

After the collapse of the monarchy the building was re-named several times, mirroring the turbulent history of the country. It was initially the "Liquidating War Ministry", and then the "National Department of Military Affairs", then the "Federal Ministry for Military Affairs" and, in 1934, the "Federal Ministry for National Defence". During the Nazi era it was the "Defence Commando XVII". Austria's stony path from an autocratic monarchy to a democratic member of the European Union cannot be better documented than in the naming of the ministry responsible for external security.

The last building on the Ringstrasse is an Art Nouveau edifice. The **Urania** **52** (1909–10) by Max Fabiani was erected with the sole aim of furthering the education of the populace. There is even an observatory within the dome. When it was dedicated on 6 June 1910, it was derisively referred to as a "scientific theatre",

BELOW: bust of Georg Coch (who invented the modern banking system) in front of the Post Office Savings Bank

Map, page 90

designed to make accessible to the general public the new medium of film. The 20-cm (8-inch) telescope in the dome is equipped with a comet tracer, and there is a central time-keeping unit where you can check the time by telephone. The lectures on popular scientific themes opened new horizons to the Viennese public.

To finish off, we move into the present for what is one of Vienna's most unusual edifices, as well as one of its most popular tourist sights alongside Schönbrunn and St Stephen's Cathedral: the **Hundertwasser-Haus** ❸ (3 Löwengasse/Kegelgasse). To get there you'll need to leave the Ring system and wander into the narrow streets of District 3. The colorful façade of this residential building is impossible to miss – it consciously breaks with every known tradition and convention around. Designed by Friedensreich Hundertwasser, it was built in 1983–6 with the aim of bringing more variety and humanity to the cityscape. Lots of curves, colours, tiles and wood rather than reinforced concrete, ceramics rather than plastics, and plants growing all over the niches and balconies are just a few of the distinctive characteristics of this unique building.

The Hundertwasser style has been the trademark of this entire area for quite some time now. To distract visitors' attention from the building and give the residents some peace and quiet, the small shopping centre opposite, known as the Village, was built.

In 1991 the **KunstHaus Wien** ❺ (3 Untere Weissgerberstrasse 13, open daily 10am–7pm), not far from the Hundertwasser-Haus, first opened its doors. This enormous gallery space, in a former furniture factory, was converted to the Hundertwasser style and now stages temporary exhibitions of works by famous 20th-century artists as well as a permanent exhibition of works by Hundertwasser himself.

TIP

Those tired of all the walking can take a tram to the Hundertwasser-Haus. The N line, right next to the Urania and parallel to the Danube Canal, will take you straight there.

BELOW: the colourful Hundertwasser-Haus

SHOPPING IN VIENNA

Vienna's high-class stores and boutiques offer the last word in rarified elegance, whilst the bustling antiques and junk markets are great fun

First of all, don't be under any illusions that Vienna is a paradise for bargain hunters; it isn't. There has always been a wealthy elite with expensive tastes who have kept prices high; in the old days it was the Imperial household, the aristocracy and the upper classes, while today these have given way to large numbers of diplomats, UN personnel, politicians and bankers. So everything has its price, though you won't find better quality or variety, particularly when it comes to crafts, fashion and design.

EXCLUSIVE STREETS

The most upmarket stores are in Kohlmarkt, Graben, and parts of Kärntner Strasse. Here, some of the shop signs still proudly bear the initials KUK, short for *kaiserlich und königlich*, which means they were once suppliers to the Imperial and royal households. But if you can't cope with the crowds of shoppers between the Opera House and St Stephen's Cathedral, there are lots of equally tempting and expensive shops lurking down the side streets. Here, you will find the kind of helpful and patient service that makes shopping an experience in itself.

Perhaps the best place to go, if you're in the buying mood but are not sure precisely what you want, is the antiques district bounded by Kohlmarkt, Spiegelgasse, Graben and Augustinerstrasse. Here, the endless succession of antique shops and art galleries are a museum of bygone Vienna.

But if your credit card can't take the strain, try Mariahilfer Strasse or, further out of the centre, Favoritenstrasse, Landstrasser Hauptstrasse and Meidlinger Hauptstrasse. Alternatively, you'll find a huge range of more affordable wares at Shopping City Süd, on the southern edge of the city.

△ **SOLD TO THE GENTLEMAN IN THE LEDERHOSEN...**
Formerly a pawnbroker's, the Dorotheum (I, Dorotheergasse 17) is now one of the world's leading auction houses.

◁ **DISPLAY HORSES**
Model Lipizzaner horses, the most famous of all Viennese souvenirs, can be found at the Augarten porcelain factory (I, Stock-im-Eisen-Platz).

◁ HIDDEN DELIGHTS

Apart from the lively and chaotic flea market on Naschmarkt, another paradise for treasure-seekers is the art and antiques market on Donaukanalpromenade, between Schwedenplatz and Schottenring U-Bahn stations. A wide variety of prints, books, jewellery and other antiques are on sale from May to September (Saturdays from 2pm to 8 pm and Sundays from 10am to 8pm).

△ MAKING AN ENTRANCE

Da Retti (I, Kohlmarkt 10) sells extremely elegant candles, fashion clothing and clocks. The entrance to the store was designed by the leading Viennese architect Hans Hollein.

◁ ANCIENT AND MODERN

Reinhold Hofstätter (I, Bräunerstrasse 12) has the city's biggest range of *objets d'art*, designer furniture and paintings.

ONE CAREFUL OWNER

Can we interest you in this sauce-boat with a slightly damaged handle? Or this delightful silver-plated sugar bowl, guaranteed to be over 100 years old? How about this extensive collection of candlesticks, so many and so varied you'll wish you didn't have electric light? Plus there's this beautiful old doll – though we must admit its clothes have seen better days – and here's a real find: a 1906 edition of the complete works of Goethe, uncut and slightly foxed, yours for only 1,200 Schillings!

You'll find the city's biggest collection of junk at the wonderful flea market in Naschmarkt, which takes place every Saturday from 8am to 6pm to the west of the daily gourmet food market. But there are few bargains to be had here; the market is always packed with tourists, so prices are high. However, you may still find some good deals if you turn up first thing in the morning or last thing at night.

Whether you discover a hidden bargain or don't buy anything at all, it is worth a visit just for the atmosphere. This is unique, partly because of the extraordinary assortment of people buying, selling and haggling, and partly because of the bizarre range of ancient relics that pass for merchandise each week.

◁ EVERYDAY CRAFTS

The Österreichischen Werkstätten (Austrian Workshops) (I, Kärntner Strasse 6) are a product of the Viennese Art Nouveau movement. Unusual pieces include some by the founding artists.

DRESSING IN STYLE ▷

Trachten-Tostmann (I, Schottengasse 3a) offers traditional Austrian costumes in high-quality fabrics, as well as young fashions.

WHERE TO EAT, DRINK AND BE MERRY

Jutta Kohout leads a tour of "living Vienna", a window on its social life. Find out – and experience – where the Viennese hang out at night, are entertained, shop or take a Sunday stroll

It must have happened around the mid-1970s, although no-one can remember the exact date or year. Vienna had been quietly languishing under a canopy of cobwebs, stuck in a corset of cliché and tradition. A thousand years of history weighed down the former capital of the Austro-Hungarian Empire, the present didn't exist. And then, suddenly and unexpectedly, the town woke up.

It started in the oldest part of Vienna, in small narrow streets with cobblestones and wrought-iron street lamps. To be precise, it happened between St Rupert's Church and the Rabensteig. Curious new bars and *Beiseln* – a cross between a pub and a restaurant – opened. Loud music filled the streets, neon lights flickered over Baroque façades. A whole city rubbed its sleepy eyes.

The "joy of living" proved to be a fever that spread as rapidly as the plague. Elderly ladies of good family fled to the safe, dusty pastry shops. Chrome instead of velour, punk instead of pomp – the smell of decay was replaced by the aura of modernity. Some said it would pass. They were wrong. The new-found life force was here to stay, proof against spoilsports. And, according to official statistics, it even lowered the suicide rate.

PRECEDING PAGES: a *Heuriger* inn; inside a coffee house; interior of the Rote Engel bar.
BELOW: an evening out.
BELOW RIGHT: wine bar on the Bäckerstrasse

Not so long ago, Vienna had one of the highest suicide rates in the world, but today it is down to an "acceptable" rate: only 28 Viennese in every 100,000 take their own lives. Most of the others prefer to seek a solution to their problems in the famous (and infamous) **"Bermuda Triangle"**, the former Jewish textile quarter around St Rupert's Church. Here, the Viennese in-crowd rules, a colourful mixture of amateur performance artists, jokers, heavy drinkers, top-class hairdressers and honorary gurus.

A lot of paths cross at **Oswald und Kalb** (1 Bäckerstrasse 14; tel: 512 2371; reserve) the nocturnal centre for the latest hot gossip. Most tourists ignore the old, unassuming exterior in the Bäckerstrasse, but inside, the media people and their victims communicate over a glass of wine at the wooden counter in front of the mirrored bar.

The wine is poured by expert Yugoslav waiters. The main choice is between an extremely palatable dry white wine and the famous Schilcher Rosé, produced in Styria. The salads, dressed with dark pumpkin seed oil, are delicious, and if you are lucky you will find fresh Slovak goose liver on the menu. Having dined, quenched your thirst and gathered information, the journey continues. Cross the road and enter **Alt Wien** (1 Bäckerstrasse 9; tel: 512 5222), only a few steps away. During the day, Alt Wien is a quiet, rather shabby café with a few snooker tables. At night, it undergoes a transformation. A guide book warns outsiders: "If you enter a bar in this city, you must be prepared to be stared at, critically assessed, have the mickey taken and be generally tested. But you will also be accepted once you have passed these tests."

The less daring never make it past the billowing tobacco fumes and babble of voices at the entrance, the brave are well rewarded. There is always at least

BELOW: an artist's *Kneipe* (pub) in the 1890s

Wherever you stand in the Bäckerstrasse, within a hundred yards there are bars and restaurants to satisfy every taste, pocket and frame of mind. After midnight, this small quiet street looks more like a fairground.

BELOW: interior of the KIX bar, designed by Oskar Putz

one love-sick figure, huddled in a corner, drowning his sorrows. An intoxicated unrecognised genius recites his poetry, and there's a harmless squabble at the bar. It's not surprising that Alt Wien was the favourite of Helmut Qualtinger, the late actor and cabaret artist, who used to celebrate here nightly and throw out anyone who didn't "look right", that is anyone whose clothes suggested middle-class aspirations. These rejects normally take refuge in the **Weincomptoir** (1 Bäckerstrasse 6; tel: 512 1760) across the street. Here you can enjoy some of the best wines in "civilised" company. Top quality bottles are stacked in wooden racks. The handwritten menu offers snacks, or a fattening meal such as spinach dumplings fried in lots of butter and sprinkled with Parmesan. The Viennese who prefer Italian food frequent the **Cantinetta** (1 Jasomirgottstrasse 3–5; tel: 535 2066), renowned for its excellent fish dishes.

Die Bar (1 Sonnenfelsgasse 9; tel: 513 1499) is frequented by ever-so-cool intellectuals who know it all and have seen it all. They just stare knowingly past each other. The tourist, not used to the pace of Viennese night life, usually gives up, but this is where it all begins!

The Bermuda Triangle

Walk down Rotenturmstrasse, past **Daniel Moser** (1 Rotenturmstrasse 14; tel: 513 2823) (rendezvous of the sons of the upper classes and ambitious transvestites), then follow the noise. You can't miss it.

Rabensteig is a small square, surrounded by very old houses. On a warm summer's evening, it becomes one big garden. If you are lucky enough to get a seat, you can sit in the middle of the city, enjoy the mild evening, flirt a little and comment on the passers-by. Or you can go into **KrahKrah** ("Croak Croak")

(1 Rabensteig 8; tel: 533 8193), choose between 40 kinds of beer and eat a hot meat sandwich in garlic rye bread. In the **Rote Engel** (Red Angel) (1 Rabensteig 5; tel: 535 4105) there's only bread and cheese to go with wine by the glass, but there's live music every night. The Rote Engel enjoys near-museum status nowadays, for it was the spark that ignited the Bermuda Triangle in the mid-1970s.

From this point, bars and restaurants spread like wildfire along the Seitenstettengasse as far as St Rupert's Church. The **Ma Pitom** (1 Seitenstettengasse 5; tel: 535 4313) is famous for its Italian and Jewish specialities.

The top address on the Ruprechtsplatz is the **Salzamt** (Salt Trading Post) (1 Ruprechtsplatz 1; tel: 533 5332). The interior was designed by the star architect Hermann Czech, and has been photographed for international decorating magazines. Plain wooden boxes hide the ventilation shafts under the ceiling, and among them hang elaborate Venetian chandeliers. The clientele is one of the chicest in the city. The food is superb – the yuppie palate thrives on chicken livers fried in red wine on a bed of lettuce, or terrine of broccoli with shrimps in herb sauce. Even the Austrian racing driver, Niki Lauda, drops in occasionally.

One of the brightest stars in the Viennese night sky is the café-restaurant **Engländer** (1 Postgasse 2; tel: 512 2734), diagonally opposite the famous traditional cabaret restaurant, Simpl. Every morning international newspapers rustle and bread rolls crunch; at noon there are open sardine sandwiches and other light meals; and at night the creative and beautiful people of Vienna meet after the cinema or theatre for a midnight snack of roast beef and horseradish.

Another popular meeting place is **Panigl** (8 Josefstädter Strasse 91; tel: 406 5218). A blood-red painting by artist Hermann Nitsch, no stranger to scandal, hangs in the dining room. The guests are mostly art and media types who

Ma Pitom's Hebrew name means "Why Suddenly?"

BELOW: people drinking outside the Herkner

communicate cheerfully at the long refectory-style tables. It's elegant but comfortable, and the Italian cuisine is worth coming back for.

In Vienna there are hundreds of bars, cafés, *Beiseln* and restaurants; it is impossible to list them all. We recommend drifting with the crowd and trying this or that restaurant for yourself. No-one, we can assure you, has ever died of thirst during this pleasant exercise.

Most revellers still awake in the early hours end up in the Linke Wienzeile in the **Café Drechsler** (6 Linke Wienzeile 22; tel: 587 8580), opposite the Naschmarkt. There is always a mixed clientele here – regular clubbers, elegant theatre-goers, the odd down-and-out or scrounger. You can have a hot meal as early as four in the morning. Many a potential hangover has been held at bay by a steaming risotto or a small goulash plus a *Pfiff* (a small glass of beer).

ABOVE: Stadtbeisl waiters.

BELOW: waiter in the Glacisbeisl

The *Beisel*

A good *Beisel* is made up of a handful of simple ingredients: a panelled bar with wooden floorboards and brightly polished taps for draught beer, where you can drink a quick glass of wine standing up; a "parlour" with chequered tablecloths and a few withered plants struggling to survive in the tobacco smoke; and a grumpy, hasty waiter, usually addressed as "Herr Franz". There is a handwritten menu with a different main dish every day, and a landlady who is usually the best advertisement for the nourishing food her kitchen prepares.

A certain Ignaz Castelli, nicknamed "Professor of the Science of Frivolity" by the Viennese, said this of the *Beisel* in 1800: "There are small and rather shabby inns in the suburbs, called *Beiseln* by the lower classes, whose innkeepers keep one or two pretty, cheeky wenches and where two or three musicians play dance

tunes every evening. There is no great variety of food – sausages, cheese, occasionally pork. During the day, the mostly rather buxom wenches pose outside the entrance and offer their services to the passing menfolk. Over their bosoms they wear silk kerchiefs, which reveal more than they cover."

Today the wenches, with or without kerchiefs, advertise their services in the personal columns of newspapers, and the shabby inns long ago became an honourable institution. Employees and pensioners, students and professors, dog owners and their pets all eat here. In a *Beisel* you get a good plain meal, none of the fancy stuff. A clear soup (with pancake, liver or semolina dumplings) for starters, followed by goulash or roast beef with vegetables, fish on Fridays or maybe even homemade noodles, followed by sweet plum or apricot dumplings. The worst enemy of these traditional inns is success. Once a *Beisel* has a reputation for good food, people start crowding in at lunchtime. Then the *Beisel* is "promoted" to a restaurant. Plain good cooking becomes internationally interesting with garnishes of pineapple or kiwi fruit. Fortunately, the landlord is usually brought to his senses again when his regulars all disappear.

The name *Beisel* sometimes appears on the front of some pseudo-rustic snack bars – avoid these traps. It's better to queue for a table at the **Pfudl** (1 Bäckerstrasse 22; tel: 512 6705). Here, you can still enjoy a delicious traditional Viennese meal. Not very far away is another good tip for fans of Viennese cuisine, **Zu den drei Hacken** (1 Singerstrasse 28; tel: 512 5895). In August, when the temperature rises, the Viennese flock to either the **Silberwirt** (5 Schlossgasse 21; tel: 544 4907) or the **Altes Fassl** (5 Ziegelofengasse 37; tel: 544 4298). Their courtyards are shaded by enormous chestnut trees, and sparrows fight over the crumbs on the gravel. Opposite the cemetery in Ottakring is another favourite

At the Pfudl, the preparation of traditional Viennese dishes is closely supervised by the landlady (the Pfudl-wirtin). In November a crispy-roasted goose with red cabbage and dumplings marks the feast of St Martin.

BELOW: the formidable landlady of the Pfudl

Beisel with a typically Viennese atmosphere, the **Zur Witwe Bolte** (16 Gallitzinstrasse 12; tel: 46 3165). The quiet drinker, sitting here with a quarter litre of *Heuriger* and a juicy piece of roast pork, soon realises that life is well worth living – as long as you're still alive.

Beisel on the fringe

To have fun at somebody else's expense, to eat well and to drink well – these are the three favourite pastimes of the Viennese. And nowadays they can indulge in all three at once. The fringe *Beiseln* (mainly cabaret) are in great demand, and it is advisable to reserve a table well in advance. If you visit the established Viennese theatres, you'll probably have to follow custom and squeeze yourself into a little black dress or half-choke yourself with a bow tie. Here, you can sprawl in jumper and jeans, and providing you can cope with the language, enjoy the abrasive cabaret on the stage. Eating, drinking and even smoking (unless the performer is still a bit hoarse from yesterday) are of course permitted. The waiters and waitresses, balancing plates and beer tankards, have perfected their timing to fit in with the performance. Strengthened in body and soul, guests leave the pub at closing time with the comfortable feeling of having indulged in physical and mental pleasures. (Most of the *Beiseln* mentioned below are very busy and it is recommended that visitors make reservations and buy a ticket before setting out for the evening.)

The first of these busy establishments to spring up was the **Kulisse** (17 Rosensteingasse 39; tel: 485 3870), in an old, converted suburban theatre. The repertoire includes Nestroy as well as social satire. Cabaret artists who manage to fill all the Kulisse's 220 seats can call themselves successful. A competitor to be reckoned with is the **Spektakel** (5 Hamburger Strasse 1; tel: 587 0653) near the Naschmarkt. There is less space, but the food is better. One of its stars is the wickedly ingenious Lukas Resetarits, known to the Viennese as Inspector Kottan, the anti-hero of a TV detective series. He reveals that the Viennese heart of gold is lead, while the guests devote themselves to the food – laughing gives you an appetite.

BELOW: the Bierbeisel at night

Other high points of the cabaret scene are the **Metropol** (17 Hernalser Hauptstrasse 55; tel: 407 77 407), a former dance café, and the **Kabarett Niedermaier** (8 Lenaugasse 1a; tel: 408 4492). The young woman who runs the latter organises three "talent spotting" evenings a year for young entertainers. The **Simpl** (1 Wollzeile 36; tel: 512 4742) offers traditional jokes and is frequented by politicians trying to prove they don't take themselves too seriously. The Simpl is the last survivor of the Golden Age of Viennese cabaret, the inter-war years and just after World War II, when popular favourites Karl Farkas and Ernst Waldbrunn indulged in repartee at New Year. There is a Viennese saying: "When times are bad, the cabaret's good". Between the wars you could choose between 25 cabaret establishments (mostly in cellars). Helmut Qualtinger, that colossus of the German stage, revived cabaret after 1945. Georg Kreisler, tinkling harmlessly at the piano, fired many an acid remark which later found its way into the language as a proverb.

Cabaret declined in popularity during the economic boom. People took work seriously, trying to grab their share as living standards rose. Today, cabaret is once more part of Viennese life. There is something for everyone, from the blackest of humour to feminist sketches.

Coffee houses

At the crack of dawn the Viennese coffee houses open their doors. There is a delicious aroma of freshly ground coffee; baskets on marble tables overflow with a vast variety of bread, buns and rolls; newspapers from all over the world are waiting, neatly sorted, for the guests. Vienna's coffee houses are a much-loved institution. The writer Camillo Schaefer said they represented "an oasis of comfort in the desert of life", essential for quenching the thirst of every age and social class.

The most colourful mixture of people can be found in the **Café Museum** (1 Friedrichstrasse 6; tel: 586 5202) in the Karlsplatz. Seated on red leather sofas and armchairs, councillors and students read or play chess, while painters and sculptors from the nearby Academy of Fine Arts discuss their work. The walls are yellowed with cigarette smoke and covered with theatrical and art posters. The waiters take care of their guests over and above the call of duty depending on the size of the tip. If you are lucky enough to get one of the window seats, you can enjoy a marvellous view of the gilded dome of the Secession building across the street.

The Secession also houses, in its cellar, a coffee house, the **Café in der Secession** (1 Friedrichstrasse 12; tel: 586 9386), which presents a daring mixture of styles (traditional coffee-house furniture, the walls tiled with garish Italian

BELOW: on stage in the Metropol

tiles). On warm summer evenings, you can dance the tango on the lawn outside, with the traffic roaring around you and St Charles' Church silhouetted against the darkening sky like a Baroque mirage.

The atmosphere in the **Landtmann** (1 Dr. Karl Lueger-Ring 4, next to the Burgtheater; tel: 533 9128) is much more subdued at lunchtime. It is probably the most splendid of the coffee houses, and it tends to be packed with politicians (the Parliament Building and Town Hall are close by). Amongst them sit journalists with ears pricked for a good story and actors waiting to be recognised. The food is excellent, the prices reasonable.

Prückel (1 Stubenring 24; tel: 512 4339) thrives on that slightly worn Viennese charm. Bridge is played here every Saturday afternoon, whilst the piano often inspires guests to an impromptu recital.

Other coffee houses in the inner city which follow the old Viennese tradition are the **Diglas** (1 Wollzeile 10; tel: 512 8401), with gigantic cakes on display, the **Frauenhuber** (1 Himmelpfortgasse 6; tel: 512 4323) and the **Bräunerhof** (1 Stallburggasse 2; tel: 512 3893). If you want culture with your coffee, you could try the **Zartl** (3 Rasumofskygasse 7; tel: 712 5560). They hold poetry readings and concerts in the evenings. The **Old Bakehouse** (Alte Backstube) (8 Lange Gasse 34; tel: 406 1101) in Josefstadt is coffee house and museum in one.

The **Hawelka** (1 Dorotheergasse 6; tel: 512 3291) looks back on a glorious past. Here, you should ask for a *Buchtel,* a kind of pastry only served hot after ten in the evening. If you prefer savoury to sweet, go to the **Trzesniewski** opposite (1 Dorotheergasse 1; tel: 512 3291) and try their rolls with spicy fillings.

The *Konditoreien* (patisseries) are temples to the sweet tooth. There is no clear distinction between a *Kaffeehaus* and a *Konditorei,* except perhaps that the clien-

While drinking hot chocolate with whipped cream at the Old Bakehouse café/museum, you can admire old flour measures, bakery utensils and an oven that was first used 250 years ago.

BELOW: the entrance to Figlmüller

tele differs. Elegant ladies, reminiscing about the times when the black forest gateau was simply *enormous*, meet at **Lehmann** (1 Graben 12; tel: 512 1815) or **Gerstner** (1 Kärtner Strasse 15; tel: 512 4963), once suppliers to the imperial court. **Heiner** (1 Kärtner Strasse 21–23; tel: 512 6863) lures hungry passers-by with decorative meringue. At **Sluka** (1 Rathausplatz 8; tel: 405 7172) you will find mountains of strudel and roulades.

The mecca for everyone with a sweet tooth, however, is the **Demel** (1 Kohlmarkt 14; tel: 535 1739). It was founded 200 years ago. Its cakes, gateaux, confectionery and delicate salads are still among the finest on offer. Guests are still addressed in the third person – "Is Madam ready to be served?" – and waitresses in monasterial black serve *crème de jour* and keep the rowdier tourists in check with a withering look. Cakes in the window are decorated with likenesses of well-known Austrians such as Emperor Franz Josef or Bruno Kreisky, the former chancellor.

Where the *Schnitzel* are largest

A bit of frivolity is essential, even when it comes to food. Restaurants are given amusing names such as **Zum Hungerkünstler** (The Expert Dieter) (6 Gumpendorfer Strasse 48; tel: 587 9210; reserve) or the **Gulaschmuseum** (1 Schulerstrasse 20; tel: 512 1017; reserve). The battle for the biggest *Schnitzel* has been won in style by **Figlmüller** (1 Wollzeile 5 (in the passage between Stephansplatz); tel: 512 6177; reserve), where the *Schnitzel* are bigger than the plates.

Disgusted vegetarians take refuge in the **Wrenkh** (15 Hollergasse 9; tel: 892 3356; reserve) and enjoy a healthy meal in a smokeless atmosphere, eating desserts sweetened with honey from Burgenland. This menu would lead to a revolt among the guests in the "authentic" Viennese pubs. Good roast pork just isn't a light meal, and chicken should be crisply fried in plenty of butter or oil. The traditional accompaniment is live zither music and *Heuriger* songs, occasionally a gypsy violinist.

The most popular places are **Piaristenkeller** (8 Piaristengasse 45; tel: 406 0193; reserve) in Josefstadt, **Augustinerkeller** (1 Augustinerstrasse; tel: 533 1026; reserve) and **Zwölf-Apostel-Keller** (1 Sonnenfelsgasse 3; tel: 512 6777; reserve) in the inner city.

Art

If you want to walk off some of those calories afterwards, take a look round some of the many Viennese art galleries. The exhibits range from Biedermeier watercolours to the products of the Jungen Wilden. The **Galerie nächst St Stephan** (1 Grünangergasse 1) promoted *avant-garde* art in the 1960s. Video art can be seen at **Galerie Grita Insam** (1 Köllnerhofgasse 6). The **Galerie Krin-zinger** (1 Seilerstätte 16), with its exhibition area of over 600 sq. metres (6,666 sq. feet), could perhaps more rightly be called a museum.

Do not miss the **Dorotheum** (1 Dorotheergasse 17; tel: 515 60212), a pawn shop and auction house in one. Its popular name is Pfandl (from the German verb *verpfänden*, to pawn). The exhibits displayed on several floors range from period furniture to paintings, jewellery, porcelain, clothes and all sorts of nick-nacks.

BELOW: outside seating on the Am Hof

Nostalgia fans can admire themselves in the decorative old mirrors, search wormy old desks for secret drawers, or sink into velour armchairs.

Gifts and souvenirs

The little antique shops between the Dorotheum and the Hofburg, around the Café Bräunerhof, fill their windows with glittering Jugendstil jewellery. The largest selection of Imperial paraphernalia is found at **Alt-Österreich Kuriositäten** (1 Himmelpfortgasse 7; tel: 513 4870). **Duschek & Schreed** (1 Dorotheergasse 13; tel: 512 5885) in the Plankengasse is the place to look for old watches, while **Zetter** (1 Lobkowitzplatz 1; tel: 513 1416) specialises in Art Nouveau *objets d'art* and **Kovacek** (1 Spiegelgasse 12; tel: 512 9954) in antique glass. Music lovers will love browsing through the antique sheet music at **Doblinger** (1 Dorotheergasse 10; tel: 515 030). There are paintings and curios galore at **Reinhold Hofstätter** (1 Bräunerstrasse 12; tel: 533 5069), and furniture and glass at **Monika Kaesser** (1 Krugerstrasse 17; tel: 512 2805).

Vienna offers souvenirs for every taste and pocket, from fine Augarten porcelain (preferably shaped into pirouetting Lipizzaner horses) to *petit-point* spectacle cases. The great traditional confectioner **Altmann & Kühne** (1 Graben 30; tel: 533 0927) produces superb miniature confectionery. They pack it into chests of drawers, boxes, cases and dolls' hatboxes and export it all over the world. But the Viennese, too, like to spoil themselves by buying a little nougat or bitter chocolate drops here.

Elegant, handmade leather shoes are the speciality of **Scheer & Söhne** (1 Bräunerstrasse 4; tel: 533 8084) and **Materna** (1 Mahlerstrasse 5; tel: 512 4165), both in the inner city. Stacked up on their shelves are the wooden models

A delicious gift to bring back from Vienna is the "métre of love" – a fancy box, exactly one metre (39 inches) long and containing tiny, hand-made pieces of confectionery.

BELOW: inside the Dorotheum, Vienna's equivalent of Sotheby's or Christie's auction house

made to measure for many prominent personalities. The beautiful and rich shop at the elegant boutique **Schella Kahn** (1 Singerstrasse 6; tel: 513 2287), which offers modern classics in quiet colours, with first-class materials and workmanship.

Spectacles to suit for the cosmopolitan couple can be found round the corner in the Liliengasse, at **Hartmann** (1 Singerstrasse 8; tel: 512 1489). Here the aids to vision are made of horn or super light pear or maple wood. You can also buy perfectly shaped combs, brushes and hair slides. Exquisite fine jewellery can be found at **Schullin** (1 Kohlmarkt 7; tel: 533 9007) or **Skrein** (1 Spiegelgasse 5; tel. 513 2284); both have workshops where you can place orders for individual and original pieces. Both fine jewellery and the latest craze are available at the **Galerie V & V** (1 Bauernmarkt 19; tel: 535 6334) in the city centre. If you've lost your rocks (or had to take them to the Pfandl), there is a vending machine outside selling necklaces made of plastic diamonds.

If you're looking for a bargain piece of furniture or nick-nacks as souvenirs you might try the **Vienna Flea Market** (Flohmarkt) (U4 Kettenbrückengasse) on Saturday mornings. There is also an **Antiques Market** (Kunst- und Antiquitätenmarkt) by the Danube Canal near the Schottenring at weekends (Saturday afternoon and all day Sunday). Competing with each other are two other events, held on the first Saturday and Sunday of every month: the **Arts and Crafts Fair** (Kunsthandwerksmarkt) (7 Spittelberggasse) and the **Art Market** (Kunstmarkt) (1 Heiligenkreuzerhof).

Shop fronts are typically ornate in Vienna.

From the casino to the theatre

Having completed your shopping trip and bought a few glittering things for yourself, you might fancy an evening of drinking champagne at one of Vienna's casinos. In the elegant atmosphere of the **Cercle** (1 Kärtner Strasse 41; tel: 512 4836), a casino, you can lose a fortune – or watch someone else losing theirs, if you prefer. Next door is the boutique of the famous dressmaker **Adlmüller** (1 Kärtner Strasse 41; tel: 512 6650), where the wives of politicians and primadonnas alike have themselves fitted in figure-flattering style with yards of taffeta for the annual Opera Ball. A visit to one of the nightclubs between St Stephen's Cathedral and the Opera House can be as expensive as an evening in the casino.

In the **Moulin Rouge** (1 Walfischgasse; tel: 512 2130) guests often wait in vain for the voluptuous striptease show they expected. The landlord, Heinz Schimanko, perhaps the best known bald head in Vienna, is a fervent patron of the arts. Thanks to a few courageous individuals, Viennese fringe theatre has been transformed from a dull desert to fertile meadow. In the very shadow of the Opera, the Burgtheater and the Theater in der Josefstadt, young ensembles have been formed that fearlessly blow the cobwebs off the classic pieces. The well-known and dedicated actress Emmy Werner was one of the courageous performers who formed her own group, the Theater in der Drachengasse, in the 1980s. She was so successful that she was offered the post of director of the Volkstheater, the first woman in Vienna to be made director of one of the big theatres.

BELOW: mouth-watering display of confectionery at the Heiner

Fitness

Well, we have found out that the Viennese like to eat and drink well, that they like to go out, display themselves and conduct intrigues. But what about keeping fit in order to survive all this good living? The Viennese, truth be told, are not very fond of sports activities. This is often to the visitor's advantage. As one travel writer ironically put it: "There will be plenty of space in the swimming pools, especially in the water."

If you want relaxing exercise, try the spectacular swimming pool, the **Amalienbad** (10 Reumannplatz 23; tel: 607 4747). You can splash around in the Jugendstil hall and watch the milky light fall through the glass roof onto the Turkish tiles. Also recommended is a visit to the steam baths with their mosaic decorations. Snobs, fresh air fanatics and those who like betting head toward the Prater. There is trap racing in **Krieau** and horse racing in **Freudenau**. Freudenau, once the meeting place of high society under the imperial and royal monarchies, is still considered one of the most beautiful racecourses in the world. You can get the best view of the start from the white-painted covered stands.

The parkland around the racecourse is a **golf course**, the only one in Vienna. On the **Alte Donau**, the old course of the Danube, is another favourite recreation centre. With the skyline of the UNO City in the background, you can surf, row, swim and go ice skating in winter. The only drawback is the mosquitoes. The favourite sport of the Viennese, however, has always been and still is simply going for a walk. On a Sunday afternoon, when the weather is good, couples, families and individuals stroll through the park of Schloss Schönbrunn, along the Danube Canal or along the Ring in the inner city. In Imperial times the flower show in the Prater was one of the most important social events in spring.

At the end of every race at Freudenau there is a confetti snowstorm of torn-up tickets tossed away by disappointed losers. Elegant old gentlemen of the turf console themselves with champagne. The atmosphere recalls a long-lost world.

BELOW: boats for hire on Heustadelwasser in the Prater

Today, the most important spring event is the **Vienna Festival** (Wiener Fest-wochen) in May and June. Traditionally it starts off with an open-air concert in the Rathausplatz, unless it's a "washout" because of the weather. For a few weeks the city belongs to the artists and street performers. There are open-air theatre performances and concerts, the traditional and *avant-garde* side by side. Vienna officially becomes one single stage.

Fasching – the season of balls

Vienna is at its liveliest when it's cold and wet, or *ungemütlich,* outside. From November to February's Ash Wednesday, all the music and concert halls with their bygone imperial splendour are filled again with the rhythm of the waltz, and they become again playgrounds where the Viennese soul unfolds, where class, clan and family are forgotten, where joy, gaiety, merriment and frivolity reign supreme.

There is the Champagne Ball, the Emperor's Ball, the Hunter and Chimney-sweep's Ball, the Thief Ball and the Opera Ball. People who normally work to-gether meet to dance, drink and laugh.

If you don't own the essential ball dress, there are places where you can hire one. The tailcoat for the Opera Ball can be rented for US$200 a night. But the real Viennese doesn't mind paying – for him, the rest of the year is there to prepare for the Ball Season, for the time when he can finally be what he was born for and when all these lifeless majestic structures of the city come to life again.

The ordinary Viennese, however, used to be more restricted in his leisure activities, for the Habsburgs did not always have the common touch that nostalgia awards them. For instance, they strictly forbade their subjects to enter the

The Prater golf course is the only one in Vienna.

BELOW LEFT: ice-skating at the Alte Donau.
BELOW: a fitting hairdo for the Opera Ball

woods and meadows outside the city walls, as day-trippers would only frighten away the game, thus spoiling their pleasures in the Imperial sport of hunting. This lasted until well into the 18th century. Not until the liberal Joseph II succeeded his mother Maria Theresa, was the **Prater** opened (in 1766) to all Viennese. Criticised for this decision by the aristocracy, he calmly retorted: "If I wanted to stay among my peers, I'd have to spend all day walking in the Crypt of the Capuchins" (where the Habsburgs are buried). The Viennese enthusiastically came *en masse* from the first day. They spread out over the meadows and filled the shady corners. Shrewd businessmen sought an Imperial licence to sell coffee, tea and ice cream. The first simple merry-go-rounds, swings and bowling alleys were set up. On one stall "mechanical birds" were on display.

The Prater's giant ferris wheel was erected in 1897, when the World Exhibition was held in Vienna. Some 67 metres (200 feet) high, at the time it was the highest ferris wheel in the world.

Growth of the Prater

The Viennese desire for the sensational led to the rapid growth of the Prater. Comic revues and shooting-galleries sprang up, there were firework displays, and dwarfs and freaks – real or fraudulent – were exhibited. In 1855, the famous *Calafatti*, a wooden figure of a Chinese mandarin (9 metres/30 feet high, with a long narrow pigtail) was set up in the centre of one of the merry-go-rounds. The true symbol of the Prater, however, has always been the figure of Punch, lovingly known as *Wurstel* ("Sausage") in Vienna. The Viennese look upon this tragicomic figure as a soulmate. Ill-treated by life, pursued by a crocodile, he is pitted from one adventure to the next and ends up as the winner after all.

The Prater was not only noise and public entertainment, but also peace and quiet. The secretive little lanes away from the commotion of the fairground were, and still are, favoured by lovers.

BELOW: ghost train at the Prater

In the last days of World War II, the Prater was badly damaged by fire. Reconstruction began in 1948, and it recovered enough to be the location for Carol Reed's brilliant movie *The Third Man*. Today, the Prater is in danger of turning into an American-style theme park. Amusement arcades and peepshows have replaced the old-fashioned merry-go-rounds with their brightly painted wooden horses. Traditional delicacies such as pickled cucumber have given way to fast-food bars.

But in Vienna, as in many other Western countries, there are recent signs of a return to the lifestyle of earlier times. All classes of society share this nostalgia. The renaissance of the city's coffee houses owes much to their new-found popularity amongst the younger generation, who have discovered that the unique charm and traditions of one of Europe's great metropolises still have much to offer contemporary society. So we can be hopeful that the special atmosphere of the Prater will survive to give pleasure to generations to come.

If you want to catch something of the old atmosphere, take a trip on the Liliputbahn, a miniature train, and rattle along the narrow-gauge track into the tangled greenery. Or stroll along the main avenue of the Prater, a splendid boulevard lined with giant trees, used every Sunday by thousands of Viennese for a cycling tour. Afterwards, go to the Lusthaus (despite its name, "house of pleasure", it's a highly respectable establishment) and take a break, replenishing yourself with a satisfying snack such as a *guglhupf* and a *melange*.

The Prater has everything – even a church.

The Bohemian Prater

In the south of Vienna, on the very edge of the tenth district of Favoriten, lies a very special street: the **Bohemian Prater** (Böhmischer Prater). On a clear day, the view of Vienna from the gently rolling slopes of the Laaerberg is superb. The sky above the sea of roofs and church towers is dotted with the colourful kites flown by children.

Until well into the last century, Bohemian brickmakers worked in this idyllic place under appalling, slave-like conditions. They fired bricks made from the dry clay soil for half the Habsburg empire and mostly slept in the open, using a brick for a pillow. The Bohemian immigrants provided plentiful cheap labour in the factories and served as cooks and maids in upper-class households. Many a touching song was written about them, but they were mercilessly exploited. Today, many pages of the Vienna telephone directory still read like the telephone directory of Prague. The lyrics of one popular song of the post-war years were written with the help of the telephone directory. It consisted entirely of a list of names beginning with V – with such tongue-twisters as Vaclavik, Vrbka and Vlk.

The Bohemian Prater is one of the few relics of the days when Bohemian immigrants lived here. Tucked away among allotments and birch woods are the old-fashioned flimsy wooden stalls. A smell of candy floss and Turkish delight floats in the air. The oldest carousel in Europe is here, under a wooden canopy dating from 1840. It was placed under a conservation order in 1985. The carved wooden horses all have names: Elfi, Herbert and Karli.

BELOW: the ferris wheel

VIENNESE CAFE LIFE

In Vienna's old coffee houses you can fantasise about debating with famous figures who once sat in your place. In Konditorei, *just concentrate on the cakes*

Some of Vienna's cafés are famous landmarks, like the Café Landtmann, the Griensteidl, the Central,

the Hawelka, and of course the Sacher. Others are less well known, but remain more authentic. There are still a vast number of them, but they are a pale imitation of Viennese café culture at the turn of the century. The superb coffee, rich assortment of cakes, and wide range of newspapers can still be enjoyed, but they have lost their old intellectual buzz.

No longer do their patrons sit at the same marble tables each day to discuss, and in many cases shape the future of international politics, literature, medicine, psychoanalysis or music. No longer do they draw up party manifestoes and plot revolutions as they play chess, indulge in slanderous gossip about one another, or stave off imminent starvation by persuading the waiter to supply food on credit. All the big names in Vienna in the early 20th century had their own particular favourites (*see The Viennese, page 74*).

END OF AN ERA

This highly sophisticated form of popular culture was destroyed by the Nazis because it was dominated by Jewish intellectuals, and it never recovered from this terrible blow. But in one respect at least, Vienna's cafés are in a stronger position than they were 100 years ago: they are havens of tranquillity in contrast to the frenetic pace of life outside, and are greatly envied by visitors. A bonus is to sit outside in summer and watch the world go by while sipping a speciality coffee.

CAFE DEMEL ▷
The traditional and elegant Demel *Konditorei* is famous for the elaborate formality of its waiters (I, Kohlmarkt 14). But be warned: in season it's always packed with tourists.

◁ **KURKONDITOREI OBERLAA**
Opinion is divided: is the Oberlaa (I, Neuer Markt 16) or the Demel the best café in Vienna?

HOW TO ORDER COFFEE

◁ CAFE CENTRAL

At the turn of the century, this was the haunt of the Viennese literati; a lot has changed since then, including the prices. However, it still has one famous regular: the writer Peter Altenberg, who died in 1919 and is represented by a papier mâché model (I, Herrengasse 14).

△ DAZZLING CREATIONS

Apple strudel, *Sachertorte*, mini-pralines, "bishop's bread", cream cakes... Everything on display is of exceptional quality at the Demel, which used to be the official supplier to the Imperial court. This fabulous café is still a place of pilgrimage for foodies.

◁ CAFE HAWELKA

The owner of this former artists' café, Mr Hawelka, has been serving customers himself for decades. Today, its wonderful (though smoky) atmosphere makes it especially popular with students and tourists (I, Dorotheergasse 6).

FOOD AND FRESH AIR ▷

Here is a typical summer scene outside St Stephen's Cathedral. Each year, the café waiters put tables and chairs on the pavement or on pedestrianised streets. When consumed outdoors, the coffee and *Torte* seem to taste better than ever.

Since the first Viennese cafés opened in the late 17th century, coffee-drinking has practically become a religion. You don't just go into a café to slurp down a quick cup of coffee and scoff a slice of cake. You go there to gossip, exchange *bons mots*, read the paper, play chess, come up with brilliant ideas, show what a cultured person you are, and not least to refuel before returning to the fray. Therefore, although the coffee may seem somewhat expensive, you are also paying for the privilege of sitting in pleasant surroundings and enjoying the unique and unhurried atmosphere.

Ordering a coffee is a rather more complicated process than you might expect. It is important to get it right to maintain your credibility in the eyes of the waiter! Rather than asking for a *Kaffee* (Austrians stress the first syllable), try getting your mouth around a *kleiner* or *grosser Brauner* (small or large white coffee), a *Kapuziner* (coffee with cream, sprinkled with cocoa or chocolate), an *Einspänner* (black coffee with whipped cream, served in a glass), or one of any number of other varieties. Any good café will automatically serve you with a glass of water as well, and you can ask for this to be refilled for free as many times as you like.

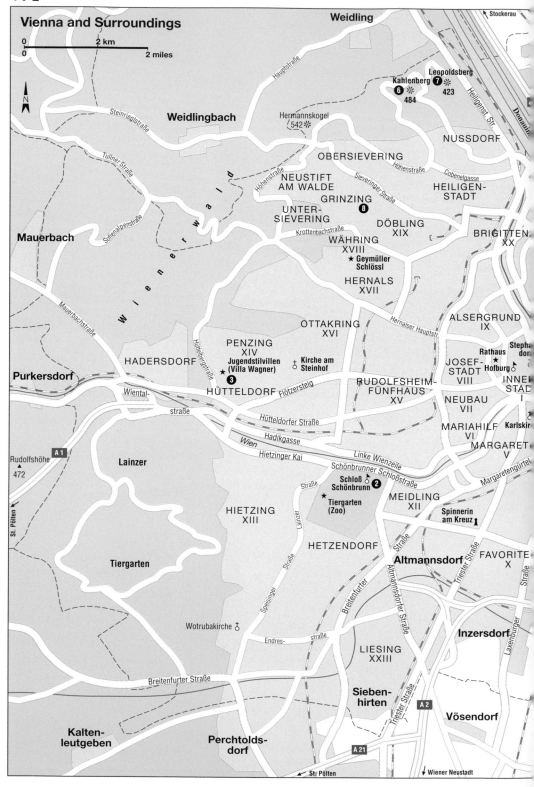

Vienna and Surroundings

Weidling

0 — 2 km
0 — 2 miles

N

Stockerau

Leopoldsberg
Kahlenberg **7** ☀
6 ☀ 423
484

Heiligenst. Str.

Donau...

Hauptstraße

Steinriegistraße

Weidlingbach

Hermannskogel
542 ☀

NUSSDORF

OBERSIEVERING

Höhenstraße

Cobenelgasse

**NEUSTIFT
AM WALDE**

Höhenstraße

Sieveringer Straße

HEILIGEN-
STADT

Mauerbach

W i e n e r w a l d

Schenalpenstraße

Tullner Straße

UNTER-
SIEVERING

GRINZING
8

Krottenbachstraße

DÖBLING
XIX

BRIGITTEN-
XX

WÄHRING
XVIII

★ Geymüller
Schlössl

HERNALS
XVII

ALSERGRUND
IX

Mauerbachstraße

OTTAKRING
XVI

Hernalser Hauptstr.

Rathaus
★ Stepha...
dor...

Purkersdorf

Hüttelbergstraße

PENZING
XIV
Jugendstilvillen
(Villa Wagner)
3

✝ Kirche am
Steinhof

RUDOLFSHEIM-
FÜNFHAUS
XV

JOSEF-
STADT
VIII

★
Hofburg ♂

INNE...
STAD...

HADERSDORF

HÜTTELDORF

Flötzersteig

NEUBAU
VII

Wiental-

Wien

Hütteldorfer Straße

MARIAHIL...
VI

Karlskir...

straße

Hadikgasse

Hietzinger Kai

Linke Wienzeile

MARGARET...
V

A 1

Rudolfshöhe
▲
472

Lainzer

Schönbrunner Schloßstraße

Schloß ♂
Schönbrunn **2**

MEIDLING
XII

Margaretengürtel

St. Pölten

Straße

★ Tiergarten
(Zoo)

Spinnerin
am Kreuz **1**

FAVORITE
X

**HIETZING
XIII**

Lainzer

Straße

HETZENDORF

Altmannsdorf

Straße

Altmannsdorfer Straße

Triester Straße

Tiergarten

Speisinger

Straße

Breitenfurter

Inzersdorf

Wotrubakirche ♂

Endres-

straße

LIESING
XXIII

Laxenburger

Straße

**Kalten-
leutgeben**

**Perchtolds-
dorf**

Breitenfurter Straße

**Sieben-
hirten**

Triester Straße

A 2

Vösendorf

A 21

← St. Pölten

↓ Wiener Neustadt

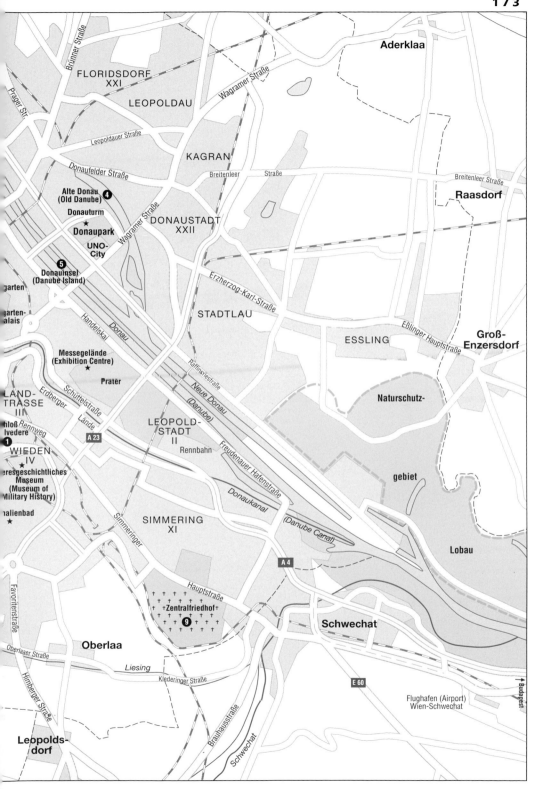

Aderklaa

FLORIDSDORF
XXI

LEOPOLDAU

Brünner Straße

Prager Str.

Wagramer Straße

KAGRAN

Leopoldauer Straße

Donaufelder Straße

Breitenleer   Straße

Breitenleer Straße

Raasdorf

Alte Donau
(Old Danube) **4**

Donauturm

★ Donaupark

UNO-
City

5
Donauinsel
(Danube Island)

Wagramer Straße

DONAUSTADT
XXII

Erzherzog-Karl-Straße

garten

garten-
alais

Handelskai

Donau

STADTLAU

ESSLING

Eßlinger Hauptstraße

Groß-
Enzersdorf

Messegelände
(Exhibition Centre)
★ Prater

Raffineriestraße

Neue Donau
(Danube)

Naturschutz-

LAND-
TRASSE
III

Erdberger

Schüttelstraße

Lände

A 23

hloß
lvedere

Rennweg

1

WIEDEN
IV
★

eresgeschichtliches
Museum
(Museum of
Military History)

nalienbad
★

LEOPOLD-
STADT
II

Rennbahn

Freudenauer Hafenstraße

gebiet

Donaukanal
(Danube Canal)

Lobau

Simmeringer

SIMMERING
XI

A 4

Favoritenstraße

Hauptstraße

† † † † †
† † † † †
† †Zentralfriedhof†
† † † † † †
† **9** † †
† † † † †

Schwechat

Oberlaa

Oberlaaer Straße

Liesing

Klederinger Straße

E 60

Himberger Straße

Leopolds-
dorf

Brauhausstraße

Schwechat

Flughafen (Airport)
Wien-Schwechat

Budapest

DISTRICTS AND SUBURBS

Vienna's suburban development is a tale of growth, contraction and class divisions. Life outside the old walls is recorded in grand palaces as well as the homes of artisans and labourers

Map, page 172

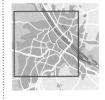

One of the many paradoxes that add to rather than diminish the charm of the Austrian capital is that Vienna consists of 23 districts. The "town" district (Stadt) is the inner city area, the 1st district, but you will have difficulty finding anyone who refers to it as that.

The Stadt is the old part of town, once ringed by fortifications and today surrounded by the ring road ("Ringstrasse"), and thus in a way still something of an enclave. The remaining districts surround the centre in concentric circles. Vienna has grown from the centre outwards – the higher the number of a district, the later the date of its integration into Greater Vienna. But expansion was not always at a moderate pace. Once it dawned that Vienna had exceeded a reasonable size, there occurred something quite remarkable and previously unheard-of. This city of millions shrank, de-corporated some districts and reduced itself to a smaller, more easily administrated area.

Vienna is still a great city, but it is not particularly large. It has no cancerous excretions eating away at the surrounding countryside. Vienna has kept itself to itself, and is a city on a human scale. Over the past 75 years, Vienna has been the first city of over a million people whose population has gone down – it has decreased by a good 30 per cent. Outside the walls of the city there has always been a wide belt of settlements, some of them older than Vienna itself.

These agricultural and wine-growing settlements were often fortified with earthworks and ditches. They formed the hinterland of Vienna, and their peaceful, natural growth over the centuries was only twice rudely interrupted, both times by the Turks (in 1529 and 1683) laying siege to Vienna. In order to clear the surroundings so that they would have an uninterrupted view of the attackers, the defenders of the city ruthlessly burnt down every farmhouse and vineyard outside the town's fortifications. Thus, in the suburbs, there are few buildings over 300 years old.

After the Turks were finally beaten in 1683 and Austria was fast becoming one of Europe's super-powers, construction fever broke out. The surrounding villages and the suburbs were rebuilt. The aristocracy built summer palaces just outside the town, quite a few of which have been preserved. The most beautiful of these is without doubt the palace "Belvedere" (Schloss Belvedere), the former residence of Prince Eugene of Savoy.

With the economy booming, tradesmen and artisans began to settle in the suburbs. From 1704, these lay inside a wall. Everything beyond the fortifications was considered to be outside Vienna. This outer "Linienwall" served as a kind of customs barrier, and the roads leading to and from Vienna were guarded by customs officials. For example, a tax was levied on all foodstuffs

PRECEDING PAGES: Schöbrunn Palace in winter. **LEFT:** plant-holding sign in Nussdorf. **BELOW:** a Biedermeier washer-woman

to be taken into Vienna and this had to be paid at the checkpoints. This so-called consumption tax law was enforced until the end of the 19th century.

In compliance with the traditions of their respective guilds, the tradesmen established themselves in certain areas – the 7th district, for example, was once the domain of silk-spinners. In those days, people referred to it as the "Diamond Mine", an indication of the incredible wealth amassed by the silk-spinners who enjoyed a monopoly over the European market for decades.

As everywhere else, the Jewish people had their own quarter. It lay on the other side of what is now the Danube Canal in Leopoldstadt (District 2). They were forced to settle there in the 17th century, only to be driven out 50 years later. In the late 19th century, Leopoldstadt became home to poor Jewish immigrants from the Eastern provinces. Over 50,000 Jews lived here until 1938.

So by the middle of the 19th century Vienna sat tightly corseted by its walls, not having grown since the Middle Ages. This inner core was ringed by the suburbs, which were expanding and thus growing ever closer together. Outside the wall that held the suburbs together lay the loose ring of small towns and villages where the factories and mass housing were being built.

This large but compact economic unit had no central government. It was made up of 35 independent administrative bodies, a situation as anachronistic as the two fortifications in the age of industrialisation. In 1850, the suburbs sandwiched between Vienna's walls and the Linienwall were incorporated into Vienna.

The walls come tumbling down

Over the next century another burst of development hit Vienna. The bastions were demolished in 1857, signalling the start of the Ringstrasse Era, the splendid

BELOW: Vienna before the demolition of the city fortifications

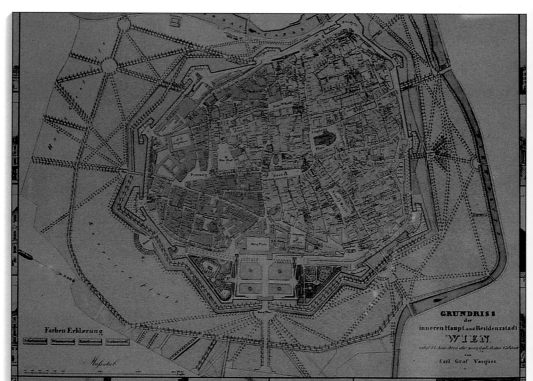

construction of the ring road. The outer suburbs also benefited from this building boom. The Danube was regulated, the canal built, and two mountain springs provided Vienna with the purest drinking water of all major cities in the world.

The next boost for developers came at the turn of the century. In 1890, in another expansionist move, the suburbs outside the Linienwall were incorporated (Districts 10–19). In 1910, the town reached across the Danube and Florisdorf became the 21st district.

During the term of Mayor Lueger (1897–1910), Vienna became a cosmopolitan city. It was primarily the inner city area, the Stadt, which had been beautified during the Ringstrasse Era. During the Lueger Era it was the turn of the outer districts. Vienna had over two million inhabitants at the turn of the century and was one of the six largest cities in the world. The "General Construction Plan" of Lueger's administration connected the inner city with its districts and suburbs. It was a large-scale, forward-looking and successful concept. Tramways were built, and the River Wien (a tributary of the Danube) and the Canal were straightened. A comprehensive land-use policy was evolved. Mayor Lueger also saw to it that the four million inhabitants were able to enjoy the benefits of proper gas, electricity and water supplies.

The last monarch having abdicated, the Social Democrats took over. Today, as 50 years ago, the monuments to "Red Vienna" are undoubtedly the imposing public buildings in the outer districts. Although Lueger's revolutionary social achievements are admirable, he had, nevertheless, ignored the housing sector. In this matter the Social Democrats deserve all the praise for their pioneering work.

After the enforced union with Germany in 1938, the *Anschluss*, yet more suburbs were incorporated into Greater Vienna. At the peak of incorporation, the

Map, page 172

Karl Lueger, mayor of Vienna at the turn of the 20th century, presided over rapid modernisation of municipal services.

BELOW: the Belvedere today

city had no fewer than 26 districts. Some of these were partly de-corporated after World War II.

Schloss Belvedere

In the past few decades, Vienna's population has steadily shrunk. At present, it stands at 1.6 million. This, however, has not stopped the town expanding – higher standards of living demand more space.

In 1693, when he was still a young Field Marshal in the army, Prince Eugene of Savoy acquired a building site outside the city gates where he planned to have his summer residence. Twenty years later, at the height of his career as general and statesman, he started building. Johann Lukas von Hildebrandt designed one of the most magnificent palaces not only in Austria but in the world. Schloss Belvedere ❶ was a masterpiece of the Baroque style. Strictly speaking, the name Belvedere (beautiful view) originally only applied to that part of the building used for official functions – the **Oberes (upper) Belvedere**, built in 1721–2. The name is justified – here, on top of the hill, you get the best and most beautiful view of Vienna and of the Vienna Woods (Wienerwald) in the distance.

The main building of the palace, the **Unteres (lower) Belvedere**, was built in 1714–16; it served as the prince's residence and also housed his magnificent

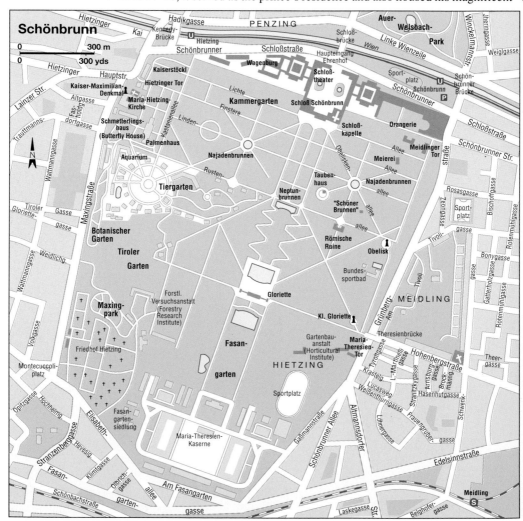

art collection. The two main buildings of the palace are connected by the park with its ornamental fountains, statues and terraces. Unfortunately only parts of its original splendour remain. The Belvedere has been called a "paraphrase in stone" of the congenial, almost Mediterranean landscape around Vienna.

Above all, the Belvedere complex is a homage to the prince who in his day was glorified as Hercules and Apollo in one – the man of action and the god of the arts. After Prince Eugene's death, the Emperor bought Schloss Belvedere. Before World War I, it was the home of the heir to the throne, Franz Ferdinand. Today, it is the home of several museums: the **Austrian Gallery** (Österreichische Galerie), Oberes Belvedere, the **Barockmuseum** (Unteres Belvedere), and the **Museum of Austrian Medieval Art** (Museum mittelalterlicher Österreichischer Kunst) in the Orangery. (All Belvedere museums open Tues–Sat 10am–5pm.)

Map, page 172

The Belvedere contains bronze and marble sculptures by Georg Raphael Donner.

Schloss Schönbrunn

The palace of Schönbrunn (beautiful fountain) ❷ (open daily: apartments 8.30am–4.30pm, in summer until 5pm) exceeds even the Hofburg as an embodiment of the power and wealth of the monarchy, and it is no accident that the imperial summer residence was designed to resemble Versailles. In Vienna, Schloss Schönbrunn is closely connected with the reign of the "old" Emperor Franz Joseph and, of course, with that of the Empress Maria Theresa, who first made it a summer residence, although the palace itself is much older than that.

Maria Theresa (1740–80), the daughter of Karl VI, was famous throughout Europe not only because of the Pragmatic Sanction, which permitted her to inherit the throne, but also because of the wars she waged against Frederick II of Prussia to defend her realm. Her domestic reforms only added to her renown.

BELOW: Napoleon at the gates of Schönbrunn

Schönbrunn Zoo, the oldest in Europe, contains Baroque animal houses. Besides the main zoo there is a safari park and nature reserve.

At the heart of the latter lay a series of administrative, legal system, policing, economic, financial and monetary changes that helped turn Austria into an absolute monarchy with a centralised government. These in turn were crucial in determining Vienna's position within the empire. Among Maria Theresa's advisors were Kaunitz, Haugwitz and Sonnenfels. Her consort, Emperor Franz I (1745–65) supported the expansion of the economy by founding and encouraging manufacturing industries, as well as encouraging the arts and sciences by summoning to court French artists and scholars to whom he entrusted the task of enlarging the royal collections.

In the 16th century the Habsburgs had built a hunting lodge near a "beautiful spring" some distance from the city gates. It was destroyed during the Turkish siege of 1683. Emperor Leopold I decided he wanted an official residence built here, so in 1696 he commissioned Johan Bernhard Fischer von Erlach to design a new palace. The resulting plans drawn up by the architect would have made Versailles look insignificant – if they had been realised. The main building was to have been built high on the hill where today only the *Gloriette* remains.

Construction of Schönbrunn began in 1700 after Fischer's second, more modest draft had been approved. Under the later influence of Maria Theresa, this finally became, more or less, what you see today. It is still an impressive building, with its wide ceremonial courtyard and two massive staircases, one on each side of the façade. The surrounding gardens were magnificently landscaped in the formal French style with geometrically arranged flower beds, hedges trimmed into shapes and perfectly straight lines of trees.

BELOW: in the park at Schönbrunn

Empress Maria Theresa commissioned Nikolaus Pacassi to redesign and enlarge the castle in order to transform it into a summer residence. His most important and splendid contribution is the well-preserved and magnificent small Galleries in the central wing.

By abandoning the highly stylised symmetry typical of the High Baroque, Pacassi was able to give the palace a remarkable dynamism. The harmony between room layout and furnishings makes Schönbrunn one of the finest examples of Austrian Rococo architecture. Pacassi's successor, Johann Ferdinand von Hohenberg, added the royal theatre, which has a typical late Rococo interior. His design of the palace gardens made him famous, however, as the leading architect of the late Baroque combined with neo-classical style. Schönbrunn's well preserved and magnificent interior places it amongst the finest and most elaborate examples of the era.

High above the castle stand the ornamental and airy colonnades of the **Gloriette** (open daily 9am–5pm; park daily 6am–sunset), built in 1765. Another interesting part of the castle is the **Wagenburg** (open daily 10am–4pm, closed on Mon Nov–Mar), which houses a collection of state coaches.

How the Viennese live

The Viennese are notorious for their lack of desire to move house once they have settled down. It is, nevertheless, quite astonishing to discover that the lifestyle of many modern Viennese still bears a close resemblance to that of their ancestors.

Until 1918, the districts of Vienna were strictly divided into social classes: There were the "aristocratic districts", the "bourgeois" and the "working-class districts". Modern building policies have done little to change this distribution.

Artisans and merchants, and to some extent civil servants, used to live in the former suburbs between the old city fortifications and the Linienwall, in what are now Districts 3–9. Most buildings in these districts were constructed at the turn of the last century, although there are a few (mainly in Districts 7 and 8) which date back to the early 19th century, the so-called "Biedermeier" era. These houses are very typical of their time; they are small and no more than two storeys high, the living area limited to what was thought to be reasonable and necessary, and with minimal ornamentation. Most of them originally had gardens. Some of these houses have become museums – like the house in which Haydn died, or the houses in which Schubert was born and passed away.

An example of the grander lifestyle of the upper middle class is the Geymüller-Schlössel (*Schlössel* means "little palace") in District 18.

All the suburbs outside the Linienwall were, and still are, the domain of the working classes, with the exception of the "aristocratic districts" in Hietzing, Währing and Döbling, and the vineyard communities at the foot of the Wienerwald. It was here too, at the edge of town, that the factories were built when Vienna became industrialised.

Thus, the thousands who came to work in the factories not only lived close to their work places, but also avoided having to pay consumption tax levied on foodstuffs being taken into the town. In many cases this meant that the cost of living for a working-class family was reduced by as much as one third. The housing conditions, however, were deplorable.

Map, page 172

Map, page 172

TIP

Schönbrunn is packed with visitors during the summer months – but to really appreciate the beauties of the grounds undisturbed, come here as early as possible. The gates to the park open at 6am!

BELOW: Schönbrunn Palace from the Gloriette

"Beautiful" buildings were the privilege of the inner city area. Out in the suburbs, houses only had to serve the purpose of providing people with a roof over their heads – thereby packing as many as possible into one building. It was almost the norm for a family of ten to be living in a one-room flat. The flats were damp, dark and overlooked dreary streets with no trees. Parks simply did not exist. However, Vienna never developed the kind of appalling slums that were so characteristic, for example, of Victorian England.

Slowly but gradually over the past decades, these tenement blocks have been replaced by more pleasant housing. Some of them still remain, however, and even today, the grey and depressing façades are still a prominent feature of these working-class districts.

Aristocratic districts

The landed and monied gentry, as well as the upper classes with real estate, had settled in the elegant flats in the inner city district, in the "diplomatic districts" (Districts 3 and 4), and in the suburban villas in Hietzing and Währinger and Döblinger Cottage – and, once again, this state of affairs is little changed. Houses in these areas fetch the highest prices and the highest rents, and are the most sought after in Vienna.

In the district of Penzing there are two monumental **Art Nouveau villas** (Jugendstilvillen) ❸ which are definitely worth a visit. Built by Otto Wagner between 1886 and 1888 and 1912–13 respectively, they are located at Hüttelbergstrasse 26 and 28. The older of the two today houses the private museum of the painter Ernst Fuchs, and if you enjoyed the work of the Viennese Secession architects, take one of the weekly guided tours of the church at the Steinhof

There was no tap water in suburban working-class flats; water supplies were fetched at the Bassena, the tap installed on each floor, which also served as a meeting point for the women.

BELOW: public housing: the Karl-Marx-Hof

(14 Baumgärtner Höhe 1; open Sat for tours at 3pm). This symbolic counterpart to the ornate Baroque style of St Charles' Church is the high point of Otto Wagner's creative output.

Some of the districts have lost a little of their appeal, others have only recently acquired the status of being "aristocratic". **Grinzing** is one of them. The traditional home of the *Heuriger* inns has also become an exclusive residential address.

Vienna and the Danube

It is not all that easy to assess whether or not Vienna actually lies on the Danube. Even if it does so now, it certainly was not so until well into the 19th century. In those days, the Danube and its many tributaries wound its way through meadows and farmland, and only one tributary actually flowed directly past the town.

In 1875, great efforts were undertaken to stop the devastation caused by heavy and frequent flooding. The bed of the Danube was straightened, the tributary flowing past Vienna made into a canal. But this meant that the navigable stream was now many miles from the town. On the left bank of the Danube a broad space was left free of buildings. This formed a flood plain that could be deliberately inundated when the river was high, removing the danger of flooding from Vienna itself.

One part of the Danube, which was cut off when its bed was straightened, became known as the **Old Danube** (Alte Donau) ❹. It still remains, fed by underground springs, and is now a haven for water sports lovers.

Between the two world wars, the Viennese discovered another beauty spot with natural broad meadows along this part of the Old Danube, the **Lobau**, and

Map, page 172

Vienna's first open-air swimming pool, the Gänsehäufel, was built along the Alte Donau in 1907. It can accommodate as many as 33,000 people.

BELOW LEFT: Art Nouveau interior: a church in Steinhof.
BELOW: the first Wagner villa

they made it into an early nudist colony. In 1981, another river bed was cut into the flood plain, running parallel to the main river. It was intended to carry excess water. This development formed the **Danube island** (Donauinsel) ❺, which is about 21 km (13 miles) long and 200 metres (220 yards) wide.

The island, which can be reached in less than 10 minutes by underground from the centre of Vienna, has become another favourite recreation area. There is a 40-km (25-mile) long beach, also mooring places and marinas, training centres for diving and surfing and many other water sports facilities.

Other cities envy Vienna with its leisure parks along the river. When thousands of city dwellers, starved of fresh air and sunshine, swarm out of the inner city and take over this El Dorado of leisure seekers, then you really could say that Vienna lies on the Danube.

The Danube island is covered by a network of cycling tracks, and in winter the Viennese flock there to practise cross-country skiing.

Tales from the Wienerwald

Ever since Strauss and his waltzes, Vienna and the Vienna Woods have been thought of as one entity. The **Vienna Woods** (Wienerwald) are the very last foothills of the Alps, which reach the borders of the city. They make a perfect setting for the beauty of Vienna. The city lies in the curve of the hills like a pearl in an oyster, and the trees make a picturesque backdrop and a boundary to the sea of houses.

It is mainly due to the idealism and stubbornness of the first of Vienna's "greens", the former member of parliament, Josef Schöffel, that this green belt survived. For years he fought a lonely but successful battle to prevent the clearing of the woodland intended by a consortium of profit-seeking stock-brokers. When at last he succeeded in drawing public attention to his campaign in 1873,

BELOW: view of the Kahlenberg hill

the permission (already granted) to cut down the trees was withdrawn. Schöffel was later elected mayor of Mödling. Thirty years later, during Mayor Lueger's term of office, steps were taken to preserve this nature resort and to extend it into a belt of woods and meadows around the city.

At one point, the Wienerwald almost touches the banks of the Danube. This beautiful spot – with its vineyards, lush meadows and tranquil beech groves – is much favoured by the Viennese when they want to leave behind the hustle and bustle of the town behind. Standing on top of the **Kahlenberg** hill ❻, you get a breathtaking view of Vienna. From here, you can walk or drive to the other favourite hill of the Viennese, **Leopoldsberg** ❼, via the **Höhenstrasse** that runs between Hütteldorf and Klosterneuburg.

Map, page 172

The Church of St Leopold

The Leopoldsberg marks the end of the Vienna Woods where they reach out towards the banks of the Danube in the east. As long ago as the first millennium AD this was the site of a Celtic acropolis, which was later replaced by a medieval fortress. In 1529, before the first Turkish siege, the fortress was blown up along with the first church on the site, a chapel dedicated to St George, in order to prevent its being captured by the approaching Turkish army. Construction of the present chapel, with its rich historic associations, did not begin until 1679, after the city had survived the plague. The resulting domed church was dedicated to St Leopold. Construction was interrupted in 1683 because of the second Turkish invasion.

Marco d'Aviano, the Papal Legate and a Capuchin priest, read a now-famous mass in the half-finished building. His incendiary sermon kindled in the

BELOW: Döbling district view, with Vienna in the distance

defensive troops, despite their inferior numbers, the courage and determination to go into the attack in an apparently hopeless battle. Although they believed that their city had already been lost, the Christian army charged down the hill and snatched from the Turkish invaders the "Golden Apple", as the Osman forces called the city of Vienna, referring to the golden dome of St Stephen's Cathedral. Had this crucial battle ended differently, then Baroque Europe, as we know it from our history books, would not have developed as it did.

In 1693 the church was finally completed and gave its name to the hill on which it stood. Until that year it was known as *Mons Calvus*, the "Bare Mountain" (Kahlenberg). Its name was then transferred to the neighbouring twin peak. And thus it was that the Battle of the Kahlenberg did not take place on the hill which now bears this name, but on the neighbouring Leopoldsberg.

Vienna and wine

One cannot be separated from the other: Vienna and wine is like Tom and Jerry or Laurel and Hardy. There are hundreds of Viennese songs which tell of this partnership. Every tourist wants to visit a *Heuriger* inn, and the well-oiled tourist machine ensures that they all get something to drink. The *Heuriger* goes back to a very old tradition. Vintners would announce the arrival of their new wines by hanging a wreath of pine twigs over the door of the inn.

From these modest beginnings a vast industry has arisen. All too often, the quiet enjoyment of a glass of new wine has turned into a noisy affair, where Viennese songs are bawled in an atmosphere of fake bonhomie.

Vienna was, until very recently, surrounded by extensive vineyards. The Church of St Charles and the "Belvedere", for example, were erected right in

Vineyards survive in Vienna's "green belt".

BELOW: entrance to a *Heuriger*

their midst. Gumpendorf (District 6), once famous for its wine, is today a densely built-up area, and it is only at the foothills of the Vienna Woods and on the other side of the Danube ("Bisamberg") that wine is still grown these days. The fact that wine is still being cultivated within the borders of Vienna is another achievement of Mayor Lueger, protector of Vienna's green belt.

Many of the former suburbs of Vienna – like Grinzing, Sievering, Neustift am Walde, Nussdorf and Heiligenstadt, as well as Stammersdorf on "the other side" – were and still are the domain of the vintners and have kept their rural taverns, even if they have long since lost their innocent village character.

Grinzing ❽, in particular, is famous for its *Heuriger* taverns. Not only countless songs, but also hundreds of films have portrayed the village as the heart of this essential element of Viennese life. Those on a short visit who are in search of this atmosphere will surely find it, albeit in a commercialised form. And yet, Grinzing's fame as the home of the *Heuriger* is relatively recent. Before the development of modern transport it lay too far from the city, and the Viennese would have been in no state to find their way back home after the consumption of the odd quarter (litre) or so. It was not until the electric tram line was extended to Grinzing at the turn of the century that the little village became accessible for wine-loving citizens of the capital.

Grinzing's history, however, stretches back over a thousand years. The names of the medieval families who lived there have been preserved. Only a few of them, however, survived the battles which were fought in the region surrounding Vienna. King Corvinus of Hungary as well as the armies of the Turkish Sultans Suleiman and Kara Mustapha pitched their tents on the strategically important slopes of the Vienna Woods. Not much remained of the village by the

Map, page 172

Vienna is still one of the largest vine-growing areas in Austria. Today, just as in the early 19th century, anyone looking out from the Kahlenberg will see the familiar view of a city bordered by vineyards.

BELOW: musical entertainment at a *Heuriger*

BELOW:
Sievering parish
church.
BELOW RIGHT: "the
biggest corkscrew
in the world"

River Nesselbach. Only Grinzing Parish Church, built in 1425 and renovated at regular intervals, survives to bear witness to this era. Even during the 18th and 19th centuries Grinzing was no more than a tranquil, sleepy village on the slopes of the Vienna Woods, eventually becoming a popular destination for excursions from the city. Mozart, Schubert and Beethoven all visited the place.

In the hearts of Viennese citizens everywhere, the atmosphere of this bygone age still lives on today. If you look you will find it too – if not in the bustle of Grinzing, then perhaps in one of the smaller, less famous wine-growing villages. Their atmosphere is still there for you to enjoy, a mixture of light-heartedness and melancholy echoing the mood of many a Viennese song.

Unfortunately, many of the genuine *Heuriger* inns – where you brought along your own picnic (bread, sausage and cheese) and sampled the new wines – are disappearing. In their place, restaurant owners have set up their own versions of *Heuriger*, providing hot food and offering other wines as well.

In recent years **Sievering**, too, has become a favourite *Heuriger* haunt. It is as old as Grinzing, and its medieval name "Suuveringen" can be found in records from 1150. Sievering's church dates from a time when the villagers wanted to save themselves the long and dangerous journey to hear mass in Heiligenstadt. In those days wolves still roamed throughout the region. Some remains of the Turkish siege can be seen in the house at Sieveringer Strasse 99. In Sievering you will even find a few *Heuriger* which are patronised by local residents.

Posthumous display

If, the morning after a lengthy visit to a *Heuriger*, you find yourself entertaining sober thoughts, you might want to seek out one of Vienna's renowned cemeter-

Grösster
Korkenzieher
der Welt!
in Grinzing

Weingut Reinprecht

ies, or "depositories of mourning", as André Heller called them. A *"schöne Leich"* (a beautiful funeral) is taken very seriously in Vienna. Many Viennese pay into special savings accounts in order to leave enough money behind for a grand funeral.

The main cemetery in Vienna, the Central Cemetery (**Zentralfriedhof**) ❾ (open daily 8am–5pm, in summer until 7pm) is an important item on the sightseeing programme of every Japanese tourist group. **St Mark's Cemetery** (St Marxer Friedhof), District 3, is also worth a visit, as its "Biedermeier" look has been very well preserved. The Jewish cemetery at the Währinger Gürtel is closed now, but still evokes shameful memories. The graves and the cemeteries in the "aristocratic districts" – for example in Hietzing, Plötzleinsdorf, Döbling or Grinzing – are beautifully situated.

Most Viennese, however, are buried in the Central Cemetery which was built in the southern suburbs in 1874, and later nicknamed "Europe's most lively graveyard". It is a vast place, covering an area of a good 200 hectares (500 acres), where almost 2.5 million Viennese lie buried (considerably more than the city's live inhabitants).

There are separate sections for the Protestants, Greek Orthodox Christians and Jews. The two Jewish sections occupy almost a third of the total area. There are also **state tombs** for the great sons and daughters of the city. (A detailed plan of the vast cemetery is available from the supervisor at Gate 2, main entrance.)

There are two quite remarkable buildings in the Central Cemetery: the church that was erected in memory of Dr Lueger (1911) and the crematorium (built by Clemens Holzmeister in 1923) on the site of the former Renaissance palace of Emperor Maximilian II.

Map, page 172

To find one of the last true Heuriger, avoid going on an organised Heuriger crawl but set out on your own and find an inn where no coaches are parked nearby. It will be well worth your while.

BELOW: avenue in the Central Cemetery

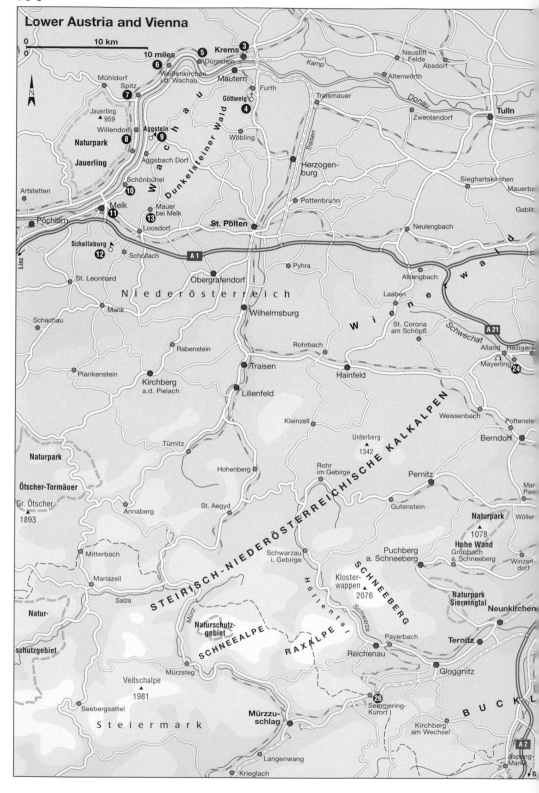

Lower Austria and Vienna

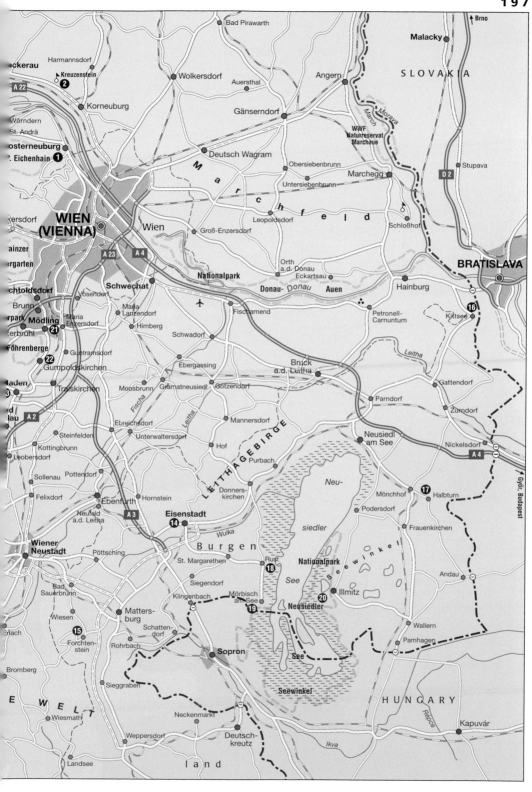

↑ Brno

Malacky

S L O V A K I A

Bad Pirawarth

ckerau

Harmannsdorf

Kreuzenstein ②

A 22

Wolkersdorf

Angern

Korneuburg

Auersthal

Wörndern

St. Andrä

Gänserndorf

March

Morava

osterneuburg

. Eichenhain ①

Deutsch Wagram

Obersiebenbrunn

WWF
Naturreservat
Marchaue

Stupava

D 2

Untersiebenbrunn

Marchegg

M a r c h f e l d

Leopoldsdorf

Schloßhof

BRATISLAVA

**WIEN
(VIENNA)**

Wien

Groß-Enzersdorf

ersdorf

ainzer

rgarten

Orth
a.d. Donau

Eckartsau

Schwechat

Nationalpark

Hainburg

htoldsdorf

Vösendorf

Donau- Donau Auen

Kittsee ⑯

Brunn

rpark

Maria
Lanzendorf

Fischamend

Petronell-
Carnuntum

Mödling ㉑

erbrühl

Maria
Enzersdorf

Himberg

Schwadorf

Leitha

Gattendorf

Föhrenberge

Guntramsdorf

Schwadorf

㉒

Gumpoldskirchen

Ebergassing

**Bruck
a.d. Leitha**

Parndorf

Zurndorf

aden

Traiskirchen

Moosbrunn

Gramatneusiedl

Götzendorf

3

Fischa

A 2

Ebreichsdorf

Mannersdorf

**Neusiedl
am See**

Nickelsdorf

Steinfelden

Leitha

A 4

d

au

Kottingbrunn

Unterwalterstorf

Hof

Neu-

⑰

Leobersdorf

Purbach

L E I T H A G E B I R G E

Mönchhof

Halbturn

Sollenau

Pottendorf

Donners-
kirchen

Podersdorf

Felixdorf

Ebenfurth

Hornstein

siedler

Frauenkirchen

Neufeld
a.d. Leitha

A 3

Eisenstadt

Andau

Györ, Budapest

**Wiener
Neustadt**

Pöttsching

⑭

Wulka

B u r g e n

St. Margarethen

Rust

Neu-

Nationalpark

siedler

Bad
Sauerbrunn

Siegendorf

⑱

See

Illmitz

Wiesen

Klingenbach

Mörbisch
am See

⑳

Wallern

Mattersburg

Schatten-
dorf

⑲

Neusiedler

Pamhagen

Forchten-
stein ⑮

Rohrbach

See

erlach

Sopron

Bromberg

Sieggraben

Seewinkel

H U N G A R Y

E W E L T

Wiesmath

Neckenmarkt

Répce

Kapuvár

Weppersdorf

**Deutsch-
kreutz**

Ikva

Landsee

l a n d

AROUND VIENNA

Imposing monasteries and castles are within easy reach of the capital in unspoilt Lower Austria. Insight recommends a tour along the Danube and to the wildlife-rich Neusiedler Lake

Map,
page 196

Vienna is not only a beautiful city, it is also beautifully located. There are not many European cities of comparable size which can combine surrounding landscape of such beauty with a wealth of art treasures. One favourite spot, the Vienna Woods, has already been mentioned. Others are the Danube valley and the "Burgenland" (land of castles) to the south-east of the city.

The Danube valley

Following the Danube upstream, you will presently see the towers and domes of **Klosterneuburg ❶**, the largest and most easterly of the many monasteries dotted along the Danube throughout Austria. Klosterneuburg, an Augustinian establishment, was founded by the margrave of Babenberg, the saintly Leopold III. In around 1100, Leopold had his residential palace built here which became known as the "new castle" (Neue Burg). Next to it he founded a monastery (Kloster) – hence the name "Klosterneuburg". Leopold was buried in the chapel within the monastery. The enamel Verdun altar (12th century) in the chapel is one of Austria's most precious works of art.

Klosterneuburg did not remain the capital of the kingdom for very long. In 1156, this title was transferred to Vienna – and stayed there.

During the Baroque era, in the 17th and 18th centuries, lavish designs were drawn up to rebuild the monastery. The initiator was Karl VI, Maria Theresa's father, who wanted to build a monumental burial place for the Austrian kings which was to be modelled on the Escorial Palace near Madrid (built by Philip II, 1563–86).

The building was started, yet never completed – like so many grandiose plans in Austria. However, even the remaining rump conveys an impression of the intended flamboyancy and Baroque grandeur of the place. The two impressive domes are decorated with the imperial crown and the "duke's hat", symbol of the Austrian dukes.

Saint Leopold III, the patron saint of Lower Austria, is still very much a part of Klosterneuburg life today. Every year in November, the Austrians remember their saint with lively celebrations. These reach a climax on the feast day of Saint Leopold, every November 15, when people flock to Klosterneuburg in their thousands to slide down the gigantic barrel (with a capacity of 56,000 litres) that stands on the site. This barrel is a very large reminder that the monastery is still one of the biggest wine producers in the country.

A little further upstream, on the opposite bank, stands the massive castle **Burg Kreuzenstein ❷**, built in the Historicist style during the 19th century. It was constructed from hundreds of bits and pieces that were taken from

PRECEDING PAGES:
Aggstein Castle ruins;
Klosterneuburg
monastery; the
monastery library
at Melk.
LEFT: vineyard
above old Stein.
BELOW: entrance to
the Klosterneuburg

other castles and monuments, and it still looks like a knight's castle out of a fairy tale – or one constructed by crazy history freaks, as some critics like to claim.

The Wachau

This is the name of the section of the Danube valley between Melk and Krems. It is said that these 35 km (22 miles) cover the most beautiful region of Austria. The Wachau is indeed one of the most romantic and almost magical river landscapes in the world.

Both man and nature had a hand in creating this beautiful spot. The gentle rolling hills that border the broad river shelter the valley from unfavourable winds without restricting the view. Man used the fertile soil *(Loess)* to his advantage by carving vine terraces and orchards out of the hillsides, and he adorned the area with a wealth of artistic and architectural treasures.

Many mythological, legendary and some historical events are connected with the Wachau and add to its romantic charm. Armies of crusaders must have passed this spot on their way down the Danube and into the Holy Land. Before them, the Burgundian knights who were the heroes of the medieval German epic, the *Nibelungenlied,* must also have passed through on their way to the kingdom of the Huns. **Pöchlarn** (which was once called Bechelaren), a few miles from Melk, is said to have been the residence of the margrave Rüdiger, one of the most noble figures to live on in Germany's heroic legends.

Krems ❸ (and its twin town **Stein,** which is now effectively part of Krems) has one of the best preserved old town centres in central Europe. Krems survived the drastic changes that came in the wake of the industrial revolution during the 19th century because it lay off the beaten track. But its role as an important trading

Wachau is perhaps at its most enchanting in spring when the slopes are covered with a sea of white blossom from the many apricot trees (Marillen).

BELOW: historic Krems

centre ceased with the coming of the railways, which led to a decline in the importance of the Danube as a transport route. The town's prosperity had always been closely linked with the river as an inland waterway, so it became too poor to be able to afford major building projects. Nowadays a restoration policy ensures that old buildings are preserved as far as possible.

The city walls, (with an impressive entrance gate, the "Wiener Tor", and the even more impressive tower – the "Pulverturm" – where gunpowder was once stored) are more or less still intact, enclosing houses from five different centuries. The dominant features of the town are its arcades and courtyards, gables, turrets and gates, ornamented façades and wrought-iron window balconies.

The most notable buildings include the 13th-century Gozzoburg, one of the oldest private residences in Austria, a Gothic church (Bürgerspitalkirche), as well as two other beautifully restored churches – the Dominican Church in central Krems and the Church of the Minorities (Minoritenkirche) in Stein. Both are used as exhibition halls today.

If you cross over the old bridge connecting Stein with Mautern and climb up the hill you come to an imposing Benedictine monastery. **Göttweig ❹**, founded in 1083, is one of the most splendid examples of Baroque monastery architecture in Austria, together with the monasteries of St Florian and Melk.

The complex was erected in 1719–24. Its frontage is more than 196 metres (650 feet) long, and the whole complex looks more like a palace than a monastery. This is not altogether surprising once you know that it was designed by Johann Lukas von Hildebrandt, the architect who created the palace of Belvedere in Vienna. His original and grandiose design, however, which allowed for the monasterial buildings to be spread across the entire hilltop, was never completed.

Map, page 196

BELOW: view of Göttweig monastery

The so-called "imperial staircase" ("Kaiserstiege") is one of the most striking staircases ever to be built in the Baroque style in Austria. Göttweig houses an important collection of copper engravings.

Pearl of Wachau

A few miles further upstream, on the Krems side of the Danube (the communities in the Wachau are almost exclusively situated on the northern banks of the river), lies the "pearl" of the Wachau, the village of **Dürnstein** ❺. There is no doubt that it really is the most beautiful and picturesque place in the entire region. On a rock jutting out into the Danube sits a chapel which once belonged to an Augustinian monastery. Together with Aggstein, it is certainly the most frequently photographed building in the Wachau. Along with the monastery at Melk, it is the prime example of perfect harmony between architecture and natural setting.

The former monastery's Baroque spire overlooks the Danube and can be seen from afar. When the façade of the building was restored, experts decided the spire should be painted blue because the original coat of paint had been blue. Some traditionalists would have much preferred the customary white coat for ancient buildings, or the yellow of the Schönbrunn palace.

Lionheart and Blondel

BELOW: Dürnstein.
BELOW RIGHT:
national costumes
in the Wachau

Dürnstein's hour of glory came about 800 years ago when the hero of Christendom, King Richard the Lionheart, was captured on Christmas Day, 1192, near Vienna. Richard was returning from the Third Crusade, and was held in the stronghold of Kuenringer-Veste as prisoner of Leopold V of Babenberg. Leopold wanted

to settle an old score with the king of England: two years before, at Acre in the Holy Land, Richard had apparently insulted Duke Leopold and his native country, Austria.

And now legend takes over. When the king did not return from his crusade, his loyal servant, Blondel, set forth to seek his master. He took his lute with him and played his familiar tunes in distant lands, wandering from castle to citadel in hope of finding the king of England. When he reached the dungeon of Dürnstein, his tunes were at last answered. Blondel speedily returned to England, raised the king's ransom and freed his master.

Only two parts of this touching story are true: Richard the Lionheart was a prisoner in Dürnstein for three months, and the ransom money was paid. The entire operation was nothing less than a blatant kidnapping: Richard owned vast domains in the south of France that posed a threat to the French crown, which was allied to the German emperor, who in turn was an ally of the Babenberg duke of Austria. Richard was, however, a great patron of the *Minnesingers* (troubadours).

Map, page 196

From Dürnstein to Melk

Fortified churches – in **Weissenkirchen** ❻ and **St Michael** near Wösendorf – are reminders that the people in the Wachau had to be constantly alert to enemy invasions. The Turks and the Swedes were amongst the hostile armies who pitched their tents here during their military campaigns. The monumental Gothic church in Weissenkirchen consists of three churches built into one. The "Wachau-Museum", housed in the Teisenhofer Hof, a splendid Renaissance building with an arcaded courtyard and pergolas, is well worth a visit. St Michael, first documented in the 10th century, is the oldest parish in this region.

ABOVE: Wösendorf village.

BELOW: Dürnstein and the Danube from the air

The Stone Age figurine known as the "Venus of Willendorf" was found in the village in 1906.

BELOW: typical alley in the Wachau

A little further upstream we find **Spitz** ❼, which throughout the centuries has always been an important market town. Have a look at the beautiful late Gothic church with its wonderful stucco figures in the choir loft and the unusual choir stalls in the nave.

Willendorf ❽, the next stop, is the home of the oldest Austrian lady, the famous "Venus of Willendorf". The statue dates from Palaeolithic times (approximately 22,000 BC). It is only about 10 cm (4 inches) high and is thought to have been a symbol of fertility. It can be seen in the Natural History Museum in Vienna.

On the other side of the Danube towers **Aggstein Castle** ❾ which was once the safest stronghold along the Danube. The ruins are still impressive, defiant and awe-inspiring. More stories and legends surround this castle than any other, but hardly any of them are based on fact. Aggstein Castle was the main stronghold of the Kuenring clan, one of the most powerful families in the Danube region in the Middle Ages. They are thought to have been thieves, although this has never been proven.

Terror in the Forest

Later, Aggstein Castle was part of the domains of a powerful knight known as Georg Schreck im Wald (the "Terror in the Forest"). Schreck im Wald's enemies grotesquely exaggerated his efforts to make his subjects abide by the rules of law and order. The most famous of the many stories about him relates how he locked the Danube with a chain and demanded a toll from everyone wanting to cross over – something he was legally entitled to do. Another tale, almost certainly apocryphal, tells of the "rose garden". This was a ridge of rocks jutting out over the rapid stream, where prisoners were put and given the choice of either dying by starvation or jumping to their deaths.

On the south side of the Danube is another castle of quite a different kind, **Schloss Schönbühel** ❿. It stands on a rocky terrace on the south side of the Danube and is an impressive rectangular building with a tower reaching into the sky. Behind it, clinging to a cliff, stands a monastery church.

The highlight of a trip through the Wachau must be the monastery in Melk (**Stift Melk**)⓫, one of Jacob Prandtauer's masterpieces and one of the loveliest of all Baroque buildings (1702–39). It is over 30 metres (100 ft) long and towers high above the Danube on a protruding rock. The main west front is turned towards the river like the bow of a ship, whilst the south front rises with serene harmony above the little village, with the massive dome and towers of the monastery church dominating the scene. The façade of the church itself is constructed on a type of balcony overhanging the water, and is flanked by the famous library and the splendid marble hall. The imperial rooms are now a museum. The lawn in front of the garden pavilion serves as an open-air theatre during the summer months.

Melk was a Roman outpost along the *Limes*, the boundary of the empire, and later became the residence of the Dukes of Babenberg who built the Benedictine monastery in 1089.

Schloss Schallaburg ⑫ is one of the most remarkable Renaissance buildings in Austria. Some parts of the castle date back to the Middle Ages (the keep and the fortification walls, for example). The arcaded courtyard is littered with terracotta objects dating from 1573: busts, masks, escutcheons and other items. The buildings have lovingly been restored in the past few years and today provide a splendid setting for art exhibitions.

The tiny village of **Mauer ⑬**, near Melk, possesses one of the most remarkable carved altars (1515) in Austria. The little Gothic pilgrimage church was unfortunately never finished, but the altarpiece, which dates from 1515, foreshadows the Renaissance.

The idyllic region of the Wachau lies to the north-west of Vienna. It is in marked contrast to the flat, steppe-like countryside of the Burgenland found to the south-east, which presages the stretching plains of Hungary.

The Burgenland

The town of **Eisenstadt ⑭** was formed by the merging of three settlements which until 1938 had been autonomous communities. All three have retained their individuality and are still separated by invisible borders. The so-called "free town" has kept a lot of its Baroque and rural charm. Oberberg grew around the churches and the monastery which had been built by the Esterházys. Unterberg became the official district of the Jews in 1671. The first Jews had arrived in this area in the 13th century.

The history of Eisenstadt, like the history of the whole of the Burgenland, is inextricably interwoven with the history of the princes and dukes of Esterházy. Their main residence, **Schloss Esterházy**, still dominates the centre of Eisenstadt

Map, page 196

The park surrounding Schloss Esterházy is so vast – approximately 50 hectares (120 acres) – that it would easily accommodate a football stadium.

BELOW: Melk monastery from the river

– a town, by the way, that looks much more like a village. Originally a rather clumsy looking but massive square fortress constructed around a central courtyard, it was rebuilt in 1663 as a Baroque castle with a tranquil façade and squat corner towers. Today, it houses the offices of the federal government of the Burgenland. There is a splendid English garden, in which the first Austrian steam engine was put on display in 1803.

The (unfinished) building complex of the "Mount Calvary" and the "Mountain Church" in the district of Oberberg are two truly remarkable and original constructions. The **Mount Calvary** (Kalvarienberg) is a notable architectural achievement. This artificial mountain was built around 1700 and pays homage to Christ's sufferings along the Way of the Cross. The path, partly built through the mountain, is lined with pictoral representations of the stages of Christ's progress to Calvary. It leads past niches, fantastic grottos and chapels and is a marvellous example of romantically idealised popular Christianity. A similar, if smaller, complex can be found at the **Church of Our Lady** (Frauenkirche) in Frauenkirchen, Seewinkel.

ABOVE: the composer Haydn, who hails from Burgenland.

BELOW: the church in Eisenstadt

Joseph Hadyn and Eisenstadt

The **Mountain Church** (Bergkirche), a circular building which was later surrounded by a square outer wall, is the last resting-place of the composer Joseph Haydn, and is usually referred to as "**Haydn's Church**". The composer and the town are almost inseparable. Haydn was born in 1732 in Rohrau in Lower Austria, on the edge of the Burgenland. For almost 30 years, from 1761 to 1790, he conducted the orchestra at the court of Prince Nikolaus Esterházy, performing both in Eisenstadt and the prince's castle, Esterháza, in what is now Hungary. The house

he lived in during those years is a small museum today. The street was renamed in his honour and is now called Haydngasse. The summer-house, where he preferred to work, has also been preserved.

The beautiful Baroque **Wertheimer House** in Unterberg, the former Jewish district, once housed the synagogue and is now a museum. A few steps away is the former home of the Austrian merchant and amateur folklorist Sandor Wolf. Its modern extension houses the Burgenland's regional museum.

The Seven Communities

Burgenland was the domain of Jewish people until the persecution of the Jews accelerated in 1938. For centuries the expression *shewa kehillot*, or the "Seven Communities", was familiar to every Jew living outside Israel.

According to tradition, the first Jewish settlements in this most western part of the kingdom of Hungary date back to the 13th century. Jewish immigrants were first documented just before 1500, after they had been driven out of Styria and Carinthia in 1496. For centuries in this region that lay just outside the Austrian border, the Jews were granted great religious and economic tolerance. Their individual feudal overlords granted them charters of rights.

It was under the far-sighted sovereignty of the Esterházys, who owned (and still own) most of the northern part of Burgenland, that the Seven Communities were founded: Eisenstadt, Mattersdorf (later renamed Mattersburg), Kobersdorf, Lackenbach, Deutschkreuz (Zelem in Hebrew), Frauenkirchen and Kittsee. Further to the south, where the Hungarian princes of Batthyány reigned, three more Jewish communities were established, in Güsing, Rechnitz and Stadtschlaining.

Map,
page 196

TIP

Eisenstadt vintner Erwin Tinhof is highly recommended by specialists in the wine trade. His astonishingly good wines have apparently made it to the wine cellars of the European Parliament in Brussels. Visits by arrangement. Gartengasse 8, Eisenstadt, tel: 02682/62648.

BELOW: Haydn's grave

These "chartered Jews", most of them craftsmen and tradesmen, enjoyed the sovereign's protection and were granted a large degree of autonomy within their own communities. The excellent teaching at the Talmudic school in Eisenstadt (based on the fundamental code of Jewish law) had become renowned beyond the borders of Austria as early as the 18th century. Many an eminent scholar came to study here.

In 1848, the Jewish communities became autonomous municipalities with a governing body consisting of a mayor and a bailiff. They were also allowed their own school and even their own fire brigade. These autonomous governments were dissolved again in the course of the 19th century. Only Mattersdorf retained its self-governing body until 1903, and Eisenstadt-Unterberg until the First Republic came to a sudden end in 1938.

Then, in 1938, the Holocaust brought this era of peaceful co-existence to an end. The only reminders today of the prosperous and peaceful times enjoyed by the Jews who lived here are a few neglected graves and tombstones.

The Esterházy dynasty is still the largest landowner in the Burgenland. Their castles and former strongholds are scattered throughout the region.

Forchtenstein ⓑ is one of the most imposing fortresses in the region. It was built in about 1300 high up on a limestone rock of the Rosalien Mountain. In the first half of the 17th century it came into the hands of the Esterházys, who rebuilt it during the years 1635–7 and gave it the appearance which it has retained until this day. The castle rock was surrounded by a wall of almost impenetrable fortifications and bastions. Its main features are the two towers which are starkly contrasting: a round medieval keep on the western side, and a Baroque tower with a bulbous spire on the eastern side. There is a well which is more than 142 metres

Obeying an old tradition, the Jewish community of Unterberg was "secured" daily at nightfall, when a chain (below) was put right across the main street.

BELOW: entrance to the Jewish ghetto in Eisenstadt-Unterberg
BELOW RIGHT: textile in the Jewish Museum

(470 ft) deep and which was dug by Turkish prisoners of war during 30 years of slave labour. Castle Forchtenstein houses a remarkable collection of Turkish art and an equally splendid collection of weapons dating from the 16th to the 19th centuries.

Kittsee Castle ⑯, in the most northeasterly part of the state, is another of the Esterházy castles. This Baroque building, which was designed in the shape of a horseshoe, now houses one of the departments of the Austrian Folklore Museum in Vienna.

Halbturn Castle ⑰, situated in the Seewinkel, is also used as a museum (temporary exhibits) today. An elegant Baroque manor house, it was designed around 1710 by Johann Lukas von Hildebrandt. The castle was badly damaged by the occupying forces after World War II, as well as by a devastating fire in 1949. The extensive restoration works lasted until 1964. Luckily, the fresco on the ceiling of the so-called garden hall, an important Rococo painting by Franz Anton Maulpertsch (1765), was not destroyed by the fire.

The Viennese seaside

The centre of Burgenland is not really the provincial capital but is rather the shallow Lake Neusiedler, fondly known as the "Viennese Sea". It lies in a gently sloping hollow in flat, treeless grassland.

Many riddles surround the **Lake Neusiedler** (Neusiedler See). The most puzzling one is the question of where all the water comes from, and where it gets its vital oxygen from as it is fed by only one river, the Wulka, and has no outflow whatsoever. The normal water level is around 1 metre (3 feet), but varies considerably depending on rainfall.

Map, page 196

BELOW: countryside near Lake Neusiedler

TIP

Beware of stormy
weather on Lake
Neusiedler. It is a
mistake to
underestimate the
lake, as even
experienced sailors
sometimes struggle
with incredibly high
waves, despite the low
water level.

BELOW: harvesting
the reeds outside
the village of Rust

Usually, one can wade across the lake (at its narrowest point, between Mör-bisch and Illmitz, an annual "lake-crossing" party is held), but very often heavy storms, which are not unusual in this area, literally just push the water aside and reveal the mud at the bottom of the lake. Several times, the lake disappeared all together – once, in 1866, for as long as 10 years. During those years, farmers used the lake as farmland. As suddenly as it had disappeared, Lake Neusiedler came back again in 1876.

A paradise for sailors

Lake Neusiedler, dotted with sailing boats manoeuvring past the numerous islands of reeds, usually presents a peaceful picture and is one of the most popular sailing areas in Austria. The calm is deceptive, however, for it can change very suddenly with the approach of a storm.

The lake, the only example in Europe of a steppe-type lake, is without doubt Burgenland's biggest attraction. It is also its most endangered environment. Lake Neusiedler was first discovered by natural scientists who were fascinated by its extraordinary and rare vegetation and animal life. It is one of the largest bird sanctuaries in Europe. The heron colony is unique.

No-one and nothing endangered the wildlife and vegetation until fairly recently. The natural environment provided by the reeds formed an ideal habitat for plants and animals alike and was only disturbed once a year, when the reeds were harvested in winter.

After World War II, the lake became a tourist attraction. At the same time, the surrounding farms were modernised and many were converted into vineyards. For some years, the lake was polluted by insecticides and pesticides, as

well as by the garbage which thousands of tourists leave behind. Happily, much stronger controls are now in place, and the cleanliness of the water is much improved.

Map, page 196

Storks and wine

The tiny town of **Rust** ⓘ, which also has some well preserved houses dating from the 16th to 18th centuries, is famous for its storks. They have lived and bred there for centuries and have always been lovingly looked after by Rust's human inhabitants.

The chimneys, on which they build their nests, are constructed in a way that takes account of their nest building habits (the nests can weigh up to 100 kg/ 220 lb). The alarming decline in the stork population, despite all these efforts, is due to the disappearance of the marshes, which are the natural feeding grounds of these birds, and the pollution through modern farming. The enormous nests high up on the chimneys remain, but more and more of them remain empty.

Rust is also famous beyond the regional boundaries by virtue of the wine produced from the local vineyards.

The Austrian Puszta

In **Mörbisch am See** ⓘ, a stage has been built into the lake. Each summer, operetta festivals are held here, which are not only attended by the regular fans, but also by millions of mosquitoes! The operetta enthusiasts don't seem to mind. For them, the stage and the closeness of the Hungarian "Puszta" provide the perfect setting for such popular "Puszta-operettas" as the *Czardasfürstin* and *Gräfin Mariza*.

ABOVE: sunset on Lake Neusiedler.

BELOW: horses grazing on the Puszta

**Map,
page 196**

TIP

The Neusiedler See-
Seewinkel National
Park House can
provide you with plenty
of information, both on
the flora and fauna and
practical matters.
Tel: 02175/34420.

BELOW: farmer in
Podersdorf.
RIGHT: watersports
on Lake Neusiedler

Where the lake gently curves is the region called **Seewinkel**, one of the most deserted areas in the whole of Austria. This almost classical "Puszta" landscape gives one the impression of actually being in Hungary.

Here, you can still see a number of old and rusty draw-wells. The villages are spread far apart. Some just consist of a row of houses on each side of the main road, often for a stretch of several miles. The houses are limewashed, with wide entrance gates, and only the reed-thatching of the roofs has been replaced by modern materials.

The many shallow lakes (with no outflows), some small, some large, are also characteristic for this area. They are called *Lacken*. Some are protected areas. The World Wildlife Fund created a nature reserve at the "Lange Lacke" which has become a haven for many rare plants and animals. This is now the heart of the **Neusiedler See-Seewinkel National Park ⓴**. At the centre of the park is the town of Illmitz which has a National Park House at the entrance (on your right if you arrive from the south).

A peaceful paradise, but the signpost "Andau, 6 km" is a grim reminder to Central Europeans of the 1956 uprising in Communist Hungary, which was so close to the Austrian doorstep. The Iron Curtain and the ominous watchtowers guarding the frontier have since disappeared. Gone are the days when you could stand here and imagine you were at the very edge of Europe – fortunately. Once upon a time, the entire region was like a dead end, a place you came to visit but where you would have to turn back at the border.

Nowadays it is not a dead end but a bridge. Vienna – and in particular the Burgenland bordering Hungary – has regained its traditional place as a link between Central and Eastern Europe.

SOUTH OF VIENNA

The fragrant Vienna Woods and spectacular mountains once inspired Vienna's creative elite. Now visitors come to Baden to cure their aches and to Mayerling to learn about a Habsburg tragedy

Map, page 196

T he first few minutes are the worst. Driving out along the Triester Strasse, through the ugly industrial zone which spreads out to the south of Vienna, you will find yourself confronted in the first instance with a sea of shopping centres and garages. And then, quite suddenly, the view changes and the concrete and factories give way to gently rolling hills. A hint of the South overcomes the traveller and even the air seems gentler, milder, reminiscent of a warm spring day.

Walks and wineries

The section of the Vienna Woods described below has a particular charm all of its own. Dark Scots pines clothe the mountain slopes, and as you walk beneath the trees the needles crunch under your feet. The air is fragrant with their scent. During the Romantic era artificial ruins were erected here and there. The wild gorges and vertical cliffs create a setting perfect for a tale of chivalry.

The footpaths around the little town of **Mödling** ㉑ are particularly attractive. During the 19th century it was a favourite retreat of novelists and painters. Ferdinand Waldmüller and Rudolf von Alt, Richard Wagner, Franz Grillparzer, Johann Nestroy and Ferdinand Raimund all loved the area. Ludwig van Beethoven lived here for years, composing not only his *Missa Solemnis* but also the *Mödlinger Tänze* for itinerant musicians who earned a living by travelling from inn to inn. Mödling today is a pretty town with a pedestrian zone bordered by lovingly restored rows of historic houses.

A pleasant afternoon walk is to stroll across the Eichkogel to **Gumpoldskirchen** ㉒, another favourite destination of the Viennese. It lies in a gentle hollow, a village where the *Heurige* stand cheek by jowl and where each seems to have a shady inner courtyard with pink and white oleander blossoming in wooden tubs, and a refreshing white wine to accompany the typical grilled chicken. On all sides stretch the green vineyards, whilst a narrow path leads to an ancient grape press tucked away in the mountains. Through the mist you can just make out the Pannonian Plains, and you sense the Hungarian Puszta which must begin somewhere beyond.

The flair of the monarchy

Since excursions to the region south of Vienna are usually linked with an extended wine-tasting session, it is better on the whole not to travel by car. There is an attractive alternative means of transport in the form of the blue-painted "Baden Train" (Badner Bahn), which departs from the stop in front of the Vienna State Opera and covers the route in about an hour with frequent stops.

Arriving at the terminus, the Josephsplatz in **Baden** ㉓ some 25km (16 miles) from Vienna, some of the finer guests have been known to wrinkle their noses in disgust,

PRECEDING PAGES: enjoying the sun in Baden bei Wien.
LEFT: a foot-path through the Vienna Woods.
BELOW: Heiligenkreuz monastery

for an unmistakable smell of sulphur lingers in the air. Every day, more than six million litres of hot spring water (36°C/97°F) bubble from the town's mineral springs. They are used (and were in Roman times too) for the treatment of rheumatism, sports injuries and other conditions. The town has an array of lovely old public baths and hotels which invite you to take the waters.

Baden is a spa town which has retained the flair of the Imperial and royal epochs, when ladies with flimsy parasols strolled through the rose garden past the famous sundial, and the court made its summer residence out here "in the country". Following in their footsteps came the aristocracy, the wealthy bourgeoisie and sophisticated *bons vivants*. Even today you can sample the atmosphere of that bygone era as you listen to the spa orchestra playing in the white-painted pavilion, spend an evening at the gambling tables in the casino or a Sunday afternoon on the wooden grandstand at the trotting course. You can round off the day in style with a coffee in one of the traditional cafés – a sweetened Imperial Blend, perhaps, topped with whipped cream.

Baden is worth a short visit in its own right, but it also makes an ideal base for excursions and walking tours in the area. You can head for the much-sung Helenen Valley, for example, or choose between Hinterbrühl and Heiligenkreuz. Each setting has its own charms, as broad and inviting landscapes suddenly give way to narrow ravines, empty and enchanted, as if a forgotten secret awaits you around the next bend. Such nostalgic intimations are especially strong in Mayerling.

ABOVE: plague monument in Baden's Hauptplatz.

BELOW: the City Club

Mayerling

On 30 January 1889, Crown Prince Rudolf, heir to the Austro-Hungarian throne and only son of Emperor Franz Joseph and Empress Elisabeth, apparently shot

his young mistress, Baroness Mary Vetsera, and then turned the pistol upon himself at the hunting lodge at **Mayerling** . Attempts were made at court to hush up the scandal, but it was not long before rumours circulated through the city, the kingdom and finally throughout Europe. Some maintained that the Crown Prince had been poisoned, or that the Baroness bled to death following a botched abortion and the grief-striken prince committed suicide.

There are also numerous anecdotes describing Prince Rudolf's dissipated and unhappy life. His father had attempted to have him brought up as a perfect soldier and had had him subjected to horrible privations and torture as a child. Little Rudolf was a sensitive, musical boy whose talents in this sphere were not appreciated. Even as an adult he had no chance of putting his liberal ideas into political practice. His father would not allow him to take part in affairs of state. And so the Crown Prince was forced to publish his theories under a pseudonym.

On top of this came the catastrophe of his private life. For political reasons he was obliged to marry Princess Stephanie of Belgium. It was an unhappy marriage and Rudolf's nightly tours of the city suburbs to drown his sorrows, visiting the dance halls and *Heurige*, and his affairs with common women, soon became notorious. The tragedy of Mayerling was the predictable conclusion to this sorry tale.

Mary Vetsera, who acquired so much importance by virtue of the incident, was actually no more than a casual acquaintance of the Crown Prince. Her effusive naiveté made her the perfect victim. After just a few meetings Rudolf confided in her about his depression and plans to commit suicide. Mary felt flattered. On 28 January 1889 they met at the hunting lodge at Mayerling, where they spent their last days together, writing suicide letters and listening to the Viennese songs of the famous *Fiaker* driver Bratfisch.

Map, page 196

TIP

On a warm day be sure to visit "Eis-Peter" in Baden's Beethovengasse for the best ice cream north of the Alps.

BELOW: the spa park in Baden

ABOVE: the monastery at Mayerling.

The 30-year-old heir to the Habsburg throne was buried in state. Masses were said for his soul throughout the Empire, whilst his 18-year-old mistress was quietly buried at Heiligenkreuz.

In her two best-selling novels, *Elisabeth, Kaiserin wider Willen* (Elisabeth, the Reluctant Empress) and *Rudolf, Kronprinz und Rebell* (Rudolf, Crown Prince and Rebel), Brigitte Hamann has researched the events in great detail and described the roots of the tragedy. Countless legends have grown up around Mayerling, and a never-ending succession of new theories and clues constantly hit the headlines.

On 22 December 1992, Mr Flatzelsteiner, a businessman from Linz, unlawfully removed the body of Mary Vetsera from its tomb in the cemetery at Heiligenkreuz – with the best of intentions, of course. He wanted finally to get to the bottom of the most mysterious affair of the House of Habsburg. Standing by the open grave, he announced that world history would have to be re-written. But even this grave-robbery and the subsequent examination of the skull of Mary Vetsera using computer techniques was only able to confirm the previous consensus.

A far more interesting sight is actually the **Heiligenkreuz Monastery** ㉕ (guided tours Mon–Sat 10am, 11am, 2pm, 3pm and 4pm; Sun and public holidays from 11am) next door, which dates from the Babenberg period. Margrave Leopold invited twelve French Cistercian monks to the Vienna Woods in 1333, and the three-aisled Roman pillared basilica with its Gothic altar was duly built at the centre of the impressive old monastery here.

Vienna's own mountains

BELOW: Archduke Rudolf and his mistress, Baroness Mary Vetsera

The six-lane motorway leads southwards past Baden and Wiener Neustadt, the roaring of the traffic echoing across the countryside like an approaching thunder-

storm. But even those incorrigible knights of the modern highway, who cover vast distances without batting an eyelid, like to glance to the right about half an hour after leaving the built-up area. This is the point where Vienna's mountains suddenly appear on the horizon.

The **Rax** and the **Schneeberg** rear up like sleeping giants above the plain. Their summits are mostly snow-covered even in summer. Both are more than 2,000 metres (6,600 ft) high, and their proximity to the capital adds to their appeal. They are popular destinations for climbing and hang gliding, for hunting chamois and searching for gentian – and sampling Enzian schnapps, of course. A rack-and-pinion railway on the Schneeberg and a cable car on the Rax make such experiences accessible even for tourists who insist on making the ascent in high heels. Caution is needed, for both mountains are often underestimated even by experienced mountain walkers, turning an excursion into yet another emergency exercise for the rescue teams.

Favourite summer haunts include **Payerbach** and **Reichenau** on the Rax as well as **Puchberg am Schneeberg**, which has a range of pistes for alpine skiers as well as tracks for cross-country fans.

Continuing in a southwesterly direction, you will soon reach the highlight of this little journey. Even in the Middle Ages the route across the **Semmering Pass** (Semmering-Kurort) ❷⑥ was one of the few safe Alpine crossings. Pious pilgrims journeyed through the passes on their way to Venice, where they embarked on a ship for the Holy Land. During the 18th century the road was widened and modernised. It became a "commercial path" as well as a "war path". Venice was no longer the main destination; the traffic was all heading for Trieste, and the road was re-christened Triester Strasse.

Map, page 196

BELOW: memorial chapel in Mayerling

The Semmering Railway

The Semmering Pass hit the international headlines in 1842 with the start of an epoch-making project – the construction of a railway line through the mountain. The Imperial railway company commissioned Carlo Ghega, a civil engineer from Venice, with the planning and execution of this major undertaking. An army of 20,000 workers from all corners of the empire was employed to dynamite millions of cubic metres of granite, constructing 31 tunnels and viaducts. Over 40 km (25 miles) long, the track climbed no less than 400 metres (1,312 ft) to the top of the pass, 895 metres (2,936 ft) above sea level.

At the time it was the highest point to be reached by a railway anywhere in the world. Even the building site drew foreign visitors and Austrian holiday-makers, who gazed in amazement at the vast scaffolding supporting the viaducts. In 1854, only five years after construction started, the Semmering Railway was commissioned. Its builder was later knighted as Carl Ritter von Ghega; but he ended up with a back-seat job in the Ministry of Finance and died young, disillusioned.

Even today, a trip southwards on the Semmering Railway is an exciting experience. The landscape flashes past the carriage windows, a succession of green slopes, dizzy ravines and mountain peaks alternating, whilst the villages on the distant plains look like dolls' houses. Rattling across the two-tier "Kalte Rinne" viaduct and plunging into the next tunnel turns the journey into a ghost-train ride for the young and young at heart. Travellers with more delicate nerves can rest easy, however, for the route is equipped with the latest safety devices.

The section from Semmering to the Adriatic only takes a couple of hours, but many a sun-hungry tourist has suddenly found the wild, romantic scenery between **Gloggnitz** and **Mürzzuschlag** much more attractive than the prospect of a

ABOVE: the Semmering train in the mountains

BELOW: countryside by the Semmering

sandy beach and breaking waves. Soon after the railway was completed, the first villas and hotels appeared along the route. The architecture is typical of the region, ornate with carved wooden verandas and balconies, turrets and conservatories. The **South Railway Hotel** (Südbahnhotel), the **Panhans** and the **Palace** are miniature castles in the very midst of the mountains, which attracted an elegant clientele. The bracing climate, similar to that of Davos in Switzerland, made many of the little villages into popular mountain cure resorts.

Peter Rosegger described the region as "the healthy lung of Vienna". The art and literary scene from Vienna regarded it as a "coffee house with a balcony" and chose it as their summer retreat. Sigmund Freud and Gustav Mahler, Alban Berg and Arthur Schnitzler, Oskar Kokoschka and many other famous names lived and worked here at some stage, and found inspiration in the lovely setting. Semmering's golden age was during the years between the wars, when it was a favourite meeting place for international fashionable society. A picture of Josephine Baker in a tight white ski suit, riding on a wooden sledge, was published worldwide.

World War II brought these boom years to an abrupt end. Villas owned by Jews were confiscated, and in the salons intellectual brilliance was suddenly replaced by ponderous folklore. Like so many other places and spheres, Semmering has never really recovered from this abrupt disintegration of all it had stood for. In recent years enthusiastic attempts have been made to recreate the old atmosphere. The Hotel Panhans has had a facelift, and the villas and guest houses have also been restored and dusted down.

Slowly, the Viennese are rediscovering their summer resort, so close to the city and yet tucked away in the mountains. Whether you plan a day trip or a leisurely holiday, a detour to the south is always a worthwhile experience.

Map, page 196

BELOW: the Südbahnhotel.
OVERLEAF: the ferris wheel at the Prater

INSIGHT GUIDES

Travel Tips

Your vacation.

Your vacation after losing your wallet in the ocean.

Lose your cash and it's lost forever. Lose American Express® Travelers Cheques and get them replaced. They can mean the difference between the vacation of your dreams and your worst nightmare. And, they are accepted like cash worldwide. Available at participating banks, credit unions, AAA offices and American Express Travel locations. *Don't take chances. Take American Express Travelers Cheques.*

do more

Travelers
Cheques

CONTENTS

Getting Acquainted

The Place

Vienna is one of the nine provinces of Austria as well as being its capital city.
Area 415 sq. km (160 sq. miles). The average distance from one side of the city to the other is 25 km (16 miles).
Altitude 170 metres (558 ft) above sea level.
Population 1,591,000 (1991).
Language German.
Religion Mainly Roman Catholic.
Time zone Central European (gmt +1 hour).
Currency The national currency is the Austrian Schilling (öS), which is divided into 100 Groschen. There are notes of 20, 50, 100, 500 and 1,000 Schilling and coins of 2, 5, 10 and 50 Groschen.
   The Austrian Schilling is closely linked to the German Mark (DM).
Weights and measures Metric.
Electricity 200V are standard, as are Continental plugs.
International dialling code +43

Climate

Vienna has a temperate climate, although in summer temperatures may rise to 35°C (95°F) and in winter they may sink to –20°C (–4°F).
Average Temperatures:
January: –1°C (30°F)
February: 2°C (36°F)
March: 4°C (39°F)
April: 7°C (45°F)
May: 14°C (57°F)
June: 18°C (64°F)
July: 19°C (66°F)
August: 19°C (66°F)
September: 15°C (59°F)
October: 9°C (48°F)
November: 3°C (37°F)
December: –1°C (30°F)

Weather forecast, tel: 1556

Economy

Of the approximately 786,000 citizens who make up the city's working population, some 15 percent are self-employed or freelance workers. Fifty percent are employees or civil servants and 15 percent are manual workers.
   Vienna is the economic turntable of Austria. Its main industries are small-scale engineering, electrical and electronic manufacture and metalwork.
   Vienna is also the seat of the national parliament. The city is also a Catholic archbishopric with 150 parishes. It is also the seat of the Protestant bishop.

Government

The administration of Vienna consists of one hundred local councillors who are elected for a period of five years. The mayor is chosen amongst them and serves simultaneously as the head of the province of Vienna. Vienna is divided into 23 districts. Since 1919 it has had a predominantly socialist administration. An exemplary legislative code guarantees a high standard of living.

Districts
The "City Centre", District No. I, is demarcated by the Ringstrasse and the Danube quay (Kai).
   The former suburbs surround this inner city district in a circle and form the districts II to IX and XX. The edge of these districts is marked by the outer ring road, the Gürtel which once marked the limes or furthermost limit of the Roman Empire.

Tourism is no. 1

Vienna's biggest money-spinner is tourism, with almost two million tourists visiting the city each year. Germany accounts for the largest number (25 percent).

   Beyond the Gürtel lie the outer boroughs, Districts X to XXIII with the exception of No. XX. The latter, together with District No. II, lies between the Danube Canal and the Danube River. Main roads leading to the outer boroughs radiate in the form of a star from the Ringstrasse.
   Along the Ringstrasse and the Gürtel the houses are numbered in a clockwise direction. Along the roads leading out from the centre they are numbered from the centre outward. Even numbers are always on the right and odd number on the left-hand side.

I	City Centre
II	Leopoldstadt
III	Landstrasse
IV	Wieden
V	Margareten
VI	Mariahilf
VII	Neubau
VIII	Josefstadt
IX	Alsergrund
X	Favoriten
XI	Simmering
XII	Meidling
XIII	Hietzing
XIV	Penzing
XV	Fünfhaus
XVI	Ottakring
XVII	Hernals
XVIII	Währing
XIX	Döbling
XX	Brigittenau
XXI	Florisdorf
XXII	Donaustadt
XXIII	Liesing

The postal code is formed by adding a 1 before and a 0 after the number of the district. Thus the XII District is 1120 (but the first district is 1010).

Planning the Trip

What to Bring

Clothing
Vienna is a conservative city when it comes to dress. Full evening dress is required for the Opera Ball, and dinner jacket and evening dresses are worn for theatre premières. Apart from that, the normal Central European conventions apply.

Entry Regulations

Austria relies heavily on tourism to balance its trade deficit. For this reason, immigration and customs formalities are fairly lax. A valid passport is required to enter the country. Some nationalities must obtain a visa before arrival. Contact the Austrian embassy in your home country for details.

Animal Quarantine
If you intend to bring any animals into Austria you need a veterinary document as proof of rabies vaccination.
Emergency service, tel: 834 303.

Customs
There is no customs duty on items intended for personal use and gifts to a total value of öS 1,000. This includes two cameras, an 8mm film or video camera, a portable typewriter, a transistor radio, a portable television set, a tape recorder and a record player. Visitors over the age of 17 years may also import duty-free 200 cigarettes or 50 cigars or 250g tobacco as well as two litres of wine and one litre of spirits.

Money

Banks and *bureaux de change* exchange foreign currency at the daily exchange rate. Currencies not listed on the Vienna Stock Exchange are changed at the free market rate.

Austrian banking secrecy laws are amongst the best in the world. Overseas stocks and shares can be sold and purchased with complete anonymity. The country's economic stability and low inflation rate make it a popular place for investing money. The import and export of Austrian and foreign currency is unrestricted, although sums above öS 100,000 must be declared if they are not to be used for tourist purposes.

Eurocheques must be made out on Schilling. The main credit cards are widely accepted by the major hotels and many of the larger shops in the city centre. Cash dispensers at most banks accept Eurocheque cards.

Public Holidays

On these days institutions and businesses are closed:
New Year's Day (1 January)
Epiphany (6 January)
Easter Monday
Ascension Day (1 May)
Whit Monday
Corpus Christi
Assumption of the Virgin Mary (15 August)
National Holiday (26 October)
All Saints' Day (1 November)
Conception of the Virgin Mary (8 December)
Christmas Day (25 December)
St Stephen's Day (26 December)

Festivals

Vienna is not just a musical city. Apart from opera, ballet performances and concerts, there is a constant succession of world-famous exhibitions. However, Vienna's range of opera, operetta, classical concerts and ballet matches that of any other cosmopolitan city. A few examples are the **Viennale Film Festival** (March), **Spanish Riding School** performances (March–June) and **waltz music** and **operetta** concerts (April–October).

The **Vienna Festival** takes place in May and June and is followed by the **Vienna Summer Music Festival**, which continues until the end of August. These festivals take place in a framework of Schubert, Mozart and Haydn concerts, which are held at various times throughout the year. An international **Youth Music Festival** and **concerts of sacred music** round off the year,

Fascinating Facts

● One in four Austrians comes from Vienna.
● In Vienna there is a surplus of women of approximately 15 percent.
● About a quarter of the 800,000 flats in Vienna are owned by the council, which means it is the biggest property owner in the world.

culminating in **Advent and Christmas music**. In November, everyone gets the opportunity to indulge in a little fantasy and extravagance, for this is when the **Viennese Ball Season** begins: the Champagne Ball, the Imperial Ball, innumerable New Year Balls, the Vienna Philharmonic Ball and, in February, the Opera Ball. Tourists can buy tickets to attend these balls too.

Apart from musical events, many conferences, trade fairs and exhibitions are held in Vienna throughout the year. Two events to take note of are the **Viennese Art and Antiques Exhibition** and the **Viennese International Trade Fair**. The former takes place in spring and the latter in autumn.

The Viennese Tourist Office publishes a calendar of fairs and conferences which the visitor can use as a reference guide to look up the dates for various events.

Getting There

By Air

Vienna International Airport (Schwechat) has connections with over 60 destinations all over the world and domestic flights to Graz, Innsbruck, Linz, Salzburg and Bregenz (via Altenrhein Airport in Switzerland). The information desk is open daily between 9am and 10pm. Austria's national and international airlines are Austrian Airlines, Tyrolean Airways and Lauda Air.

Vienna Schwechat Airport is situated about 19 km (12 miles) southeast of the city centre. It can be reached in about 25 minutes via the airport motorway. In the late 1980s a new terminal was opened, enabling the aircraft to be reached directly by passenger bridges.

Branches of international banks and car rental firms will be found in the arrivals hall, alongside a large number of shops offering tax-free Austrian goods for sale.

Vienna Schwechat Airport, tel: 711 102 231.

Flight information, tel: 711 102 233.

Air Canada: I Scubertring 9 , tel: 712 4608 412.

Air France: I Kärntner Strasse 49, tel: 514 180.

Austrian Airlines: I Kärntner Ring 18, tel: 505 5757-0.

British Airways: I Kärntner Ring 10, tel: 505 7691-0.

Delta Airlines: I Kärntner Ring 17, tel: 512 6646-0.

German Lufthansa: 6 Mariahilfer-strasse 123, tel: 599 1124-0.

Qantas: I Opernring 1/R, tel: 587 7771.

Swissair: I Kärntner Ring 18, tel: 505 5757-0.

Visitors who do not rent a car upon arrival (which is not advisable anyway, because of the one-way streets and difficult parking situation in the city centre) have a number of public transport options for getting into the city centre.

By Train

Most long-distance trains arrive at and leave Vienna via the West Station (Westbahnhof) and South Station (Südbahnhof). Trains from Germany, France, Belgium and Switzerland arrive at the West Station, whilst those from former Yugoslavia, Greece, Hungary and Italy use the South Station.

There are a number of international inter-city trains linking Vienna with other countries in western Europe – Eurocity (EC) trains run between Dortmund, Bochum, Essen, Duisburg, Düsseldorf, Cologne,

Koblenz, Mainz, Würzburg, Nürnberg and Regensburg and Vienna. There is also an EC link between Munich and Vienna.

Additional International Inter-City trains:

Ostend–Vienna Express: Ostend–Brussels–Cologne–Vienna *Arlberg Express:* Paris–Basle–Zurich–Vienna *Holland–Vienna Express:* Amsterdam–Cologne–Vienna

Trains carrying cars run between Vienna and Düsseldorf, Cologne and Frankfurt.

During the summer you can take the Danube steamer from Passau to Vienna instead of travelling by train.

Railway General Information, tel: 1700.

Passenger Information, tel: 1717.

West Station Destinations, tel: 1552.

South Station Destinations, tel: 1553.

Complaints, tel: 245 512.

Local Services (Vienna–Baden), tel: 815 6532.

Reservations: Austrian Railways (Österreichisches Verkehrsbüro), I, Opernring 5, tel: 588 628.

By Car

Austria has a good motorway network linking Vienna with the western and southern provinces. It usually takes less than three hours to reach the capital from the German border near Salzburg. Most visitors from the west who arrive in Vienna by car do so via the western motorway.

Airport to City Centre Services

● **Express Coach** These operate between the airport and the City Air Terminal at the Hilton Hotel. Coaches run every 20 minutes 8am–9pm. Between 6am and 8am they run every 30 minutes. The City Air Terminal is very conveniently located.

● **Taxi** A taxi from the airport to

the city centre costs approximately öS 350.

● **Shuttle** Transport by minibus to/from the airport from every major hotel can be arranged through the concierge or by phoning, tel: 636 0190.

● **Train** A regular service leaves Wien-Nord/Praterstern via Wien-Mitte (central station),

Landstrasse, City Air Terminal for the airport. The journey time is around 30 minutes. You will require a valid ticket for the main zone plus one outer zone (öS 13).

● **Underground** Take the U3 or U4 service.

● **Tram** The S7 goes to/from the city centre.

There is a Tourist Information Centre on the outskirts of the city. There is a similar office by the southern motorway entrance to the city.

Motorway Tourist Information: **Western motorway exit** (Auhof), tel: 971 271.
Vienna South (Triester Strasse 149), tel: 674 151.

By Boat
The Austrian national shipping line is the celebrated **Danube Steamship Company** (DDSG Blue Danube Schiffahrt GmbH).

There is an **Information Office** at the Embarkation Quay by the Reichsbrücke (II, Handelskai 265, Passenger Hall, tel: 727 50440). Opening hours are 7am–6pm, May–September. A regular steamer service runs along the Danube from the beginning of May until the end of September, and through the Wachau from early April. There are ferry links with Budapest and Passau. Between Budapest and Vienna there is also an express hydrofoil service (Mahart), which leaves Vienna (Reichsbrücke) at 8am and arrives in Budapest at 1.30pm. The return trip leaves Budapest at 1pm and reaches Vienna at 7.20pm. The fare costs öS 750 single, öS 1,100 return.

The Slovakian Danube Steamship Company also operates a hydrofoil between Vienna and Bratislava. It leaves Vienna (Reichsbrücke) at 8.30am and reaches Bratislava at 9.30am. The return trip leaves Bratislava at 4pm and arrives in Vienna at 5.15pm.

The former Soviet Danube Steamship Company operates a ferry service between Vienna and Yalta.

Tourist Information

Viennese Tourist Office (Wiener Tourismusverband), II, Obere Augarten-strasse 40, tel: 211 140-1.

Overseas offices of the Austrian National Tourist Authority:
London: 30 St George Street, London WIR 0AL, tel: (171) 629 0461.
Los Angeles: 11601 Wilshire Boulevard, Suite 2480, Los Angeles, CA 90025, tel: 477 3332.
New York: 500 Fifth Avenue, Suite 2009-2022, New York, NY 10110, tel: 944 6880.
Amsterdam: (Oostenrijks Toeristenburo), Stadhouderskade 2, 1054 ES, Amsterdam, tel: 612 9682.
Copenhagen: (Ostrigs Turistbureau), Nyropsgade 37, 1602 Copenhagen V, tel: 130 432.
Frankfurt: (Österreichisches Fremdenverkehrsamt), Rossmarkt 12, tel: 206 98.
Paris: (Office National Autrichien du Tourisme), 47 Avenue de l'Opera, F-75002 Paris, tel: 47 42 78 57.
Rome: (Ente Nazionale Austriaco per il Turismo), Via Barberini 29, I-00187 Rome, tel: 481 4658.

Local Tourist Offices
Tourist Information (City): I, Kärntner Strasse 38, tel: 513 8892. Open daily 9am–7pm.
Information Süd: X, Triester Strasse 149, tel: 616 00 70. Open April–May and October daily 9am–7pm, July–September daily 8am–10pm.
Information West: XIV, Auhof, tel: 979 12 71. Open April–October daily 8am–10pm, November daily 9am–7pm, December–March daily 10am–6pm.
Official Tourist Information: I, Opernpassage, tel: 431 608, 435 974. Open daily 9am–7pm.

Austria Information, IV, Margaretenstrasse 1, tel: 587 2000. Open Monday–Friday 10am–5pm, Thursday 10am–6pm.
Lower Austria Information, I, Heidschuss 2, tel: 533 3114.

Literature on Vienna

The Viennese Tourist Office will supply you with a variety of leaflets and brochures, including:
● Vienna (illustrated brochure)
● City map
● Diary of forthcoming events
● Calendar of conferences
● Monthly diary of events
● Jewish Vienna
● Vienna Waits for You (for young people)
● List of youth hostels and camp sites
● List of museums
● List of hotels and restaurants
● List of *Heurige*
● Art Nouveau in Vienna
● Previews of programmes for the State Opera House and the Volksoper
● Programmes for the Spanish Riding School and the Vienna Boys' Choir
● Brochure of winter events, carnival and spring events
● Vienna Festival programme
● Viennese Summer Music Festival – preview and programme

Vienna Tourist Authority (Written information), II, Obere Augartenstrasse 40, tel: 211 140, fax: 216 8492.
City Information, I, Rathaus, tel: 438 989.
Programme Information for the National Theatre, tel: 531 200.
Jewish Welcome Service, I, Stephansplatz 10, tel: 533 2730.

Practical Tips

Business Hours

Banks
Open Monday–Friday
8am–12.30pm, 1.30–3pm,
Thursday until 5.30pm. Main
branches do not close during the
lunch hour.
Chase Manhattan Bank, III,
Löwengasse 47, tel: 712
28010.
Creditanstalt Bankverein, I,
Schottengasse 6–8, tel: 531
310.
Österreichische Sparkasse, I,
Krugerstrasse 13, tel: 513 15 78.
Internationale Bank für
Aussenhandel AG, I, Neuer
Markt 1, tel: 515 560.

Bureaux de Change
Stephansplatz: daily
9am–10pm.
Opernpassage: daily 8am–7pm.
Südbahnhof: daily
6.30am–10pm.
City Air Terminal: daily 8am–12
noon, 1pm–6.30pm.
Airport: daily 8.30am–11.30pm.

Credit Cards
American Express, I, Kärntner
Strasse 21–23, tel: 515 67.
Visa, III, Invalidenstrasse 2, tel:
711 110.
Diners Club, IV, Rainergasse 1,
tel: 501 355.

Religious Services

Catholic services from 6am, tel:
515 52-375.
Protestant services, tel: 512
8392.
Jewish services, Vienna Temple,
I, Seitenstättengasse 4, tel: 361
655.

Old Catholic Church, I,
Wipplingerstrasse 6, tel: 637
133.
Vienna Islamic Centre, XXI, Am
Hubertusdamm 17–19, tel: 270
1389.
Islamic Prayer Room, IX,
Türkenstrasse 13, tel: 344 625.
Anglican services, III,
Jaurésgasse 17, tel: 0049.
Mormons, tel: 373 257.
Methodists, tel: 604 5347.

Media

Cable television is firmly
established in Vienna, which
means that English, Swiss,
German, French and Austrian
television programmes can be
seen almost everywhere. The
Blue Danube radio station
broadcasts in English parallel to
the popular Ö3 programme.
   International newspapers and
magazines are available
throughout the city centre. A
wide selection of titles will be
found in particular in the
Opernpassage. The *International
Herald Tribune* and the *Financial
Times*, along with various other
foreign-language newspapers,
are available early in the
morning.
   Newsagents, called Tabak
Trafik, are recognisable by their
sign, a red ring with a cigarette
in the middle. Apart from
newspapers and magazines they
also sell tobacco, cigarettes and
stamps and bus and tram
tickets.

Tipping

In most restaurants, the
service charge will
automatically be added to
your bill. An additional tip of
10 percent, however, is
usually expected for good,
efficient service. Taxi drivers,
hairdressers and tourist
guides will also expect a 10
percent tip for their services.

Post & Telecoms

Vienna has 115 post offices
which are open Monday–Friday
8am–noon and 2pm–6pm. The
main post office and the post
offices at railway stations are
open 24 hours a day.
Main Post Office, I,
Fleischmarkt 19, tel: 51590.
Open 24 hours a day, every day.
Post Office Information: 832
101.
Telephone Exchange: Fernamt
Wien, I, Schillerplatz 4, tel: 588
440.
Directory Enquiries:
National: 16;
International: 08;
Telegrams: 190.
Courier services: Der Bote, tel:
310 7373; Blitzkurier, tel: 310
3310.

Austria has a modern
communications network and
direct dialling is available to
most countries in the world. As
well as phoning from your hotel,
you can also make international
calls from post offices or from
many telephone booths.
Australia: 0061
Belgium: 0032
Denmark: 0045
France: 0033
Germany: 0049
Hungary: 0036
Italy: 0039
Netherlands: 0031
Switzerland: 0041
United Kingdom: 0044
USA: 001

Useful Addresses

Congresses
Vienna has become one of the
most popular congress cities in
Europe: 22 Congress Centres
and 16 Congress Hotels (nine
more are under construction)
provide the right accommodation
for groups of every size. For
information contact:
Congress Office, Vienna Tourist
Association, II, Obere Augarten-
strasse 40, tel: 216 8492.

Diplomatic Representation
Australia: IV, Mattiellistrasse 2, tel: 512 8580.
Canada: I, Laurenzerberg 2, tel: 531 3830 00.
India: I, Kärntner Ring 2a, tel: 505 8666.
Ireland: III, Landstrasser Hauptstrasse 2 (Hilton Hotel), tel: 715 4246.
South Africa: XIX, Sandgasse 33, tel: 326 4930.
United Kingdom: III, Jauresgasse 12, tel: 716 13-0.
United States of America: IX, Boltzmanngasse 16, tel: 313 39-0.

Business Services
World Trade Centre, Vienna Airport, tel: 7007 6000.
Domino Bürocenter, I, Bäckerstrasse 1, tel: 515 360.
German Chamber of Trade (Deutsche Handelskammer), V, Wiedner Hauptstrasse 142, tel: 545 14170.
Vienna Chamber of Trade (Kammer der gewerblichen Wirtschaft für Wien), I, Stubenring 8–10, tel: 514 500.
Institute for the Promotion of Trade (Wirtschaftsförderungsinstitut), XVIII, Währinger Gürtel 97, tel: 476 770.
Swiss Chamber of Trade in Austria (Schweizer Handeslkammer in Österreich), I, Neuer Markt 4, tel: 512 7950.

International Agencies
Vienna is the second seat of the United Nations in Europe (after Geneva). During the 1970s the Vienna International Centre was built, known to the Viennese as UNO City. It serves as headquarters for various international bodies: the IABO (International Atomic Energy Authority), UNIDO (United Nations Industrial Development Organisation), the CSDHA (Centre for Social Development and Humanitarian Affairs), the INCB and the UNFDAC, the United Nations narcotics organisations, the UNCITRAL, the United Nations

Emergencies
● **Police:** 133.
● **Fire Brigade:** 122.
● **Rescue Service:** 144.
● **Ambulance:** 401 44.
● **Doctor** (emergency): 141.
● **Dentist** (emergency): 512 2078.
● **Chemist** (after hours): 1550.
● **Socio-psychiatric help:** 318 419 (IX, Fuchsthallergasse 18).
● **International Chemists:** 512 2825 (I, Kärntner Ring 15).
● **Poison Centre:** 434 3439 (IX, Lazarettgasse 14).

Travellers' Emergency Calls Emergency calls for travellers are broadcast by Austrian Radio in the programme "Autofahrer unterwegs" between noon and 1pm. (Latest travel news is on Ö3 every hour.)

department of international commercial law, the UNWRA, the United Nations association on behalf of Palestinian refugees and the UNHCR (United Nations High Commission for Refugees). UNO City is extra-territorial ground and even Austrians need a passport to enter.

As well as the various United Nations bodies in Vienna, the city is the headquarters of OPEC (Organisation of Petroleum Exporting Countries) and the IMZ (International Music Centre).

Health

Accident & Emergency
1. Unfallchirurgische Ambulanz des AKH, IX, Alserstrasse 4, tel: 404 00 (on uneven days)
2. Unfallchirurgische Ambulanz des AKH, IX, Spitalgasse 23, tel: 404 00 (on even days)
The Ärztenotdienst (Emergency Medical Service), tel: 141, has a list of doctors and dentists on duty at the weekend. The oral surgery department at the AKH is also available.
Universitäts-Zahnklinik (University Dental Hospital), IX,

Währinger Strasse 25a, tel: 424 636. Charge for materials only.
Psychosomatisch-Gynäkologische Ambulanz, II, Universitätsfrauenklinik, IX, Spitalgasse 23, tel: 404 000. Termination of pregnancy is legal during the first 12 weeks in Austria. Costs must be paid privately (approximately öS 4,000). For information contact **Familienplaning**, XVIII, Währinger Gürtel 141, tel: 346 561. Open Monday, Wednesday and Friday 8am–noon.
Österreichische Aids Gesellschaft, XIV, Sanatorium-strasse 2, tel: 911 2901.
Venereal Diseases: Institut für Dermato-Venerologische Serodiagnostik, Lainzer Krankenhaus, XIII, Wolkersbergenstrasse 1, tel: 801 000.

Medical Services
Allgemeines Krankenhaus (AKH), IX, Alserstrasse 4 & 9, Spitalgasse 23 & 9, Lazarettgasse 14, tel: 404 00.
Allgemeine Poliklinik der Stadt Wien, IX, Mariannengasse 10, tel: 404 09.
Kinderklinik Glanzing (Children's Hospital), XIX, Glanzinggasse 37, tel: 476 020.
Krankenhaus der Barmherzigen Brüder, II, Grosse Mohrengasse 9, tel: 211 21. Free treatment available in cases of financial difficulty.
Semmelweis-Frauenklinik (Women's Hospital), XVIII, Bastiengasse 36–38, tel: 476 150.
St Anna Kinderspital (Children's Hospital), IX, Kinderspitalgasse 6, tel: 401 700.
Acupuncture: Ludwig-Boltzmann-Institut für Akupunktur, XV, Huglgasse 1–3, tel: 981 04 261.
Homeopathy: Institut für Homöopathie, Krankenhaus Lainz, Pav. VII, XIII, Wolkersbergenstrasse 1, tel: 801 00. Can provide a list of all recognised homeopaths in Austria.

Vaccinations: Hygiene-Institut der Stadt Wien, IX, Kinderspitalgasse 15, tel: 404 90.

Useful Numbers

Telegrams: 190.
Faults: 41.
ARBÖ: 123.
Babysitting service: Vienna University 408 7046; Academic Guest Service 587 3525.
Boat services: 1537.
Bus services: 711 01.
Central hotel booking service: 424 225.
Cinema programmes: 1577.
Current temperature: 1554.
Driving information: 1527.
Flight information: 711 100.
Lost property: 313 440.
National theatre programme information: 1518.
Normal tuning pitch: (440 Hz)q 1509.
ÖAMTC: 120.
Radio taxi: 313 00, 601 60, 814 00.
Railway Information: 1717.
Towing service: 656 541.
Traffic news: 1590.
Train enquiries (West Station): 1552; (South Station): 1553.
Weather forecast: 1566.

Lost Property
Lost Property Office, IX, Wasagasse 22, tel: 313 44-9211 (general), -9205 (tram), -9202 (documents). Open Monday–Friday 8am–noon. Public transport, tel: 501 300. Westbahn, tel: 5800 2996. Südbahn, tel: 5800 35656.

Enquiries regarding lost items should first be made at the relevant police station.

Dress & Costume Hire

● **Eva Randa**, XVI, Koppstrasse 66, tel: 646 8163.
● **Faschingsprinz**, I, Wollzeile 27, tel: 512 8133.
● **Lambert Hofer**, XV, Hackengasse 10, tel: 587 8458.

Getting Around

On Arrival

You should avoid the centre of Vienna if travelling by car. There are few parking facilities in the inner city, and the network of one-way streets makes driving a nightmare. Car parks provide the best solution to the parking problem, but note that some of them are closed at weekends and during the night.

Private Transport

By Car
There are certain areas where parking is permitted for 1½ hours when a parking disk is displayed. These can be purchased at tobacco shops (Tabak-Trafik). At night, during the winter months, it is forbidden to park in streets with tram lines. Where parking is not allowed, you may only stop for a maximum of ten minutes. A parking ticket costs about öS 100. If your car is towed away, you must reclaim it at the nearest police station. Once the fine of öS 2,000 (plus a handling fee) has been paid, the car can be collected at Wienerberg or Mannswörth. The fine for exceeding the speed limit is öS 200 upwards. Below is a list of car parks in the centre of the town:
City Parkhaus, (Stephansplatz), entrance Schulerstrasse, tel: 512 2709. Open Monday–Friday 7am–9pm, Saturday 7am–2pm.
Garage am Hof, entrance Schottengasse, Freyung, tel: 635 571. Open day and night, seven days a week.

Hoher Markt Garage, entrance Marc-Aurel-Strasse, tel: 635 825. Open Monday–Friday 7am–8pm.

Breakdown Services

● **ÖAMTC:** I, Schubertring 1–3, tel: 711 990; Emergency call: 120 or 9540.
● **ARBÖ:** XV, Mariahilfer Strasse 180, tel: 853 535-0; Emergency call: 123.

Concordialplatz Garage, entrance Salzgries or Börsengasse, tel: 636 374. Open Monday–Friday 7am–7pm.
Franz-Josefs-Kai-Garage, entrance Franz-Josefs-Kai, tel: 631 521. The first floor is open day and night, seven days a week.
Garage am Beethovenplatz, entrance Johannesgasse, tel: 735 321. Open day and night, seven days a week.
Kärntner Strasse Tiefgarage, entrance Känrtnerring, tel: 571 597. Open day and night, seven days a week.
Opernringhofgarage, entrance Operngasse or Elisabethstrasse. Open day and night, seven days a week.

Petrol stations open at night:
I, Börsengasse 11
I, Franz-Josefs-Kai/Morzinplatz
III, Untere Viaduktstrasse 47–49
IV, Paulanergasse 13.

Traffic Regulations
At a roundabout you must give way to cars coming from the right. Approaching a junction you must get in lane. A rapid succession of flashing lights during the green phase indicates that the lights are about to change to red. It is forbidden to use your horn within the city limits. Drivers and passengers using the front seat must wear seat belts. Children under 12 years old may not sit at the front.

The driving licences of most other countries are recognised,

as are car registration documents. However, it is advisable to carry an international insurance card. Cars registered abroad must bear an oval nationality disk.
Speed limit: 130km (80mph) – motorways, 100km (60mph) – country roads, 50km (30mph) – built-up areas.
Traffic accidents: All traffic accidents involving injury to persons must be reported to the police. Foreigners should use the accident report form issued by the Comité Européen des Assurances. The ÖAMTC and ARBÖ maintain breakdown patrols on the main roads. Non-members may use these services upon payment of a fee.
ÖAMTC Breakdown Service, tel: 120.
ARBÖ Breakdown Service, tel: 123.
Fire Brigade, tel: 122.
Police, tel: 133.
Ambulance, tel: 144.
Traffic news: The radio station Ö3 broadcasts traffic reports in German every hour after the news. Programmes are interrupted in the case of major

Car Rental

● **Avis**, I, Opernring 5 and Schwechat Airport, tel: 587 6241.
● **Budget Rent-a-Car**, III, Am Stadtpark and Schwechat Airport, tel: 756 565.
● **Europcar**, III, Park and Ride U3, Erdberg and Schwechat Airport, tel: 799 6176.
● **Hertz**, I, Kärntner Ring 17, tel: 512 86 770.
● **Reisemobil-Vermietung Benkö**, IV, Rechte Wienzeile 21, tel: 571 19 993.
● **Rent a Bus**, XII, Assmayergasse 60, tel: 813 32 23.
● **Blecha**, Exclusive Rent a Car (Rolls Royce, Bentley, Mercedes 600), XVI, Lienfeldergasse 35, tel: 485 36 72.

hold-ups. In the Vienna area there are also traffic bulletins in English and French broadcast by Radio Blue Danube.

By Taxi
In Vienna, taxis do not cruise the streets looking for customers. They wait at fixed taxi stands. In the city centre these can be found at:
Babenbergerstrasse/Burgring
Dr Karl-Lueger-Ring/Schottentor
Hoher Markt/Marc-Aurel-Strasse
Opernring/Operngasse
Schottenring/Ringturm
Schwarzenbergplatz/Kärntner Ring
Stubenring/Dr Karl-Lueger-Platz
Radio Taxi: 313 00, 601 60, 401 00.
Airport Taxi and Overland Journeys: 312 511, 319 2511.
Radio Taxi Perchtoldsdorf: 693 929.

Public Transport

By Train
You do not need a car in Vienna. Few major cities have such a well developed public transport system. Underground (**U-Bahn**) and a variety of local and suburban trains (**Stadtbahn, Schnellbahn, Lokalbahn** and **Regionalbahn**) are complemented by a network of trams (Strassenbahn) and buses.
There are five underground lines:
U1: Kagran–Reumannplatz
U2: Karlsplatz–Schottenring
U3: Erdberg–Johnstrasse
U4: Heiligenstadt–Hütteldorf
U6: Heiligenstadt–Siebenhirten
The Baden local train (Badner Lokalbahn) runs from the State Opera House to Josephsplatz in Baden bei Wien. There are nine suburban train services (S-Bahn) connecting Vienna with the surrounding region (Neusiedl am See, Neulengbach, Wiener Neustadt, Tulln and Mödling).
The 21 regional trains provide links with other destinations in the area.

Although in many other cities the **trams** have been taken out of service, in Vienna they are still an essential part of the public transport network. Their lines do not interfere with regular traffic and progress can often be faster than by car. There are 36 lines which form a dense inner-city network, further supported by 73 **bus** routes.
The red stops are compulsory and all vehicles automatically stop here; the blue stops are request stops and vehicles stop only when hailed.
The last tram runs at about 11.30pm and 12.15am. A blue bar at the front and back indicates that this is the last one.
Special trams can be hired from the transport authorities for group excursions (reservations tel: 65930 2455). Between May and October on Saturdays, Sundays and public holidays you can also take a nostalgic trip on a historic tram (adults öS150, children öS50). Further information can be obtained at Karlsplatz underground station, tel: 587 3186.

By Bus
The best way of travelling through the narrow streets and alleys of the city centre is the **Citybus**. Three routes run on weekdays through the centre:
1A: Schottentor–Landstrasse
2A: Schwedenplatz/Petersplatz to Dr Karl-Renner-Ring
3A: Schottenring–Schwarzenbergplatz
A timetable can be obtained at transport authority offices and at tobacco shops (Tabak-Trafik).
The cheapest way of getting around Vienna is to buy one of the various season tickets:
Vienna Sampler Ticket (Wiener Schnupperkarte), valid on weekdays between 8am and 8pm on all public transport routes within the inner city zone.
24-hour or 72-hour Season Ticket, valid for all public

transport routes for the given period. Transferable.

8-day "Green" Ticket, valid for eight days (not necessarily in succession) on the entire network. Can be used by more than one person at a time, provided the correct number of strips has been cancelled.

Single Tickets can be bought individually or in blocks of at least five tickets.

Weekly Season Tickets, valid for 7 days within the central zone, and Monthly Season Tickets, are not transferable.

Senior Citizens (women over 60, men over 65), can buy Senior Citizens' Tickets which entitle them to two journeys. **Children** under six years of age travel free in the inner zone. During school holidays and on Sundays and public holidays children between the ages of six and 15 also travel free. Normally they travel for half the adult price.

Normal tickets can be bought from the conductor or at tobacco shops (Tabak-Trafik) as well as transport authority ticket offices. Such tickets are also valid for journeys into the surrounding region; an extra strip is cancelled for each zone you enter. Tickets must be cancelled when first used. Ticket machines do not give change.

The city has eight Night Bus Routes, along which the buses run during the nights Friday–Saturday and Saturday–Sunday as well as before public holidays. Tickets must be purchased on the bus.

Further information can be obtained from the Customer Service Department of the Vienna Transport Authority, tel: 501 30 2357 (open Monday–Friday 8am–3pm), or at the following underground stations: Karlsplatz, Stephansplatz, Praterstern, Philadelphiabrücke, Volkstheater, Landstrasse, tel: 587 3186.

Where to Stay

Vienna is a great centre of hospitality; few cities in the world have such a long-established tradition of looking after visitors. The Austrian hotel industry enjoys a high international reputation, with even the smallest hotels showing the same typically conservative attention to detail that marks them out from international business hotel chains.

During the high season, it is often very hard to find suitable accommodation, so early booking is highly recommended. It is also very difficult to live cheaply in Vienna. If your budget is limited, you will find much more affordable places to stay outside the city centre but still within easy reach by public transport.

The majority of hotels are in the 1st district of Vienna, which makes the best base for exploring the city on foot. This area is also home to the main theatres and concert halls, as well as the best restaurants and bars. If you come to Vienna for pleasure, you should definitely consider staying within the Ring.

All prices include value added tax, and most include breakfast. The main difference between pensions and hotels is that the former are smaller and tend to be family-owned.

Some hotels put a surcharge of up to 200 percent on telephone calls.

The **Vienna Tourist Office** (see page 229) produces a brochure with details of accommodation

suitable for disabled visitors; this is also available from *Österreich-Werbung*.

If you arrive in Vienna without having booked accommodation, you can obtain details of rooms from tourist information offices (see page 229).

Hotel Listings

LUXURY (FIVE-STAR)
Bristol
I, Kärntner Ring 1.
Tel: 5 1516-0, fax: 5 1516 550.
An Art Nouveau building dating from 1884; rather more intimate than many other five-star hotels. Its restaurant, the Korso, is popular with hotel guests and outsiders alike for its light Viennese cuisine and distinguished wine list.

Im Palais Schwarzenberg
III, Schwarzenbergplatz 9.
Tel: 7 98 47 14, fax: 7 98 45 15.
Wonderfully furnished, and located in one wing of a Baroque royal palace with a superbly romantic view of the park, all just a stone's throw from the city centre.

Imperial
I, Kärntner Ring 16.
Tel: 5 0110-0, fax: 5 0110 410.
Official guests of state, actors and leading pop stars stay in the Imperial, with its 128 elegant rooms and suites. Definitely the place to be seen, and the Zur Majestät restaurant is one of the best and most expensive in Vienna.

Sacher
I, Philharmonikerstrasse 4.
Tel: 5 14 56, fax: 5 14 578 10.
Archdukes, ministers and senior army officers used to stay here, and the Sacher is still the city's most famous hotel. Past its heyday, perhaps, but you can still be sure of top-class service.

Vienna Marriott
I, Parkring 12a.
Tel: 51 518-0, fax: 51 51 866 72.
A postmodern glass building opposite the park.

Vienna Plaza
I, Schottenring 11.
Tel: 3 13 90-0, fax: 3 13 90-160.
A recently built and very elegant
Art Nouveau-style hotel.

FIRST-CLASS (FOUR-STAR)
Astoria
I, Kärtner Strasse 32–34.
Tel: 5 15 77-0, fax: 5 15 77-82.
A civilised old hotel immediately
behind the Staatsoper.
Biedermeier im Sünnhof
III, Landstrasser Hauptstrasse 28.
Tel: 7 16 71-0, fax: 71 67 1-5 03.
A uniquely attractive set of
restored Biedermeier-style
buildings, complete with original
shopping arcade.
Clima-Villenhotel
XIV, Nussberggasse 2c.
Tel: 37 15 16, fax: 37 13 92.
Located in a villa district at the
foot of the Nussberg, well
outside the city centre; ideal for
a bit of peace and fresh air.
König von Ungarn
I, Schulerstrasse 10.
Tel: 51 58 4-0, fax: 51 58 48.
Centrally located only metres
from the Stephansdom, and over
400 years old, this hotel is full of
old-fashioned charm. It has
everything you would expect of a
four-star hotel, and the glass-
roofed inner courtyard is
particularly attractive.
Mailbergerhof
I, Annagasse 7.
Tel: 51 20 64 1, fax: 51 20 64
1-10. An old building with a very
modern interior, located in the
pedestrian area of the city centre.
Parkhotel Schönbrunn
XIII, Hietzinger Hauptstrasse 12.
Tel: 87 80 4, fax: 87 80 4-32 20.
Very close to the palace and
gardens of Schönbrunn, this
hotel formerly housed the
Kaiser's guests. It is still redolent
of the imperial past.

Vienna Penta Renaissance
III, Ungargasse 60.
Tel: 71 17 5-0, fax: 71 17 5-90.
One of the city's newest and
architecturally most striking
hotels, but slightly off the
beaten track, ten minutes by
tram from the Ringstrasse.

MID-RANGE (THREE-STAR)
Kärtnerhof
I, Grashofgasse 4.
Tel: 5 12 19 23, fax: 5 13 22 28.
Pleasantly quiet, despite its
central location.
Schild
XIX, Neustift am Walde 97–99.
Tel: 44 21 910, fax: 44 21 91 53.
This 20-room hotel is a paradise
for wine connoisseurs, since it is
surrounded by *Heurige* – bars
selling new wine made on the
premises.
Schweizerhof
I, Bauernmarkt 22.
Tel: 53 31 93 1, fax: 63 02 14.
Relatively inexpensive, despite
its very central position.
Wandl
I, Petersplatz 9.
Tel: 5 34 55-0, fax: 5 34 55-77.
Immediately behind the
Peterskirche, and thus very
much at the hub of things.
Zur Wiener Staatsoper
I, Krugerstrasse 11.
Tel: 5 13 12 74-0, fax: 5 13 12
74-15. Newly renovated and, as
its name suggests, close to the
opera and thus popular with
singers.

SIMPLE (TWO-STAR)
Cyrus
X, Laxenburger Strasse 14.
Tel: 62 25 78, fax 6 04 42 88.
Familes particularly welcome. 20
rooms, eight with bath or
shower.
Kugel
VII, Siebensterngasse 43.
Tel: 5 23 33 55, fax: 5 23 16 78.
Small, clean rooms, located in
the middle of the shopping
district.
Rathaus
VIII, Lange Gasse 13.
Tel: 4 06 43 02, fax: 4 08 42 72.
Inexpensive rooms with the
advantage of being right in the
middle of the lively Josefstadt
district, with its countless small
bars.

VERY SIMPLE (ONE-STAR)
Baltic
VIII, Skodagasse 15.
Tel: 4 05 62 66.
Family hotel with 27 rooms.

Pensions

FIRST-CLASS (FOUR-STAR)
Arenberg
I, Stubenring 2.
Tel: 5 12 52 91, fax: 5 13 93 56.
The doyen among pensions, with
a plush, elegant atmosphere
and excellent location.

MID-RANGE (THREE-STAR)
Hayd
VI, Mariahilfer Strasse 57–59.
Tel: 5 87 44 14, fax: 5 86 19 50.
Simple, mid-range pension in a
not exactly quiet area. Only a few
minutes from the centre by U-
Bahn.
Nossek
I, Graben 17.
Tel: 5 33 70 41, fax: 5 35 36 46.
Small, cosy pension in the heart
of Vienna.

SIMPLE (TWO-STAR)
Wildenauer
X, Quellenstrasse 120.
Tel: 6 04 21 53, fax: 6 02 24 85.
Family pension.

Youth Hostels

Charges per night range between öS 130 and öS 250.

Hostel Ruthensteiner
XV, Robert Hamerling-Gasse 24.
Tel: 89 34 20 2, fax: 8 93 27 96.
Open all year except over
Christmas and New Year.

Jugendgästehaus der Stadt Wien
XIII, Schlossberggasse 8.
Tel: 8 77 15 01-0, fax: 87 70 26 32. Open all year.

Jugendgästehaus Wien Brigittenau
XX, Friedrich-Engels-Platz 24.
Tel: 3 32 82 94-0, fax: 3 30 83 79. Open all year.

Jugendherberge Myrthengasse
VII, Myrthengasse 7.
Tel: 5 23 63 16-0.
Open all year.

Turmherberge Don Bosco
III, Lechnerstrasse 12
Tel: 7 13 14 94.
Open March to November.

Campsites

Campingplatz der Stadt Wien West I
XIV, Hüttelbergstrasse 40
Tel: 9 14 14 49.
Open in August only.

Campingplatz der Stadt Wien West II
XIV, Hüttelbergstrasse 80
Tel: 9 14 23 14, fax: 9 11 35 94.
Open all year except February.

Campingplatz der Stadt Wien Süd
XXIII, Breitenfurterstrasse 267.
Tel: 8 65 92 18.
Open July and August only.

Camping Rodaun
XXIII, An der Au 2, Rodaun.
Tel: 8 88 41 54.
Open March to September only.

Campingplatz Schloss Laxenburg
Münchendorfer Strasse, A 2361
Laxenburg, Nord-Österreich.
Tel: (0 22 36) 7 13 33.
Open mid-April to October.

Where to Eat & Drink

Viennese Cuisine

We have already dealt with Viennese cuisine in detail; this has been influenced over a long period by the many Italian, Czech, Yugoslavian, French and Turkish restaurants in the city. Particularly since the borders with eastern Europe have been opened, Vienna receives almost as many visitors from the east as from the west, and the range of international restaurants has grown even wider.

An up-to-date monthly restaurant guide is published in *Wiener* magazine.

LUXURY RESTAURANTS

(Set menu öS 600–1,500)
Do&Co
I, Stephansplatz 12.
Tel: 5 35 39 69-18.
Open daily from noon to 3pm and 6pm to midnight. A city-centre venue in which to see and be seen. Enjoy the superb view of the cathedral, colourful interior design, friendly service and outstanding food, with a Japanese Tepan-Yaki grill every Tuesday and Saturday.

Korso
I, Mahlerstrasse 2.
Tel: 5 15 16-0.
Open Sun–Fri from noon to 2pm and 7pm to 1am; closed at lunchtimes in July and August. The place for connoisseurs of new Austrian cuisine. Chef Reinhard Gerer offers an impressive range of dishes, from potato goulash and tripe to experimental creations like skate wings and morel ravioli, and there is a range of rare Austrian and foreign wines.

Schwarzenberg
III, Schwarzenbergplatz 9.
Tel: 7 98 45 15-6 00.
Open daily from noon to 3pm and 6pm to 11pm. An unforgettable evening's dining in the conservatory, with a superb set menu, a glass of wine and the dulcet tones of the Wiener Staatsoper orchestra wafting over from the park next door. As you might expect, this unique setting doesn't come cheap.

Zu den drei Husaren
I, Weihburggasse 4.
Tel: 5 12 10 92.
Open daily from noon to 3pm and 6pm to 1am. Good, traditional Viennese cuisine served by candlelight, complete with waltz music and a stylish interior. The starters and desserts are particularly recommended.

OLD VIENNESE SPECIALITIES

Augustinerkeller
I, Augustinerstrasse 1.
Tel: 5 33 10 26.
Traditional food in the shadow of the Hofburg. Mid-price.

Hietzinger Bräu
XIII, Auhofstrasse 1.
Tel: 8 77 70 87.
Open daily from 11.30am to 3pm and 6pm to 11.30pm. This is the place to go if you're partial to beef. If you haven't sampled the delights of Hüferl, Schulterscherzl and Meise, then now's your chance; there are over 15 different beef dishes on the menu. There are also plenty of other traditional Viennese creations to choose from. Mid-price.

Piaristenkeller
VIII, Piaristengasse 45.
Tel: 4 06 01 93-0.
Old Viennese eatery in Josefstadt, with good, wholesome food in upmarket surroundings. Mid-price.

Zum Alten Heller
III, Ungargasse 34.
Tel: 7 12 64 52.
Open Tue–Sat from 9.30am to
11pm. Very similar to the Zum
Herkner (see below), but without
the celebrity clientele. Mid-price.

Zum Herkner
XVII, Dornbacher Strasse 123.
Tel: 45 43 86.
Open Mon–Fri from 9am to
11pm. Unfortunately, the
glitterati have discovered this
little suburban bar and
restaurant, but the food is still
the kind that grandmother used
to make. Mid-price.

CHEAP AND AUTHENTIC
Schweizerhaus
II, Strasse des 1. Mai 116.
Tel: 7 28 01 52.
Open March to mid-November
daily from 10am to midnight.
Particularly recommended if
you've just been to the Prater
and the kids have spent all your
money. Leave them in the
children's playground to work off
any energy they may have left,
and relax with a draught beer in
the tree-shaded garden.
Particularly recommended:
gegrillte Stelzen (grilled knuckle
of pork).

Zwölf-Apostel-Keller
I, Sonnenfelsgasse 3.
Tel: 5 12 67 77.
Popular city-centre restaurant
offering good food and
traditional Viennese specialities.

International Cuisine

FRENCH
Salut
I, Wildpretmarkt 3.
Tel: 5 33 35 81.
Fish specialities are particularly
recommended.

GREEK
Der Grieche
VI, Barnabitengasse 5.
Tel: 5 87 74 66.
Schwarze Katze
VI, Girardigasse 6.
Tel: 5 87 06 25.

All Aboard!
Enjoy a meal on the "beautiful
blue Danube" at floating
restaurant **Johann Strauss**, I,
Schwedenplatz-Kleine Donau,
tel: 5 33 93 67. (In fact the
river is not beautiful or blue,
nor has it ever been!)

INDIAN
Demi Tass
IV, Prinz-Eugen-Strasse 28.
Tel: 5 04 31 19.
Exclusive, and the prices are
astronomical, but the food is
very, very good.
Koh-i-noor
I, Marc-Aurel-Strasse 8.
Tel: 5 33 00 80.
The strains of the sitar and the
hiss of the charcoal grill provide
a sonorous accompaniment to
meals in this smart restaurant.
Maharadscha
I, Gölsdorfgasse 1.
Tel: 5 33 74 43. Vienna's oldest
Indian restaurant, offering good,
3-star-quality food.

ITALIAN
Cantinetta
I, Jasomirgottstrasse 3–5.
Tel: 5 35 20 66.
A unique restaurant located in
the meat district but specialising
in exquisite fish dishes.
Da Gino e Marija
IV, Rechte Wienzeile 17.
Tel: 5 87 45 70.
Three stars.
Da Luciano
VII, Sigmundsgasse 14.
Tel: 5 23 77 78.
Three stars.
Firenze Enoteca
I, Singerstrasse 3
Tel: 5 13 43 74.
Three stars.
Grotta Azzurra
I, Babenbergerstrasse 5
Tel: 5 86 10 44.
Although not exactly cheap, they
don't come much better than
this superb range of antipasti,
pasta, and fish and meat dishes.
Four stars.

JEWISH
Ma Pitom
I, Seitenstettengasse 5.
Tel: 5 35 43 13.
This restaurant shows just how
well Jewish and Italian dishes go
together.

RUSSIAN
Feuervogel
IX, Alserbachstrasse 21.
Tel: 3 17 53 91.
Excellent, but expensive.

TURKISH
Kervansaray
I, Mahlerstrasse 9.
Tel: 5 12 88 43.
Five stars.

Vegetarian

Wrenkh
XIV, Hollergasse 9, tel: 8 92 33
56, and Bauernmarkt 10, tel: 5
33 15 26.
Open Mon–Sat 11.30am to
2.30pm and 6pm to midnight. At
last, a place for vegetarians and
healthy eaters. When you've had
enough of all that rich Viennese
cooking, come here instead for
first-class food, excellent wines
and a cosy atmosphere.

Fast Food, Snacks & Pizzas

Naschmarkt
I, Schwarzenbergplatz 16; 1
Schottengasse 1; 4 Mariahilfer
Strasse 85–87.
Nordsee
I, Kärntner Strasse 25; 1
Kohlmarkt 6; 4 Naschmarkt; 7
Mariahilfer Strasse 34.
Pizzeria Adriatic
I, Habsburgergasse 6–8.
Pizzeria Grenadier
I, Kärntner Strasse 41.
Pizza-Paradise
IV, Mariahilfer Strasse 85–87.
Schwarzes Kameel
I, Bognergasse 5.
Now a delicatessen, Art-
Nouveau restaurant and
sandwich bar; full of history,
since Beethoven used to eat

FAST FOOD (continued)

here, and has become distinctly trendy over recent years.

Trzesniewski
I, Dorotheergasse 1.
Filled rolls, cider and beer.

Beisel

You will find a *Beisel*, or little local bar/restaurant, on just about every street corner in Vienna. Their simplicity reflects the uncomplicated culture and traditions of Vienna; the wine is basic table wine; the food is good home cooking; and the prices won't break the bank. Unfortunately, some have developed into fashionable bars and top-class restaurants over recent years. The best way to recognise a real *Beisel* is to check whether the owners do the cooking and pull the beer themselves, and whether the menu is written on a slate.

Bei Max
I, Landhausgasse 2.
Tel: 5 33 73 59.
Closed Saturdays, Sundays and public holidays. Unusually quiet for a *Beisel*, and offering excellent food.

Figlmüller
I, Wollzeile 5.
Tel: 5 12 61 77.
The home of the city's biggest *Wiener Schnitzel*, so large that they stick out way over the side of the plate. A small *Beisel* decorated in traditional style, with the wine list and menu written on blackboards. Deservedly popular with tourists.

Oswald und Kalb
I, Bäckerstrasse 14.
Tel: 5 12 13 71.
A slightly spartan interior and a clientele of tourists, celebrities and people trying to wind down after a hard day. The food is excellent, but usually lukewarm because there are too many customers and not enough waiters.

Pfudl
I, Bäckerstrasse 22.
Tel: 5 12 67 05.
Country-style atmosphere, finely prepared traditional Viennese cuisine, and speedy service.

Salzamt
I, Ruprechtsplatz 1.
Tel: 5 33 53 32.
Closed Sat, Sun and public holidays. Beautiful interior and young, fashionable clientele, but the food is not that imaginative. However, it does serve very tasty noodle-based dishes, which is unusual for a *Beisel*.

Weincomptoir
I, Bäckerstrasse 6.
Tel: 5 12 17 60.
Sample the best in Austrian and international wines at the round bar of this three-storey building, and enjoy the finest food of any *Beisel* in Vienna.

Witwe Bolte
VI, Gutenberggasse 13.
Tel: 5 23 14 50.
Excellent traditional Viennese home cooking in the oldest and most basic *Beisel* in the Spittelberg district.

Witwe Bolte
XVI, Gallitzinstrasse 12.
Tel: 46 31 65.
After a plate of juicy roast pork and a bottle of wine here, all your cares will melt away.

Zu den 3 Hacken
I, Singerstrasse 8.
Tel: 5 12 58 95.
Closed Sun and public holidays. A veritable temple for lovers of Viennese cuisine. The menu is big, and so are the portions. Very popular with the locals, so advance booking essential.

Heurige Outside Vienna

More traditional *Heurige* and *Buschenschanken* than exist in Vienna can be found in every wine-growing town and village. These open for only a few days a year, or at weekends, and the Viennese like to keep the identities of the best ones to

Heurige

You haven't seen Vienna properly until you've paid a visit to a *Heurige*. Both *Heurige* and *Buschenschanken* are places where new wine is sold by the wine-grower, and are recognisable by the wreaths or branches hanging outside the door. They often have beautiful gardens in which you can sample the latest vintage in the shade of chestnut trees or even the grapevine itself; most have music and a buffet.

City Centre
Zwölf-Apostel-Keller
I, Sonnenfelsgasse 3.
Tel: 5 12 67 77.
Open daily 4.30pm to midnight. This well-known city-centre *Heurige* has a historic wine cellar on two floors, and serves good wines and hot food.

Grinzing
Mayer am Pfarrplatz
XIX, Heiligenstädter Pfarrplatz 2.
Tel: 37 12 87.
Open from 4pm to midnight. Beethoven wrote the *Eroica* symphony here, and today the Mayer family are continuing to compose their own award-winning wines. The wonderful garden shaded by chestnut trees and the generous buffet make this place a unique experience.

Sirbu
XIX, Kahlenberger Strasse 210.
Tel: 3 20 59 28.
Open from April to mid-October, Mon–Sat 3pm to midnight. This romantic little *Heurige* nestles

themselves. You can discover them by keeping an eye out for the branches hanging above the door. Look in Sievering, Neustift am Walde, Stammersdorf, Strebersdorf, the Wienerwald and as far south as Sooss.

amid vine-covered hillsides. It has a superb garden and a spectacular view of Vienna, particularly after dark.

Weingut Reinprecht
XIX, Cobenzlgasse 22.
Tel: 32 01 47.
Everything that a *Heurige* should be: excellent local wines, a large and varied buffet, traditional Viennese melodies in the background, and a large terraced garden.

Neustift am Walde
Fuhrgassl-Huber
XIX, Neustift am Walde 68.
Tel: 4 40 14 05.
If you prefer something a little more rustic, don't miss the earthy atmosphere of this *Heurige*. On days when it's too cold to sit outside in the magnificent garden, warm yourself indoors with a plate of sucking pig, grilled chicken and other choice items from the buffet.

Ottakring
10er Marie
XVI, Ottakringer Strasse 222–224. Tel: 4 89 46 47.
This particular *Heurige* was established in 1740, and was named after a winegrower's daughter in the 19th century.

Sievering
Braunsperger
XIX, Sieveringer Strasse 108.
Tel: 3 20 39 92.
If you have a particular interest in genuine local grape varieties, then don't miss this *Heurige*. *Weissburgunder, roter Zweigelt* and *Grüner Veltliner* are among those on offer, while *Gemischter Satz* is a blend of different grape varieties which are picked and pressed together.
Zum Heiligen Nepomuk
XIX, Sieveringer Strasse 58.
Tel: 3 20 58 51.
Named after the statue of St Nepomuk outside the building, this *Heurige* has been owned by the Schreiber family since the

17th century. The old Viennese courtyard attracts people from all over the city and the surrounding area.

Stammersdorf
Gerhard Klager
XXI, Stammersdorfer Strasse 14. Tel: 2 92 41 07.
Open Tue–Sat from 3pm to midnight. This *Heurige* is a real experience, particularly for children, who have their very own playground to play in while the grownups sample fine wines and high-quality food. If you're driving, try the delicious low-alcohol grape must instead.

Strebersdorf
Hubert Andrae
XXI, Russbergstrasse 88.
Tel: 2 90 14 76.
Wine-grower Hubert Andreas has earned widespread praise for his truly excellent wine. His vines grow on the sunny slopes of the Bisamberg, and the experience amassed by his family over the past hundred years has stood him in good stead.

Coffee Houses

The Viennese coffee-house tradition goes back 300 years. People take their coffee seriously here, and it is served in a wide variety of ways, always with a glass of water.
Alt Wien
I, Bäckerstrasse 9.
Tel: 5 12 52 22.
A café for world-weary travellers, literati, artists and philosophers, or those who think they are.
Alte Backstube
VIII, Lange Gasse 34.
Tel: 4 06 11 01.
Not so much a café as a museum, with lots of old kitchen utensils hanging on the wall, and a 250-year-old oven.
Bräunerhof
I, Stallburggasse 2.
Tel: 5 12 38 93.
Popular city-centre café with a wide selection of *Torten*. Once

Viennese Coffees

- *Kleiner/Grosser Brauner* – small/large white coffee
- *Kleiner/Grosser Mokka* – small/large black coffee
- *Einspänner* – black coffee with whipped cream, served in a glass
- *Fiaker* – black coffee with rum
- *Mokka gespritzt* – black coffee with cognac
- *Kapuziner* – small cup of coffee with a drop of cream
- *Piccolo* – small black coffee, with or without whipped cream
- *Melange* – Large cup of coffee with lots of milk

Important: Never order just "Kaffee", and if you must use the word, make sure you stress the first syllable, Austrian-style. If you get it wrong, you risk incurring the waiter's disdain.

the haunt of the famous modern writer, Thomas Bernhard.
Café Engländer
I, Postgasse 2.
Tel: 5 12 27 34.
An all-day café for anyone who's anyone in Vienna. A variety of breakfasts are served in the morning, followed by sandwiches and filled rolls at lunchtime, and hot food until late at night.
Café Museum
I, Friedrichstrasse 6.
Tel: 5 86 52 02.
Dominated by artists, students and professors from the nearby Academy of the Visual Arts.
Café in der Secession
I, Friedrichstrasse 12.
Tel: 5 86 93 86.
Distinctively decorated with brightly coloured tiles contrasting with typical café-style furniture. Beautiful view of the Karlskirche.
Diglas
I, Wollzeile 10.
Tel. 5 12 57 65-0.
Traditional old coffee house near Stephansplatz, with incredibly large *Torten* in the window.

COFFEE HOUSES (continued)

Drechsler
VI, Linke Wienzeile 22.
Tel: 5 87 85 80.
A shabby but superb place where the customers are the main attraction.

Frauenhuber
I, Himmelpfortgasse 6.
Tel. 5 12 43 23.
Everything you'd always imagined a Viennese café to be.

Goldegg
IV, Argentinierstrasse 49.
Tel: 5 05 91 62.
A place to just sit and enjoy a *Melange* in peace and quiet.

Hartauer
I, Riemergasse 9.
Tel: 5 12 89 81.
Definitely the place to be if you're an opera fan.

Hawelka
I, Dorotheergasse 6.
Tel: 5 12 82 30.
Still stylish and studenty, though its great days as an artists' café with celebrity customers are long since past, and the tourists have moved in. The *Buchteln* (baked yeast dumplings) are legendary, but are served only after 10pm.

Hohlnstein & Schellmann
IX, Währinger Strasse 6.
Tel: 3 17 14 73.
Young academics come here to engage in heated discussion.

Landtmann
I, Dr-Karl-Lueger-Ring 4.
Tel: 5 32 06 21.
Right beside the Burgtheater, and a rendezvous for actors, politicians and publishers.

Prückl
I, Stubenring 24.
Tel: 5 12 43 39.
Popular 1950s café with piano music at weekends.

Schlosscafé Parkhotel Schönbrunn
XIII, Hietzinger Hauptstrasse 10–14, tel: 8 78 04-0.

Zartl
III, Rasumofskygasse 7.
Tel: 7 12 55 60.
Evening events include music and literary readings.

Cake Shops

A traditionally more family-oriented place than the *Kaffeehäus* in Vienna is the *Konditorei* (patisserie). Among the best are:

● **Demel**, I, Kohlmarkt 14, tel: 5 35 17 17-0. An absolute must if you have a sweet tooth.

● **Gerstner**, I, Kärntner Strasse 11–15, tel: 5 12 49 63-0. The former patissier to the Imperial and royal courts; there's still not much you can teach them about making fine pastries.

● **Heiner**, I, Kärntner Strasse 21–23, tel: 5 12 68 63. Particularly renowned for its scrumptious meringues.

● **Lehmann**, I, Graben 12, tel: 5 12 18 15. Viennese ladies who lunch like to pop in here after a hard morning's shopping.

● **Sacher**, I, Philharmonikerstrasse 4, tel: 51 45 78 46. Cream cakes for the cream of Viennese society, if your budget and your waistline will stretch to it. Or buy some of the world-famous *Sachertorte* and have it gift-wrapped so you can send it home to impress your friends.

● **Sluka**, I, Rathausplatz 8, tel: 4 05 71 72. Excellent *Strudel*.

Nightlife

Discos

Atrium
IV, Schwindgasse 1, tel: 505 3594.

Bijou Bar im Parkhotel Schönbrunn
III, Hietzinger Hauptstrasse 10–20, tel: 878 040.

Move
VIII, Daungasse 1, tel: 406 32 78.

U4
XII, Schönbrunner Strasse 222, tel: 815 8307.

Cabaret

Cabaret Fledermaus
I, Spiegelgasse 2, tel: 512 8438.

Casanova Revuetheater
I, Dorotheergasse 6–8, tel: 512 9845.

Freie Bühne Wieden
IV, Wiedner Hauptstrasse 60b, tel: 586 2122.

Hernalser Stadttheater im Metropol
XVII, Geblergasse 50, tel: 433 543.

Heurigenkabarett "Spitzbuben"
XIX, Hackhofergasse 13, tel: 371 285.

Kabarett & Komödie am Naschmarkt
VI, Linke Wienzeile 4, tel: 587 2275.

Kabarett Niedermair
VIII, Lenaugasse 1a, tel: 408 4492.

Kabarett Simpl
I, Wollzeile 36, tel: 512 4742.

Kulisse
XVII, Rosensteingasse 39, tel: 453 870.

Spektakel
V, Hamburger Strasse 14, tel: 587 0653.

Nightclubs with Cabaret

Casanova Revue-Bar-Theater
I, Dorotheergasse 6–8, tel: 512 9845.
Eden Bar Cabaret
I, Liliengasse 2, tel: 512 7450.
Eve-Bar-Cabaret
I, Führichgasse 3, tel: 512 5452.
Fledermaus, I, Spiegelgasse 2, tel: 512 8438.
Moulin Rouge
I, Walfischgasse 11, tel: 512 2130.

Late-night Venues

Beatrixstüberl
III, Ungargasse 8, tel: 725 876.
Café Drechsler
VI, Linke Wienzeile 22, tel: 587 8580. Open until 4am.
Café Kammerspiele
I, Rotenturmstrasse 25, tel: 533 3210.
Jazzland
I, Franz-Josefs-Kai 29, tel: 533 2575.
Jazz Spelunke
VI, Dürergasse 3, tel: 587 0126.
Klimt Bar im Hilton
III, Am Stadtpark, tel: 717 000.
Porta
I, Schulerstrasse 6, tel: 513 1493.
Queen Anne
I, Johannesgasse 12, tel: 512 0203.
Tenne
I, Annagasse 3, tel: 525 708.
Wurlitzer
I, Schwarzenbergplatz 10, tel: 650 311.

Casinos

● **Spiel Casino Wien**, I, Kärntner Strasse 41, tel: 512 4836. Open daily from 5pm.
● **Spiel Casino Baden**, Baden bei Wien, im Kurpark, tel: (02252) 4496. Open daily from 4pm.

Culture

Popular Music

Jazz
Café Wortner, IV, Wiedner Hauptstrasse 55, tel: 505 3291.
Jazz-Leit, XVI, Habichergasse 15, tel: 950 721.
Metropol, XVII, Hernalser Hauptstrasse 55, tel: 433 543.
Miles Smiles, VIII, Lange Gasse 51, tel: 428 4814.
Opus One, I, Mahlerstrasse 11, tel: 513 2075.

Country
Café Verde, VII, Gardegasse 3, tel: 939 171.
Nashville, V, Siebenbrunnengasse 5a, tel: 557 389.

Latin
Arauco, III, Krummgasse 1a, tel: 715 6397.
America Latina, VI, Mollardgasse 17, tel: 597 3269.
Macondo, V, Hamburger Strasse 11, tel: 567 742.

Rock & New Wave
Blue Box, VII, Richtergasse 8, tel: 932 682.
Szene Wien, XI, Hauffgasse 26, tel: 743 341.
Arena, III, Verlängerte Baumgasse, Franzosengraben, tel: 788 596.

Classical Music

Some twenty classical ensembles live and work in Vienna. If they are not away on tour, they perform in the various concert halls and churches

throughout the city. During the "Musical Summer" there are also open-air concerts on historic squares and in the city's parks.
Bösendorfer Saal, IV, Graf-Starhemberg-Gasse 14, tel: 504 6651.
Konzerthaus, III, Lothringer Strasse 20, tel: 721 211.
Musikverein, I, Bösendorferstrasse 12, tel: 505 8681.
Sophiensäle, III, Marxergasse/Blattgasse, tel: 722 196.
State Opera House, I, Opernring 2, tel: 51444 2959.
Volksoper Wien, IX, Währinger Strasse 78, tel: 51444 2959.
Vienna Boys' Choir, II, Obere Augartenstrasse 1, tel: 588 04141.
Wiener Kammeroper, I, Fleischmarkt 24, tel: 513 6072.

Theatre

Ticket Sales
The Vienna Tourist Office produces a monthly programme magazine listing all events which will take place in the city during that period: theatre, concerts, cabaret, lectures, readings, symposia and exhibitions. However, the office does not sell tickets for the various events. At least 14 days in advance, non-residents can order tickets either by telephone or in writing from the **National Theatre Association**, Hanusschgasse 3, A-1010 Vienna (fax: 51444 2969). Applications must reach the association at least seven days before the event in question. Holders of credit cards (Air Plus, Amex, Diners, Visa, MasterCard and Eurocard) can book from six days before the performance by phone, tel: 513 1513. **Daily programme information** can be obtained by tel: 1518.

   The **Vienna Ticket Service** sells tickets for the **Music Association**, the **Konzerthaus**, the **Theater an der Wien** and the **Raimundtheater** (tel: 534 1363, fax: 534 1379).

Tickets for the Vienna Boys' Choir performances in the Imperial Chapel and for dramatic and musical performances in private theatres can be obtained from **ticket offices** (see below) or on the evening of the performance at the box office.
American Express, I, Kärntner Strasse 21–23, tel: 515 110.
ATT Reisen, I, Josefsplatz 6, tel: 512 4466.
Kartenbüro Alserstrasse, tel: 405 13 72.
Karten-Insel am Naschmarkt, I, Lobkowitzplatz 3, tel: 512 36 43.
Kartenbüro Kehleudorfer, I, Krugerstrasse 3, tel: 512 6312.
Kartenbüro Hoberg, I, Schottenring 3, tel: 319 7840.

State Theatre
Akademietheater, III, Lisztstrasse 1, tel: 51444 2959.
Burgtheater, I, Dr. Karl-Lueger-Ring 2, tel: 51444 2959.
Staatsoper (State Opera), I, Opernring 2, tel: 51444 2959.
Volksoper (Folk Opera), IX, Währinger Strasse 78, tel: 51444 2959.

Private Theatre
Dramatisches Zentrum, VII, Seidengasse 13, tel: 961 556-0.
Ensemble Theater am Petersplatz, I, Petersplatz 2, tel: 535 3200.
Kammeroper, I, Fleischmarkt 24, tel: 513 6072.
Kammerspiele, I, Rotenturmstrasse 20, tel: 533 2833.
Raimundtheater, VI, Wallgasse 18–20, tel: 599 7727.
Theater an der Wien, VI, Lehargasse 5, tel: 588 30265.
Theater Gruppe 80, VI, Gumpendorfer Strasse 67, tel: 565 222.
Theater in der Josefstadt, IX, Josefstädter Strasse 26, tel: 402 5127.

Volkstheater, VII, Neustiftgasse 1, tel: 932 776.

Small Stages
Ateliertheater, VI, Linke Wienzeile 4, tel: 587 8214.
Auersperg 15, VIII, Auerspergstrasse 15, tel: 430 707.
Drachengasse-2-Theater, I, Fleischmarkt 22, tel: 513 1444.
Experiment am Liechtenwerd, IX, Liechtensteinstrasse 132, tel: 314 108.
Graumanntheater, XV, Graumanngasse 39, tel: 535 1245.
International Theater, IX, Porzellangasse 8, tel: 913 6272.
Kleine Komödie, I, Walfischgasse 4, tel: 512 4280.
Pradler Ritterspiele, I, Bibergasse 2, tel: 512 5400.
Spielraum, XIV, Palmgasse, tel: 713 0460.
Theater am Schwedenplatz, I, Franz-Josefs-Kai 21, tel: 535 7914.

Theatre Prices

Approximate prices are:
● **Vienna State Opera** (Staatsoper): category I up to öS 800, category VI up to öS 1,800.
● **Folk Opera** (Volksoper): category I up to öS 250, category IV up to öS 500.
● **Vienna State Theatre** (Burgtheater): up to öS 500.
● **Akademietheater**: up to öS 500.
● **Theater in der Josefstadt**: up to öS 490.
● **Kammerspiele**: up to öS 440.
● **Volkstheater**: up to öS 470.
● **VT Studio**: up to öS 125.
● **Theater an der Wien**: up to öS 540.
● **Raimundtheater**: up to öS 520.
● **Academy of Music**: öS 40 to 450.
● **Konzerthaus**: öS 60 to 750.
● **Burgkapelle**: öS 50 to 120.

Theater Brett, VI, Münzwardeingasse 2, tel: 587 0663.
Theater Die Tribüne, I, Dr. Karl-Lueger-Ring 4, tel: 533 8485.
Vienna's English Theatre, VIII, Josefsgasse 12, tel: 402 1260.

Marionette & Puppet Theatres
Arlequin Marionettentheater, I, Maysedergasse 5, tel: 341 9043.
Urania Puppenspiele, I, Uraniastrasse 1, tel: 712 8191.

Galleries

Vienna has a lively gallery scene; the selection listed below will help you to gain an impression of the city's artistic life. Most galleries lie in the district behind St Stephen's Cathedral.
Galerie Ariadne, I, Bäckerstrasse 6, tel: 512 9479.
Galerie Contact im Palais Rottal, I, Singerstrasse 17, tel: 512 9880.
Galerie Julius Hummel, I, Bäckerstrasse 14, tel: 512 1296.
Galerie Krinzinger, I, Seilerstätte 16, tel: 513 3006.
Galerie nächst St Stephan, I, Grünangergasse 1, tel: 512 1266.
Galerie Peter Pakesch, I, Ballgasse 6, tel: 512 4814.
Galerie Würthle, I, Weihburggasse 9, tel: 512 2312.

Literary & Cultural Institutes

Afro-Asian Institute, IX, Türkenstrasse 3, tel: 310 51 45.
Albert Schweitzer House, IX, Schwarzspanierstrasse 13, tel: 425 265.
Alte Schmiede (Vienna Artists' Association), I, Schönlaterngasse 9, tel: 408 06 95.
Amerlinghaus, VII, Stiftgasse 8, tel: 523 64 75.
Astro Box, VII, Burggasse 9, tel: 526 11 47.

Buddhist Centre, I, Fleischmarkt 16, tel: 513 98 36.
Café America Latina, VI, Turmburggasse 7, tel: 597 92 69.
International Cultural Institute, I, Opernring 7, tel: 586 7321.
International Meditation Society, I, Biberstrasse 22, tel: 512 7859.
Jerry's Verein für kulturelle Kommunikation, IX, Widerhofergasse 5, tel: 310 73 35.
Musisches Zentrum, VIII, Zeltgasse 7, tel: 408 3250.
Österreischischer pen Club, I, Bankgasse 8, tel: 533 4459.
Shakespeare & Co., I, Sterngasse 2, tel: 535 5053.
Theosophical Society of Austria, XVI, Erdenweg 21, tel: 979 22 11; line open until 7pm.
Women's Communication Centre, IX, Wühringer Strasse 9, tel: 408 5057.

Libraries

Austrian National Library (Österreichische Nationalbibliothek), I, Josefsplatz 1, tel: 534 10.
Graphic Collection (Albertina), I, Augustinerstrasse 1, tel: 534 830.
Library of the Austrian Academy of Science (Bibliothek der Österreichischen Akademie der Wissenschaft), I, Dr. Ignaz-Seipel-Platz 2, tel: 515 81-257.
University Library (Universitätsbibliothek), I, Dr. Karl-Lueger-Ring 1, tel: 401 03-2376.

Museums

Vienna has over 50 museums, and no visitor to the city is likely to see them all. Most of them, however, will have at least one exhibition of interest.
Albertina Graphic Collection (Graphische Sammlung Albertina), I, Augustinerstrasse 1, tel: 534 830. Open Monday, Tuesday and Thursday

Museum Opening on Public Holidays

The following museums are open on Easter Sunday, Easter Monday, Whit Sunday and Whit Monday:
● Museum of the History of Art (Kunsthistorisches Museum)
● Schönbrunn Palace
● Imperial Apartments of the Hofburg
● Capuchins' Crypt.

Most museums are closed on:
● Election days
● January 1
● Good Friday
● Easter Sunday
● May 1
● Whit Sunday
● Corpus Christi
● November 1 & 2 (All Saints),
● December 24 & 25.

10am–4pm, Wednesday 10am–6pm, Friday 10am–2pm, Saturday, Sunday 10am–1pm; closed July and August.
Artists' Association (Alte Schmiede), I, Schönlaterngasse 9, tel: 512 44 46. Open Monday–Friday 9am–3pm.
Austrian Film Museum (Österreichisches Filmmuseum), I, Augustinerstrasse 1, tel: 533 7056. Screening of historic films October–May, Monday–Saturday 6pm and 8pm.
Austrian Folklore Museum (Österreichisches Museum für Volkskunde), VIII, Laudongasse 15–19, tel: 406 8905. Open Tuesday–Friday 9am–4pm, Saturday 9am–12 noon, Sunday 9am–1pm.
Austrian Gallery (Österreichische Galerie), III, Prinz-Eugen-Strasse 27 (Management), tel: 795 570. Open daily except Monday 10am–5pm.
Austrian Gallery of the 19th and 20th Centuries (Österreichische Galerie des 19. und 20. Jahrhunderts), IV, Oberes Belvedere, Prinz-Eugen-Strasse 27, tel: 795 570. Open daily except Monday 10am–5pm.
Austrian Museum for Applied Arts (Österreichisches Museum für angewandte Kunst), I, Stubenring 5, tel: 711 360. Open daily except Monday 10am–6pm, Thursday 10am–9pm.
Austrian National Library (Österreichische Nationalbibliothek), I,

Josefsplatz 1, tel: 534 100. Open Monday–Saturday 10am–4pm (11am–noon November–April), Exhibitions: Monday–Saturday 10am–4pm.
Austrian Theatrical Museum (Österreichisches Theatermuseum), I, Hanuschgasse 3, tel: 512 2427. Open Tuesday and Thursday 11am and 3pm.
Bell Museum (Glockenmuseum), X, Troststrasse 38, tel: 604 3460. Open Wednesday 2pm–5pm.
Cathedral and Diocesan Museum (Dom- und Diözesanmuseum), I, Stephansplatz 6, 1st floor, tel: 51 552-598. Open Wednesday–Saturday 10am–4pm. Sunday and public holidays 10am–1pm.
Circus and Clown Museum (Zirkus- und Clownmuseum), II, Karmelitergasse 9, tel: 211 061-27. Open Wednesday 5.30pm–7pm, Saturday 2.30pm–5pm, Sunday 10am–noon.
Clock Museum of the City of Vienna (Uhrenmuseum der Stadt Wien), I, Schulhof 2, tel: 533 2265. Open daily except Monday 9am–4.30pm.
Collection of Court Porcelain and Silver (Hoftafel und Silberkammer), Hofburg, I, Michaelerplatz, tel: 523 4240-99. Open Tuesday–Friday and Sunday 9am–1pm.
Collection of Popular Religious Art (Sammlung Religiöse Volkskunst), I, Johannesgasse 8, tel: 512 1337. Open

MUSEUMS (continued)
Wednesday 9am–4pm, Sunday
9am–1pm.

Criminal Museum of Vienna
(Wiener Kriminalmuseum), II,
Grosse Sperlgasse 24, tel: 214
4678. Open 10am–5pm.

**Crypt of the Habsburgs in the
Church of the Augustinians**
(Herzgruft), housing the burial
urns containing the hearts of the
Habsburg family, I,
Augustinerstrasse 3, tel: 533
7099. Open Monday, Tuesday,
Thursday 9am–12 noon,
Wednesday and Friday 10am–12
noon.

Esperanto Museum (Esperanto-
Museum), I, Hofburg,
Michaelertor, tel: 535 5145.
Open Monday and Friday
9am–4pm, Wednesday
10am–6pm.

**Federal Museum of Pathology
and Anatomy** (Pathologisch-
Anatomisches Bundesmuseum),
IX, Spitalgasse 2, tel: 406 86
72. Open Wednesday 3pm–6pm,
Thursday 8am–11am, closed on
the first Saturday in the month
and during August.

Fiaker Museum
(Fiakermuseum), XVII,
Veronikagasse 12, tel: 432 607.
Open on the first Wednesday of
the month, 10am–12 noon.

Fire Brigade Museum
(Feuerwehrmuseum), I, Am Hof
7, tel: 531 99. Open Saturday
10am–12 noon, Sunday and
public holidays 9am–noon.

Funeral Museum
(Bestattungsmuseum), IV,

Goldegasse 19, tel: 50195-227.
Open Monday–Friday 12
noon–3pm by prior arrangement.

**Gallery of Painting and Fine
Arts** (Akademie der bildenden
Künste, Gemäldegalerie), I,
Schillerplatz 3, tel: 588 160.
Open Tuesday, Thursday and
Friday 10am–2pm, Wednesday
10am–1pm and 3pm–6pm,
Saturday, Sunday and public
holidays 9am–1pm.

Gallery of the 19th Century
(Stallburg), I, Reitschulgasse 2,
tel: 526 480. Open Monday,
Wednesday, Thursday, Saturday
and Sunday 10am–4pm.

**Globe Museum of the Austrian
National Library**
(Globenmuseum der
Österreichischen
Nationalbibliothek), I,
Josefsplatz 1, 3rd Floor, tel: 534
102-97. Open
Monday–Wednesday, and Friday,
11am–12 noon, Thursday
2pm–3pm.

Hermesvilla (Historic Villa), XIII,
Lainzer Tiergarten, tel: 804
1324. Open Wednesday–Sunday
and public holidays
9am–4.30pm.

Historic Baker's Shop (Alte
Backstube), VIII, Lange Gasse
34, tel: 431 101. Open
Tuesday–Saturday
9am–midnight, public holidays
2pm–midnight.

Historic Clock (Ankeruhr), I,
Hoher Markt 10/11. Daily
parade of figures at noon.

**Historic Museum of the City of
Vienna** (Historisches Museum

der Stadt Wien), IV, Karlsplatz,
tel: 505 8747. Open daily except
Monday, 9am–4.30pm.

House of Art (KunstHaus Wien),
Untere Weissgerberstrasse 13,
tel: 712 0491. Open daily
9am–7pm.

**Imperial Apartments and State
Rooms** (Hofburg), I,
Michaelerplatz, tel: 587
5554/515. Open
Monday–Saturday 8.30am–noon
and 12.30pm–4pm, Sunday and
public holidays
8.30am–12.30pm.

Imperial Crypt (Kaisergruft),
I, Neuer Markt, tel: 512 6853.
Open daily 9.30am–4pm.

**Imperial Treasury of Secular and
Religious Art** (Weltliche und
geistliche Schatzkammer), I,
Hofburg, Schweizerhof, tel: 21
770. Open daily except Tuesday
10am–6pm.

**Jewish Museum of the City of
Vienna** (Jüdisches Museum der
Stadt Wien), I, Dorotheergasse
II, tel: 535 04 31. Open
Sunday–Thursday 10am–5pm.

**Museum of Austrian Medieval
Art and Austrian Baroque
Museum** (Museum
mittelalterlicher österr. Kunst
und österr. Barockmuseum),
Unteres Belvedere, IV, Rennweg
6a, tel: 784 15804. Open daily
except Monday, 10am–5pm.

Museum of Ephesian Sculpture
(Ephesos-Museum), Neue Burg,
I, Heldenplatz, tel: 521 770.
Open Monday and
Wednesday–Friday 10am–6pm.

Museum of Ethnology (Museum
für Völkerkunde), I, Neue Burg,
Heldenplatz, tel: 534 300. Open
daily except Tuesday
10am–4pm.

Museum of the History of Art
(Kunsthistorisches Museum), I,
Burgring 5, tel: 525 240. Open
daily 10am–6pm, alternate
weeks on Tuesday or Friday also
6pm–9pm, Saturday and Sunday
9am–6pm.

Museum of Lower Austria
(Niederösterreichisches
Landesmuseum), I, Herrengasse
9, tel: 531 10-3111. Open

Museum Charge Tips

● A **multiple-entry ticket** is
available at a reduced price (öS
150, representing a reduction
of approx. 28 percent) for all
national and municipal
museums.
    It has 14 sections, is
transferable and can also be
used by more than one person
at the same time. Depending
on the price category of the

establishment, between one
and four sections are cancelled
for each visit.
● **Children** under the age of six
years and school classes are
admitted free of charge.
● **Entry is free** for all visitors to
most national and municipal
museums on Friday mornings
and on the first Sunday of every
month.

Tuesday–Friday 9am–5pm, Saturday noon–5pm, Sunday 10am–1pm.

Museum of Military History (Heeresgeschichtliches Museum), III, Arsenal, Obj. 18, tel: 795 610. Open daily except Friday 10am–4pm.

Museum of Modern Art (Palais Lichtenstein), IX, Fürstengasse 1, tel: 317 69 00. Open daily except Tuesday 10am–6pm.

Museum of Natural History (Naturhistorisches Museum), I, Burgring 7, tel: 521 770. Open daily except Tuesday 9am–6pm.

Museum of Saddlery (Museum für Hufbeschlag, Beschirrung und Besattlung), III, Linke Bahngasse 11, tel: 711 55-372. Open Monday–Thursday 1.30pm–3.30pm.

Museum of the Austrian Resistance Movement (Museum des Österreichischen Freiheitskampfes), Altes Rathaus, I, Wipplingerstrasse 8/3, tel: 534 36. Open Monday, Wednesday and Thursday 8am–5pm.

Museum of the Institute for the History of Medicine (Josefinum), IX, Währinger Strasse 25/1, tel: 403 2154. Open Monday–Friday 9am–3pm.

Museum of Viticulture (Weinbaumuseum), XIX, Döblinger Hauptstrasse 96, tel: 368 65 46. Open Saturday 3.30pm–6pm, Sunday 10am–noon.

Neidhart Frescoes (Mittelalterliches Museum), I, Tuchlauben 19, tel: 535 9065. Open daily except Monday 10am–12 noon and 1pm–4.30pm.

Prater Museum II, Hauptallee, Planetarium near the Ferris Wheel, tel: 249 432. Open Saturday, Sunday and public holidays 2pm–6.30pm.

Roman Ruins, Am Hof I, Am Hof 9. Open Saturday, Sunday and public holidays 11am–1pm.

Roman Ruins, Hoher Markt I, Hoher Markt 3, tel: 535 5606.

Open daily except Monday 10am–12.15pm and 1pm–4.30pm.

Schönbrunn Palace, Carriage House, Imperial Apartments, Gloriette, Tropical Glasshouses, Sundial House and Zoo, XIII, Schönbrunner Schloss-strasse, tel: 877 1236. Open daily 8.30am–17.00 (to 16.30 winter).

The Secession (Headquarters of the Vienna Secessionist Movement), I, Friedrichstrasse 12, tel 587 5307. Open Tuesday–Friday 10am–6pm, Saturday and Sunday 10am–4pm.

Sigmund Freud Museum (Sigmund-Freud Museum), IX, Berggasse 19, tel: 319 1596. Open Monday–Friday 9am–3pm.

Sobek Clock Collection (Uhrensammlung Sobek), XVIII, Pötzleinsdorfer Strasse 102, tel: 473 139. Open Tuesday–Friday 10am–3pm by prior arrangement. There is a guided tour each Sunday at 3pm.

State Collection of Historic Furniture (Bundessammlung Alter Stilmöbel), VII, Mariahilferstrasse 88, tel: 934 240. Open Tuesday–Friday 8am–4pm, Saturday 9am–12 noon.

Technical Museum (Technisches Museum), XIV, Mariahilferstrasse 212, tel: 894 01 49. Open Tuesday–Friday and Sunday 9am–6pm.

Tobacco Museum (Tabakmuseum), VII, Messepalast, Mariahilferstrasse 2, tel: 526 171 60. Open Tuesday 10am–7pm, Wednesday–Friday 10am–3pm, Saturday and Sunday 9am–1pm.

Tram Museum of Vienna (Wiener Strassenbahnmuseum), III, Erdbergstrasse 109, tel: 790 90. Open May–October Saturday, Sunday and public holidays 9am–4pm.

Treasury of the Teutonic Order (Schatzkammer des Deutschen Ordens), I, Singerstrasse 7, tel: 512 1065-6. Open May–October Monday, Thursday, Saturday and

District Museums

Each of the 23 city districts of Vienna has its own museum with displays on local history and objects of special interest.

Sunday 10am–12 noon, Wednesday, Friday and Saturday also 3pm–5pm; November–April Monday, Thursday and Saturday 10am–12 noon, Wednesday, Friday and Saturday 3pm–5pm.

Virgil Chapel (Virgilkapelle), I, Stephansplatz Underground Station, tel: 513 5842. Open daily except Monday 10am–12.15pm and 1pm–4.30pm.

Weapons Collection and Collection of Historical Musical Instruments (Waff-ensammlung, Sammlung alter Musikinstruments), Neue Burg, I, Heldenplatz. Open daily except Tuesday, 10am–6pm.

Memorial Museums
The following are open daily except Monday, 9am–12.15pm and 1pm–4.30pm:
Beethoven: "Pasqualatihaus", I, Mölker Bastei 8, tel: 535 8905; "Heiligenstädter-Testament-Haus", XIX, Probusgasse 6, tel: 375 408; "Eroica-Haus", XIX, Döblinger Hauptstrasse 92, tel: 369 1424.
Mozart: "Figarohaus", I, Domgasse 5, tel: 513 6294.
Johann Strauss: Residence, II, Praterstrasse 54, tel: 2140 121.
Schubert: Museum (Birthplace), IX, Nussdorfer Strasse 54, tel: 317 3601; house in which he died, IV, Kettenbrückengasse 6, tel: 581 6730.
Haydn/Brahms: Residence and Memorial Room, VI, Haydngasse 19, tel. 596 1307.

Excursions

Walking Tours

Official guides, usually experts in their field, lead groups through the various districts of the city. Approved guides wear an official badge. Tours last about 1½ hours and take place in all weathers. A brochure listing the different tours is available from the Vienna Tourist Office.

Below is a selection of "Walks through Vienna": How Beethoven lived; Franz Schubert and his life; Emperor Franz Joseph and Empress Elisabeth; The Mysterious Hofburg; Composers and their Monuments and Museums; The New Treasury; Klimt, Schiele and Other Highlights of Viennese Art; Art Nouveau in Vienna; Viennese Sagas and Legends; The Habsburgs' Crypts.
Private guided tours: Charlotte Speiser, tel: 259 2535; cost for half a day: öS 1,030.

City Tours

Alternative Stadtrundfahrten, IX, Kolingasse 6, tel: 343 384.
Cityrama Sightseeing Tours, I, Börsengasse 1, tel: 534 130.
Citytouring Vienna, XV, Penzinger Strasse 46, tel: 894 1417.
Cruises on the Danube: DDSG Travel Service, tel: 72 750 222.
Fiakers: Stands by St Stephen's Cathedral, at Heldenplatz and at Albertinaplatz.
Oldtimer Tramway, tel: 587 3186 for information.
Sightseeing by Bicycle, tel: 311 258.

Sightseeing flights, Flugplatz Schwechat, tel: 679 454.
Vienna Guide Service, tel: 443 0940.
Wiener Stadtrundfahrten, I, Friedrich-Schmidt-Platz 1, tel: 712 4683-0.

Riverboat Cruises

The Austrian national shipping line, the celebrated **Danube Steamship Company** (Donau-Dampfschiffahrts-Gesellschaft/ DDSG), has an **Information Office** at the Embarcation Quay by the Reichsbrücke (II, Handelskai 265, Passenger Hall tel: 72 750 222). Opening hours are 7am–6pm, May–September.

During the summer months combined rail and boat excursion tickets are available, by which you can explore the most attractive sections of the Danube:
Hündertwasser-Tour: öS 140
Donaustrom-Tour: öS 170
Vienna–Bratislava: öS 210
Vienna–Budapest: öS 750
A combined excursion ticket Vienna–Melk (rail), Melk–Krems (boat) and Krems–Vienna (train) costs öS 380. There is a 50 percent discount for families and senior citizens. In Melk, Spitz and Krems you can hire bicycles at the railway station for öS 35 per day. You can take your own bicycle along for öS 25.

There are also discotheque and *Heurige* trips in the evenings on the Danube and the Danube Canal.

The Zoo

Schönbrunn Palace Zoological Gardens lie at the foot of Schönbrunn Hill. Of the original buildings on this site, only the central pavilion (1752, by Jadot de Ville-Issey) remains today as the café-restaurant. Animals from all over the world are on view.

Bike Tours

Pedal Power
Ausstellungstrasse 3, tel: 729 72 34. Three-hour tours around the city centre, starting at 10am from the Prater Ferris Wheel regardless of weather. Daily May–September, Tuesday, Thursday and Saturday in April and October. Also bicycle hire.

Palace Spectacle

Sound and light shows take place at Belvedere Palace, daily from 15 May until 31 August at 9pm and from 1 September until 30 September at 8pm. Tickets are available from Österreich–Haus, I, Josefsplatz 6, or at the ticket office on the evening of performance, tel: 514 4429 59.

Sport & Leisure

Participant Sports

Further information can be obtained from the **Sports Office of the City of Vienna** (Sportstelle der Stadt Wien), VIII, Friedrich-Schmidt-Platz, tel: 4000 51 and the Haus des Sports, IV, Prinz-Eugen-Strasse 12, tel: 505 32 450.

Bowling
Bowlinghalle Prater, II, Prater Hauptallee 124, tel: 346 461.
Bowlinghalle am Postsportplatz, XVII, Schumanngasse 107.

Fishing/Angling
For information, tel: 432 176.

Golf
Österreichischer Golfverband, Haus des Sports, tel: 505 32 450.
Golfplatz, II, Freudenauer Strasse 65a.

Ice Skating
Eishunstlaufuerland IV, tel: 505 75 35.

Water Sports
Donauinsel, general information tel: 428 00-3110.
Surfinsel, V, Margaretengötrel 126, tel: 544 61 610.
Schistek, Surfbrettverleih, tel: 227 730.
Freizeitzentrum Neue Donau, Surfbrettverleih, tel: 227 730.

Cycling
Radverleih Luef, tel: 388 698 (Bicycle rental).
At the following depots bicycles can be hired for öS 30 per hour or öS 70 per day. Bicycles are also available for rental at some railway stations (öS 60 per day); they may be returned to a different station.
For information, tel: 565 051 5507.
I, Franz-Josefs-Kai (near the Salzbrücke), tel: 663 422.
II, Prater 133 (near the elevated railway), tel: 240 9494.
II, Vivariumstrasse 8, tel: 266 644.
X, Waldgasse 47, tel: 641 0113.
XIX, Heiligenstädter Strasse 180, tel: 374 598.
XXII, Linkes Ufer (Weir 1), tel: 231 171.
XXII, New Danube, Reichsbrücke, tel: 236 518.

Swimming
Open-air pools open 9am–7pm, May–September:
Stadionbad, II, Prater, Meiereistrasse.
Laaerbergbad, X, Ludwig-von-Höhnel-Gasse 2.
Theresienbad, XII, Hufelandgasse 3.
Hietzinger Bad, XIII, Atzgersdorfer Strasse 14.
Schönbrunner Bad, XIII, Schlosspark.
Neuwaldegger Bad, XVII, Promenadegasse 58.
Schafbergbad, XVII, Josef-Redl-Gasse 1.
Krapfenwaldbad, XIX, Krapfenwaldgasse 65-73.
River bathing is possible along the cut-off arms of the Old Danube:
Angeliebad, XXI, An der Oberen Alten Donau.
Gänsehäufl, XXII, Moissigasse 24.
Städtisches Strandbad Alte Donau, XXII, Arbeiterstrandbadstrasse 91.
Natural bathing areas:
Lobau, accessible via the Hubertusdamm.
Donauinsel, northern and southern section.

Indoor pools with sauna:
Amalienbad, X, Reumannplatz 9, tel: 642 112.
Dianabad, II, Lilienbrunnengasse 7–9, tel: 262 516.
Jörgerbad, XVII, Jörgerstrasse 42, tel: 434 305.
Oberlaa Thermalbad, X, Kurbadstrasse 14, tel: 681 611-52.
Nude bathing is permitted on North section of the left bank of the Danube. Walled-in barbecue grills can be used free of charge.

Tennis
II, Prater 21, tel: 246 384.
II, Prater, Kriau, tel: 248 261.
III, Arsenalstrasse 1, Obj. 3–5, tel: 782 132.
III, Landstrasser Hauptstrasse 63–65, tel: 725 435.
III, Lothringer Strasse 22, tel: 736 553.
III, Sechskrügelgasse 4, tel: 738 289.
VII, Mariahllfer Strasse 80, tel: 933 0154.

Spectator Sports

● **Riding:** Spanish Riding School, I, Michaelerplatz 1: ticket reservation, tel: 533 9031-0 or through theatre ticket agencies and offices. Prices: seats öS 200–600, standing room öS 135–150. Trotting races take place at Kriau and Freudenau.
● **Football:** You can watch football in the Praterstadion.

Shopping

Where to Shop

The city's best shops are in the city centre between the Hofburg, Graben and Kärntner Strasse. Here you will also find a number of art dealers, galleries and antique shops. Business hours are Monday–Friday usually from 8am until 6pm, and Saturdays from 8am until noon.

Clothing

CLASSIC FASHIONS
E. Braun & Co., I, Graben 8.
Elmar Garzon, I, Naglergasse 19.
Erwin & Georg Grüener, I, Kohlmarkt 5.
Knize, I, Graben 13.
Etoile, I, Lugeck 3.
House of Gentlemen, I, Kohlmarkt 12.
Lady Ascot, I, Kohlmarkt 2.
Linnerth, I, Lugeck 1–2.
Striberny, I, Führichgasse 2.

AVANT-GARDE
Szekely Peter, I, Führichgasse 10/6/05.
Steinegg Anglike, I, Salzgries 18/98.
Schella Kann, I, Seilerstätte 15 and I, Singerstrasse 6/2/8.

YOUNG FASHIONS
Ciau-Ciau, I, Tuchlauben 17.
Guys & Dolls, I, Schultergasse 2.
Judengasse Drei, I, Judengasse 3.
Lilli Pilli, I, Bäckerstrasse 10.
Lord Rieger, I, Judengasse 11.
My Market, I, Singerstrasse 4.

TRADITIONAL COSTUMES
Plankl, I, Michaelerplatz 6.

Lanz, I, Kärntner Strasse 10.
Nagy, I, Wollzeile 36.

PETIT POINT EMBROIDERY
Smejkal, I, Kohlmarkt 9.
Stransky, I, Hofburgpassage 2.

Miscellaneous

ANTIQUES
Wiener Interieur, I, Dorotheergasse 14.
Alt Wien Kunst, I, Bräunerstrasse 11.
Art und Interieur, I, Seilerstätte 28.
Antiquitäten Bednarczyk, I, Dorotheergasse 12.
Antoquitäten Feldbacherm, I, Annagasse 6.

ART
Galerie Image, I, Ruprechtsplatz 4.

BOOKS
Hintermayer, VII, Neubaugasse 290 and VI, Gumpendorfer Strasse 51.
Berger, I, Kohlmarkt 3.
Braumüller, I, Graben 22.
Gerold, I, Graben 31.
Gottschalk's Bücher-Basar, I, Krugerstrasse 10.
Herrmann, I, Grünangergasse 1.
Octopus, I, Fleischparkt 16.
English Bookshop Heidrich, I, Plankengasse 7.
  Second-hand/rare books
Aichinger, Bernhard & Co., I, Weihburggasse 16.
Böhlau, I, Dr. Karl-Lueger-Ring 12.
Bourcy und Paulusch, I, Wipplingerstrasse 5.
Bücher Ernst, VI, Gumpendorfer Strasse 82.
Der Buchfreund W. Schaden, I, Sonnenfelsgasse 4.

CRAFTS
Österreichische Werkstätten, I, Kärntner Strasse 6.

DEPARTMENT STORES
Gerngross, VII, Mariahilfer Strasse 38–48.

Accessories

● **Hats:**
Cilly, I, Petersplatz 2.
● **Shoes:**
D'Ambrosio, I, Bauernmarkt 1.
Angelo, I, Seilergasse 1.
Bellezza, I, Kärntner Strasse 45.
Map-Stiefelkönig, I, Kupferschmiedgasse 2.
● **Jewellery:**
Cartier, I, Kohlmarkt 4.
Carius Binder, I, Kärntner Strasse 17.
Galerie am Graben, I, Graben 17.
Hammermüller, I, Wipplinger Strasse 31.
Schullin, I, Kohlmarkt 17.

MAGAZINES
Morawa, I, Wollzeile 11.
H. Winter (International Press), VI, Mariahilferstrasse 77–79.

MAPS
Freytag & Berndt, I, Kohlmarkt 9.

MUSIC: RECORDS
Carola, I, Albertinapassage.

MUSICAL INSTRUMENTS
Musikhaus Doblinger, I, Dorotheergasse 10.
Musik Goll, I, Babenbergerstrasse 1–3.

PRINTS & POSTERS
Art & Poster Galerie, I, Getreidemarkt 10.
Dorst, I, Schottengasse 2.

Markets

Almost every district within the city has an open-air market. There are also temporary markets, which are usually held on Tuesday and Friday. The city's most famous market is the **Naschmarkt**. There is also a **Flea Market** in the vicinity on Saturday. (During the summer months there is another flea market which is near the Schwedenplatz/Marienbrücke).

The Naschmarkt is held along the Wienzeile near Kettenbrückengasse.

At certain times of year, other traditional markets are held across the city:

All Saints' Market
(Allerheiligenmarkt) in front of gates 1–3 of the Central Cemetery (early November).
Christmas Market
(Christkindlmarkt) in December in front of the Town Hall.
Lenten Market (Fastenmarkt), XVII, Kalvarienberggassse/St-Bartholomäus-Platz (February–March).
Confirmation Market
(Firmungsmarkt) at Whitsun on St Stephen's Square.

Export Procedures

Goods in Austria are subject to VAT (20 percent) or a luxury tax (32 percent). If the purchase price is more than öS 1,000, visitors are entitled to a refund of VAT upon departure.

To claim a refund, the purchased items must be presented to the customs officials at the border and the customs form (ATS form/U34) duly stamped. This document, together with the invoice proving that VAT was paid on the goods, must be obtained when purchasing the items and presented to the customs officers for inspection. At the airport you should follow the signs "tax free for tourists".

There are no facilities for claiming a VAT refund when travelling by train.

Language

The Austrian national language is German, which is spoken by about 100 million people world-wide. As well as Austria, Germany, parts of Switzerland and some small German enclaves in eastern Europe, there are also German-speaking communities in North America, South America and South Africa. German and English both belong to the West Germanic language group, together with Dutch, Frisian, Flemish and Afrikaans, but while a Dutchman and a German may be able to communicate quite effectively, an Englishman and a German are unlikely to make much progress, despite the many similarities between the two languages. A glance at the numbers from one to ten (see page 253) will prove that point.

Anyone who learnt Latin at school will be familiar with some of the difficulties that German presents: nouns have three genders and four cases, verbs are conjugated, pronouns are followed by one of three cases, word order is governed by some complicated rules and there are five different ways of saying "the". The only compensation is that pronunciation is perfectly consistent with spelling.

Although many young Austrians speak English and are always keen to try it out on visitors, there are many parts of the country, where a smattering of German will prove very helpful.

Even if you are fairly confident in German, you may encounter some difficulties in rural Austria, as there is a remarkable diversity in regional accents and dialects. There are strong links between Austrian German and the dialects of German spoken in Bavaria, yet within Austria some dialects are not understood by fellow Austrians. While it may sometimes be difficult to understand Austrians when they are speaking to each other, almost all can switch to High German when necessary.

New Spelling Rules

As from 1 August 1998, certain amendments to German spelling will come into force. One aim of the new regulations is to make German pronunciation even more consistent with spelling, so, for example, *schneuzen* (to blow your nose) will in future be spelt *schnäuzen*. Changes will

Pronunciation

Most **consonants** are pronounced as in English with the following exceptions:
● *g* as in "get", *ch* as in the German composer Bach, *j* is like "y", *k* is always pronounced, *v* is more like an "f", *w* as the English "v" and *z* is pronounced as "ts". The *scharfes S* or *ß* is sometimes used to replace *ss*.
Vowels and vowels with *umlauts* are less straightforward:

● *a* as in "b<u>a</u>d"; *e* as in "h<u>ay</u>"; *i* as in "s<u>ee</u>k"; *o* as in "n<u>o</u>t"; *u* as in "b<u>oo</u>t"; *ä* is a combination of "a" and "e" as in "g<u>e</u>t"; *ö* combines "o" and "e" as in B<u>e</u>rt; *ü* combines "u" and "e" as in "tr<u>ue</u>".
Dipthong sounds:
● *ai* as in "t<u>ie</u>"; *au* as in "s<u>au</u>erkr<u>au</u>t"; *ie* as in "th<u>ie</u>f"; *ei* as in "w<u>i</u>ne"; *eu* as in "b<u>oi</u>l".

be made to the use of the ß symbol and, when two words such as *Schiff* and *Fahrt* are combined, all three "f"s will be written, ie *Schifffahrt*, instead of *Schiffahrt*.

Some standardisation will be introduced into the spelling of *Fremdwörter* (loan words), eg the plural of *Baby* will in future be *Babys* not *Babies*, *Mayonäse* will replace *Mayonnaise* and *Photo* will be spelt *Foto*. Other changes include the deletion of the space between certain word pairs, the use of the upper case with adjectival nouns, guidance in using commas and rules for hyphenation.

Words & Phrases

GENERAL
Hello *Gruss Gott*
Good morning *Guten Morgen*
Good afternoon *Guten Nachmittag*
Good evening *Guten Abend*
Good night *Gute Nacht*
Goodbye *Auf Wiedersehen*
Goodbye (informal) *Servus, Pfiat di*
Do you speak English? *Sprechen Sie Englisch?*
I don't understand *Ich verstehe nicht*
Could you please speak slower? *Könnten Sie bitte etwas langsamer sprechen?*
Can you help me? *Können Sie mir helfen?*
yes/no *Ja/Nein*
please/thank you *Bitte/Danke*
sorry *Entschuldigung*
How are you? *Wie geht's?*
Excuse me *Entschuldigung Sie, bitte*
You're welcome *Bitte schön*
It doesn't matter *(Es) macht nichts*
OK *Alles klar*
What a pity *Schade*
Thank you for your help *Besten Dank für ihre Hilfe*
See you later *Bis später*
See you tomorrow *Bis morgen*
What time is it? *Wie spät ist es?*
10 o'clock *zehn Uhr*

half past ten *halb elf*
This morning *heute morgen*
this afternoon *heute nachmittag*
this evening *heute abend*
Let's go! *Los!*
Leave me alone *Lass mich in Ruhe*
Clear off *Hau ab*
Where are the toilets? *Wo sind die Toiletten?*

How to say "you"

In most cases we have given the polite form for "you", which is *Sie*. The familiar form *du* can sometimes be used if talking to a younger person, but is normally reserved for close friends and family.

large/small *gross/klein*
more/less *mehr/weniger*
now *jetzt*
later *später*
here *hier*
there *dort*

ON ARRIVAL
station *Bahnhof*
bus station *Busbahnhof*
bus stop *Bushaltestelle*
Will you tell me when to get off the bus? *Können Sie mir sagen, wann ich aussteigen muss?*
Where can I get the bus to the Adler Hotel? *Wo fährt der Bus zum Hotel Adler weg?*
Does this bus go to the town centre? *Fährt dieser Bus zur Stadtmitte?*
Which street is this? *Welche Strasse ist das?*
How far is it the station? *Wie weit ist es zum Bahnhof?*
Do you have a single room? *Haben Sie ein Einzelzimmer?*
Do you have a double room? *Haben Sie ein Doppelzimmer?*
Do you have a room with a private bath? *Haben Sie ein Zimmer mit Bad?*
How much is it? *Wieviel kostet das?*
How much is a room with full board? *Wieviel kostet ein*

Zimmer mit Vollpension?
Please show me another room *Bitte zeigen Sie mir ein anderes Zimmer*
We'll (I'll) be staying for one night *Wir bleiben (Ich bleibe) eine Nacht*
When is breakfast? *Wann gibt es Frühstück?*
Where is the toilet? *Wo ist die Toilette?*
Where is the bathroom? *Wo ist das Badezimmer?*
Where is the next hotel? *Wo ist das nächste Hotel?*

TRAVELLING
Where is the airport? *Wo ist der Flughafen?*
Where is platform one? *Wo ist Bahnsteig eins?*
Can you call me a taxi? *Können Sie mir ein Taxi rufen?*
Where do I get a ticket? *Wo kann ich eine Fahrkarte kaufen?*
departure/arrival *Abfahrt/Ankunft*
When is the next flight/train to ...? *Wann geht der nächste Flug/Zug nach ...?*
to change (flights/trains) *umsteigen*

The Alphabet

Learning how to pronounce the German alphabet will enable you to spell your name:
a = ah, **b** = bay, **c** = tsay,
d = day, **e** = eh, **f** = eff,
g = gay, **h** = har, **i** = ee, **j** = yot,
k = kar, **l** = ell, **m** = emm,
n = enn, **o** = oh, **p** = pay,
q = koo, **r** = air, **s** = ess,
t = tay, **u** = oo, **v** = fow,
w = vay, **x** = icks, **y** = upsilon,
z = tset

Have you anything to declare? *Haben Sie etwas zu verzollen?*
close/far *nah/weit*
free (of charge) *kostenlos*
price *Preis*
fee *Gebühr*
Have you got any change? *Können Sie Geld wechseln?*
bridge *Brücke*

Emergencies

Help!	*Hilfe!*
Stop!	*Halt!*
Please call a doctor	*Holen Sie einen Arzt*
Please call an ambulance	*Rufen Sie einen Krankenwagen*
Please call the fire-brigade	*Rufen Sie die Feuerwehr*
Where is the nearest telephone box?	*Wo ist die nächste Telefonzelle?*
I am ill	*Ich bin krank*
I have lost my wallet/hand-bag	*Ich habe meine Geldtasche/ Handtasche verloren*
Where is the nearest hospital?	*Wo ist das nächste Krankenhaus?*
Where is the police station?	*Wo ist das nächste Polizeiwache?*
Where is the British consulate?	*Wo ist das britische Konsulat?*

Customs *Zoll*
entrance *Eingang, Einfahrt*
exit *Ausgang, Ausfahrt*
height/width/length *Höhe/ Breite/Länge*
no stopping *Halten verboten*
one-way street *Einbahnstrasse*
picnic area *Rastplatz*
travel agency *Reisebüro*

ON THE ROAD

gas (petrol) station *Tankstelle*
I have run out of petrol *Ich habe kein Benzin mehr*
My car has broken down *Ich habe eine Autopanne*
Could you give me a push/tow? *Könnten Sie mich bitte anschieben/abschleppen?*
Can you take me to the nearest garage? *Können Sie mich zur nächsten Werkstatt bringen?*
Can you find out what the trouble is? *Können Sie feststellen, was das Problem ist?*
Can you repair it? *Können Sie es reparieren?*
The road to ... ? *Die Strasse nach ...?*
left *links*
right *rechts*
straight on *geradeaus*
opposite *gegenüber*
Where is the nearest car-park? *Wo ist der nächste Parkplatz, bitte?*
over there *da drüben*
Turn left/right after the bridge *Biegen Sie hinter der Brücke links/rechts ab*

Here is my driving licence *Da ist mein Führerschein*
Here are my insurance documents *Hier sind meine Versicherungsunterlagen*
brakes *Bremsen*
bulb *Glühbirne*
by car *mit dem Auto*
dead end *Sackgasse*
diesel *Diesel*
give way *Vorfahrt beachten*
headlights *Scheinwerfer*
jack *Wagenheber*
map *Strassenkarte*
no parking *Parken verboten*
one-way street *Einbahnstrasse*
petrol *Benzin*

Shop Signs

open/closed *geöffnet/geschlossen*
bookshop *Buchhandlung*
butcher's *Metzgerei*
cake shop *Konditorei*
department store *Kaufhaus*
drugstore, chemist (not medications) *Drogerie*
fashion *Mode*
fresh every day *täglich frisch*
ladies' clothing *Damenkleidung*
launderette *Wäscherei*
magazines *Zeitschriften*
newspapers *Zeitungen*
self-service *Selbstbedienung*
shoes *Schuhe*
special offer *Sonderangebot*
stationery *Schreibwaren*
travel agent *Reisebüro*

road/street *Strasse*
slow/fast *langsam/schnell*
unleaded *bleifrei*
water/oil *Wasser/Öl*
windscreen wipers *Scheibenwischer*

ON THE TELEPHONE

I must make a phone call *Ich muss telefonieren*
Can I use your phone? *Kann ich Ihr Telefon benutzen?*
Can I dial direct? *Kann ich direkt wählen?*
Please connect me with ... *Bitte verbinden Sie mich mit ...*
What is the code for Great Britain? *Was is das Vorwahl für Grossbritannien?*
Who is speaking? *Wer spricht da?*
The line is engaged *Die Leitung ist besetzt*
A reversed charges call, please *Ein R-Gespräch, bitte*
I'll call again later *Ich rufe später wieder an*

SHOPPING

Where can I change money? *Wo kann ich Geld wechseln?*
Where is the pharmacy? *Wo ist die Apotheke?*
What time do they close? *Wann schliessen sie?*
Where is the nearest bank? *Wo ist die nächste Bank?*
Where is the nearest post-office? *Wo ist die nächste Post?*
I'd like ... *Ich hätte gern ...*
How much is this? *Was kostet das?*
Do you take credit cards? *Akzeptieren Sie Kreditkarten?*
I'm just looking *Ich sehe mich nur um*
Do you have ...? *Haben Sie ...?*
That'll be fine. I'll take it. *In Ordnung. Ich nehme es.*
No, that is too expensive *Nein, das ist zu teuer*
Can I try it on? *Kann ich es anprobieren?*
Do you have anything cheaper? *Haben Sie etwas Billigeres?*

<u>SIGHTSEEING</u>

Where is the tourist office? *Wo ist das Fremdenverkehrsbüro?*
Is there a bus to the centre? *Gibt es einen Bus ins Stadtzentrum?*
Is there a guided sightseeing tour? *Werden geführte Besichtigungstouren zur Verfügung?*
When is the museum open? *Wann ist das Museum geöffnet?*
How much does it cost to go in? *Was kostet der Eintritt?*
art gallery *Kunstgalerie*
castle *Schloss*
cathedral *Dom*
church *Kirche*
exhibition *Ausstellung*
memorial *Denkmal*
old part of town *Altstadtviertel*
tower *Turm*
town hall *Rathaus*

Produce Markets/Delis

Can I taste it? *Kann ich einmal probieren?*
That is very nice. I'll take some. *Das ist sehr lecker/Das schmeckt sehr gut. Davon nehme ich etwas.*
What's the price per kilo? *Was kostet es pro Kilo?*
A piece of that cheese, please *Ich hätte gern ein Stück von dem Käse*
About 200g ham please *Etwa zwanzig dag Schinken, bitte*
● In Austria 100g is 10 dag (Dekagramm). So 200g ham is 20 dag.

walk *Spaziergang*
Roman *Römisch*
Romanesque *Romanisch*
Gothic *gotisch*
open daily *täglich*

<u>DINING OUT</u>

Do you know a good restaurant? *Kennen Sie ein gutes Restaurant?*
A table for one/two/three *Ein Tisch für eine Person/zwei/drei Personen, bitte*

Could we order a meal, please? *Können wir bitte bestellen?*
Can we have the bill, please? *Können wir bitte bezahlen?*
evening meal *Abendessen*
lunch *Mittagessen*
children's portion *Kinderteller*
snack *Jause, Imbiss*
menu *Speisekarte*
soup/starter Suppe/*Vorspeise*
main course *Hauptgericht*
dessert *Nachspeise*
beer/wine *Bier/Wein*
bread *Brot*
bread roll *Brötchen, Semmel*
cake *Kuchen*
coffee *Kaffee*
milk *Milch*
mineral water *Mineralwasser*
mustard *Senf*
salt/pepper *Salz/Pfeffer*
sugar *Zucker*
tea *Tee*
wine list *Weinkarte*
tip *Trinkgeld*

Frühstück **Breakfast**
Brot bread
Semmel/Brötchen roll
Eier eggs
Fruchtsaft fruit juice
hartgekochtes Ei hard-boiled egg
heiss hot
kalt cold
Marmelade/Konfitüre jam
Orangensaft orange juice
Pumpernickel black rye bread
Rühreier scrambled egg
Schinken ham
Schwarzbrot brown rye bread
Speck bacon
Weissbrot white bread

Suppen **Soups**
Eintopf thick soup
Erbsensuppe pea soup
Fritattensuppe consommé with strips of pancake
Gemüsesuppe vegetable soup
Griessnockerlsuppe semolina dumpling soup
Gulaschsuppe goulash soup
Hühnersuppe chicken soup
Nudelsuppe noodle soup
Ochsenschwanzsuppe oxtail soup
Zwiebelsuppe onion soup

Table Talk

I am a vegetarian *Ich bin Vegetarier(in)*
I am on a special diet *Ich halte Diät*
What do you recommend? *Was würden Sie empfehlen?*
I am ready to order *Ich möchte bestellen*
Enjoy your meal *Guten Appetit*
What would you like to drink? *Was möchten Sie trinken?*
Hat es Ihnen geschmeckt? *Did you enjoy your meal?*
Cheers! *Prost!*

Vorspeisen **Starters**
Austern oysters
Froschschenkel frogs' legs
Gänseleberpastete pâté de foie
Geeiste Melone iced melon
Rollmops rolled-up pickled herring
Schnecken snails
Spargelspitzen asparagus tips
Strammer Max ham and fried egg on bread
Wurstplatte assorted cooked meats

Fleischgerichte **Meat Courses**
Backhuhn roast chicken
Blutwurst black pudding
Bockwurst large frankfurter
Bratwurst fried sausage
Currywurst pork sausage with curry powder
Deutsches Beefsteak minced beef/hamburger
Stelze knuckle of pork
Ente duck
Fasan pheasant
Fleischlaibchen meatballs
Fleischpastetchen rissole
Gulasch goulash
Hähnchen/Huhn chicken
Kalbsbries veal sweetbreads
Kümmelfleisch pork stew with cumin
Lamm am Spiess lamb on the spit
Lammbraten roast lamb
Leberknödel liver dumplings
Ochsenschwanz oxtail
Räucherschinken cured ham
Rehrücken saddle of deer
Rind beef
Rinderbraten roast beef

Rinderfilet fillet of beef
Sauerbraten braised pickled
beef
Schweinebauch belly of pork
Schweinebraten roast pork
Schweinefilet loin of pork
Serbisches Reisfleisch diced
pork, onions, tomatoes and
rice
Speck bacon
Szegediner Goulasch goulash
with pickled cabbage
Tiroler Bauernschmaus various
meats served with sauerkraut,
potatoes and dumplings
Truthahn turkey
Wiener Schnitzel breaded
escalope of veal
Zigeunerschnitzel veal with
peppers and relishes
Zunge tongue

Fisch Fish
Austern oysters
Barbe mullet
Bismarckhering filleted pickled
herring
Fischfrikadellen fishcakes
Fischstäbchen fish fingers
Forelle trout
Garnelen prawns
Hecht pike
Heilbutt halibut
Heringstopf pickled herrings in
sauce
Hummer lobster
Jakobsmuscheln scallops
Kabeljau cod
Krabbe shrimps
Lachs salmon
Makrele mackerel
Muscheln mussels
Sardinen sardines
Schellfisch haddock
Schwertfisch swordfish

Seebarsch sea bass
Seezunge sole
Thunfisch tuna
Tintenfisch squid

Knödel Dumplings & Noodles
Semmelknödel/Serviettenknödl
bread dumplings
Leberknödel liver dumplings
*Kasnocken/Kässpätzle/
Kasnödel* pasta balls with
cheese
Kartoffelknödel potato
dumplings
Knödel dumplings
Maultasche Swabian ravioli
Nockerl gnocchi
Nudeln noodles
Spätzle grated pasta

Gemüse Vegetables
Bohnen beans
Bratkartoffeln fried potatoes
Champignons mushrooms
Erdäpfel potatoes
Kartoffelpuree creamed
potatoes
Kartoffelsalat potato salad
Knoblauch garlic
Kohl cabbage
Kopfsalat lettuce
Kürbis pumpkin
Lauch leek
Linsen lentils
Pommes (frites) chips/French
fries
Rohnen beetroot
Salat salad
Sauerkraut pickled cabbage

Nachspeisen Desserts
Apfelkuchen apple cake
Apfelstrudel flaky pastry stuffed
with apple
Auflauf soufflé

Bienenstich honey-almond cake
Eis ice-cream
Eisbecher ice-cream with fresh
fruit
Fruchttörtchen fruit tartlet
Gebäck pastries
Kaiserschmarrn sugared
pancake with raisins
Käsetorte cheesecake
Linzer Torte cake spread with
jam and topped with cream
Marillenknödel apricot
dumplings
Mandelkuchen almond cake
Mohnkuchen poppyseed cake
Mohr im Hemd chocolate
pudding with chocolate sauce
Obstkuchen fruit tart
Palatschinken pancakes
Pofesen stuffed fritters
Rote Grütze raspberries or
redcurrants cooked with
semolina
Sacher Torte chocolate cake
with jam and chocolate icing
Schwarzwälder Kirschtorte
Black Forest gateau

Numbers

0	*null*		
1	*eins*	1st	*erste(r)*
2	*zwei*	2nd	*zweite(r)*
3	*drei*	3rd	*dritte(r)*
4	*vier*	4th	*vierte(r)*
5	*fünf*	5th	*fünfte(r)*
6	*sechs*	6th	*sechste(r)*
7	*sieben*	7th	*siebte(r)*
8	*acht*	8th	*achte(r)*
9	*neun*	9th	*neunte(r)*
10	*zehn*	10th	*zehnte(r)*
11	*elf*	11th	*elfte(r)*
12	*zwölf*	12th	*zwölfte(r)*
13	*dreizehn*/13th	*dreizehnte(r)*	
20	*zwanzig*/20th	*zwanzigste(r)*	

Days, Months & Seasons

Monday *Montag*
Tuesday *Dienstag*
Wednesday *Mittwoch*
Thursday *Donnerstag*
Friday *Freitag*
Saturday *Samstag/
Sonnabend*
Sunday Sonntag

January *Januar/Jänner*
February *Februar/Feber*
March *März*
April *April*
May *Mai*
June *Juni*
July *Juli*
August *August*
September *September*

October *Oktober*
November *November*
December *Dezember*

spring *Frühling*
summer *Sommer*
autumn *Herbst*
winter *Winter*

21 einundzwanzig/21st
  einundzwanzigste(r)
30 dreissig
40 vierzig
50 fünfzig
100 hundert/100th hundertste(r)
1,000 tausend/1000th
  tausendste(r)
1,000,000 eine Million

Slang

a right mess eine Schweinerei
bastard Arschloch, du blöde
  Kuh, du Schweinehund
bloody hell! verdammt noch mal!
gay schwul, warm
great, magic klasse, super, toll,
  Spitze, leiwand
oh my God! du lieber Gott!
pissed besoffen, fett, voll
pissed off sauer, grantig,
  angefressen
shit Scheisse, Mist
stupid doof, blöd, deppert,
  narrisch
wow! Mensch! Mah! Wahnsinn!

Loan Words

With Germany standing at the
heart of Europe, its language
has been subjected to many
foreign influences. For centuries,
there was a large Jewish
community in Germany and they
brought many Hebrew words into
regular usage. Words such as
Massel (good luck), vermasseln
(to make a mess of things),
messchugge (crazy) and
Mischpoche (rabble) are now
part of everyday language.
  During the 17th century, the
Huguenots introduced many
French words into German, such
as those used to describe food
(eg Ragout fin, Roulade,
Frikassee, Püree, Eclair, Petits
fours).

Saying the Date

● on the 20th October 1999:
am zwanzigsten Oktober,
neunzehnhundertneunundneun
zig
● yesterday gestern
● today heute
● tomorrow morgen
● last week letzte Woche
● next week nächste Woche

  More recently, English has
infiltrated the German language,
mainly in popular culture. English
speakers will be on familiar
ground in the worlds of sport,
pop music, entertainment and
computers (eg Fitness,
Feedback, Snowboard,
Mountain-bike, Disco,
Videorecorder, Groupie,
Entertainer, Software, Byte).

False Friends

False friends are words that look
like English words, but actually
mean something different. Ich
bekomme ein Baby, for example,
does not mean "I am becoming
a baby", but "I am having a
baby"; ein Berliner is a jam
doughnut and also never means
"also", but usually "so" or
"therefore".
  Some loan words can be very
confusing too. Aktuell means
"up-to-date" or "fashionable",
not "actual", and Ich komme
eventuell could mean that I am
not coming at all. A good
translation would be "I might
come".
  Ein Knicker is a scrooge and
ein Schellfish is a haddock.

Further Reading

History

Austria-Hungary and Great
Britain, 1908–14, by A.F.
Pribram. Greenwood Press,
London.
Austria, Empire and Republic, by
Barbara Jelavich. Cambridge
University Press.
Dissolution of the Austro-
Hungarian Empire, by J.W.
Mason. Longman.
Mayerling: the Facts behind the
Legend, by Fritz Judtman. Harrap
1971.
Nightmare in Paradise: Vienna
and its Jews, by George E.
Berkeley. California University
Press.

Biography/ Autobiography

The Life and Work of Sigmund
Freud, by Ernest Jones. Penguin.
Gustav Mahler – Memories and
Letters, by Alma Mahler. Collins.
Letters, by W.A. Mozart. Edited
by Hans Mersmann. Dover
Publications.
Prince Eugene of Savoy, by
Nicholas Henderson.
Weidenfeld.
The World of Yesterday, by
Stefan Zweig. New York 1943.
Maria Theresia, by Edward
Crankshaw. Constable.

Literature

Austrian Life and Literature –
Eight Essays. Edited by Peter
Branscombe. Scottish Academic
Press.
From Vormärz to Fin de Siècle –
Essays in 19th Century Austrian
Literature. Edited by Mark G.
Ward. Lochee Publications.
The Austrian Mind – An
Intellectual and Social History

Compound Words

The German language can be restructured to create new words
simply by linking words together. One of the best examples is:
das Donaudampfschiffsfahrtsgesellschaftskapitänsmützensternlein
or "the litte star on the Danube shipping company captain's cap".

1848–1938, by William M. Johnstone. University of California Press.
La Ronde and Other Plays (translations), by Arthur Schnitzler. Carcanet Press.

Art & Architecture

The Age of the Baroque, 1610–1660. Greenwood Press, London.
Baroque and Rococo, edited by Anthony Blunt. Granada.
Vienna in the Age of Schubert – the Biedermeier Interior, by Christa Witt-Dorring.
Vienna 1900 – Art, Architecture, Design, by Kirk Varnedoe.

Food

Austrian Cooking, by Gretel Beer. André Deutsch.

Other Insight Guides

The widely acclaimed Insight Guide series includes over 200 titles covering every continent.

Companion volumes to this book include *Insight Guide: Austria* and *Insight Guide: Germany*, wide-ranging guides which provide a cultural overview of these popular destinations.

Insight Pocket Guide: Vienna contains a local host's personal recommendations for wining, dining, sightseeing and much more. Complete with large fold-out map of the city.

Insight Compact Guides to *Vienna* and *Salzburg* are pocket-sized encyclopedias packed with text, pictures and maps. They're the perfect on-the-spot guides to these cities of music.

ART & PHOTO CREDITS

All photographs by **Christian Hager** except for:

AKG Photo 18, 21, 44L, 45L, 204T, 206T
Tony Anzenberger 31, 128, 181, 214/215, 216, 219
Anzenberger/Zach-Kiesling 165R
Courtesy Austrian Tourist Board 200, 201, 203B, 203T, 211T, 213, 218T, 220T, 222T
Bodo Bondzio 224
János Kalmár 46, 47, 49, 63, 69, 71, 79, 88, 101, 107L, 114, 120B, 124/125, 150/151, 152L, 154, 155, 156B, 156T, 162, 163T, 164, 165L, 165T, 167B, 167T, 186B, 202L, 204B, 208L, 208R, 211B, 212, 217, 218B, 221, 223
Wilhelm Klein 68, 206B, 207, 209, 210
Wolfgang Kraus 139
Kunsthistorisches Museum Wien 130
Mary Evans Picture Library 43, 45R, 153
Museum D. Stadt Wien 22, 26, 27
PAG-Verlag Wien 54
Mark Read/APA 52, 56, 58L, 58R, 60, 75L, 78, 80, 86/87, 93, 99R, 100T, 102T, 103, 104, 105L, 105R, 107R, 108L, 108R, 108T, 111L, 111R, 112, 113, 116B, 116T, 118, 119L, 119R, 119T, 120T, 127L, 127R, 134T, 137, 138T, 140T, 152R, 161, 174, 179T, 180T, 185, 186T, 188L, 188R, 199
Topham Picture Point 19, 34, 37, 220L, 220R
WARCH 24, 25, 28, 29, 38/39, 48, 59, 72, 179B
WFV 14, 30, 70, 96, 99L, 135, 146/147, 158, 159, 170/171, 183L, 183R, 190/191, 192/193, 194/195, 198, 202R, 205
Zach-Kiesling 36, 187

Picture Spreads

Pages 50/51 Clockwise from bottom left-hand corner: János Kalmár, Mary Evans Picture Library, János Kalmár, János Kalmár, János Kalmár, János Kalmár, Erich Lessing/AKG Photo, János Kalmár, Erich Lessing/AKG Photo.
Pages 64/65 Clockwise from bottom left-hand corner: János Kalmár, Adam Woolfitt/Robert Harding Picture Library, Christian Hager, János Kalmár, János Kalmár, János Kalmar, János Kalmár, János Kalmár, Adam Woolfitt/Robert Harding Picture Library.
Pages 144/145 All János Kalmár.
Pages 168/169 Clockwise from bottom left-hand corner: János Kalmár, János Kalmár, János Kalmár, János Kalmár, János Kalmár, Mary Evans Picture Library, Blaine Harrington III, János Kalmár.

Cover photograph
Robert Harding Picture Library
Maps **Berndtson & Berndtson Publications GmbH, Polyglott Kartographie, Huber Kartographie**
Cartographic Editor **Zoë Goodwin**
Production **Mohammed Dar**
Design Consultants
Klaus Geisler, Graham Mitchener
Picture Research **Hilary Genin**

Index

Note: page numbers in *italics* refer to illustrations

The Insight Approach

The book you are holding is part of the world's largest range of guidebooks. Its purpose is to help you have the most valuable travel experience possible, and we try to achieve this by providing not only information about countries, regions and cities but also genuine insight into their history, culture, institutions and people.

Since the first Insight Guide – to Bali – was published in 1970, the series has been dedicated to the proposition that, with insight into a country's people and culture, visitors can both enhance their own experience and be accepted more easily by their hosts. Now, in a world where ethnic hostilities and nationalist conflicts are all too common, such attempts to increase understanding between peoples are more important than ever.

Insight Guides:
Essentials for understanding

Because a nation's past holds the key to its present, each Insight Guide kicks off with lively history chapters. These are followed by magazine-style essays on culture and daily life. This essential background information gives readers the necessary context for using the main Places section, with its comprehensive run-down on things worth seeing and doing.

Finally, a listings section contains all the information you'll need on travel, hotels, restaurants and opening times.

As far as possible, we rely on local writers and specialists to ensure that information is authoritative. The pictures, for which Insight Guides have become so celebrated, are just as important. Our photojournalistic approach aims not only to illustrate a destination but also to communicate visually and directly to readers life as it is lived by the locals. The series has grown to almost 200 titles.

Compact Guides:
The "great little guides"

As invaluable as such background information is, it isn't always fun to carry an Insight Guide through a crowded souk or up a church tower. Could we, readers asked, distil the key reference material into a slim volume for on-the-spot use?

Our response was to design Compact Guides as an entirely new series, with original text carefully cross-referenced to detailed maps and more than 200 photographs. In essence, they're miniature encyclopedias, concise and comprehensive, displaying reliable and up-to-date information in an accessible way. There are almost 100 titles.

Pocket Guides:
A local host in book form

However wide-ranging the information in a book, human beings still value the personal touch. Our editors are often asked the same questions. Where do *you* go to eat? What do *you* think is the best beach? What would *you* recommend if I have only three days? We invited our local correspondents to act as "substitute hosts" by revealing their preferred walks and trips, listing the restaurants they go to and structuring a visit into a series of timed itineraries.

The result: our Pocket Guides, complete with full-size fold-out maps. These 100-plus titles help readers plan a trip precisely, particularly if their time is short.

Exploring with Insight:
A valuable travel experience

In conjunction with co-publishers all over the world, we print in up to 10 languages, from German to Chinese, from Danish to Russian. But our aim remains simple: to enhance your travel experience by combining our expertise in guidebook publishing with the on-the-spot knowledge of our correspondents.